Study Guide

Integrated Science
for CSEC®
2nd edition

Lawrie Ryan
Denise L. J. Hernandez
Victor Joseph
Bermadee McKenzie-Briscoe
Marsha Russell

OXFORD
UNIVERSITY PRESS

Great Clarendon Street, Oxford, OX2 6DP, United Kingdom

Oxford University Press is a department of the University of Oxford.
It furthers the University's objective of excellence in research, scholarship,
and education by publishing worldwide. Oxford is a registered trade mark of
Oxford University Press in the UK and in certain other countries

First published by Nelson Thornes Ltd in 2012
This edition published by Oxford University Press in 2015

British Library Cataloguing in Publication Data
Data available

978-0-19-841382-0

1 3 5 7 9 10 8 6 4 2

Printed in Great Britain by Ashford Print and Publishing Services, Gosport

Contents

Introduction 1

Section A: The organism and its environment

Unit 1 Matter

1.1	States of matter	2
1.2	Cell structure	4
1.3	Diffusion and osmosis	6
1.4	Active transport	8

Unit 2 Reproduction and growth

2.1 Reproduction 10
2.2 Sexual reproduction 12
2.3 Menstrual cycle, pregnancy and birth 14
2.4 Birth control methods 16
2.5 Pre- and post-natal care 18
2.6 Sexually Transmitted Infections (STIs) 20
2.7 Growth in plants, humans and population 22

Unit 3 Food and nutrition

3.1 Photochemical reactions 24
3.2 Crop production 26
3.3 Food chains and food webs 28
3.4 Food groups and nutrition 30
3.5 The importance of a balanced diet 32
3.6 Digestion 34
3.7 Microorganisms and food preservation 36
3.8 Teeth and digestion 38

Unit 4 Transport systems

4.1 Transport systems in plants 40
4.2 The human circulatory system 42
4.3 Blood groups 44
4.4 Immunity 46
4.5 High blood pressure and its effects 48
4.6 Drugs 50
4.7 Skeleton, joints and muscles 52

Unit 5 Respiration and air pollution

5.1 Respiratory surfaces 54
5.2 Breathing and gaseous exchange 56
5.3 Respiration 58
5.4 Air pollution 60
5.5 Effects of smoke 62

Unit 6 Excretion

6.1 Excretion in humans 64
6.2 Excretion in plants 66

Unit 7 Sense organs and coordination

7.1 The eye 68
7.2 Light and colour 70
7.3 The ear 72
7.4 The nervous system 74
7.5 The endocrine system 76

Unit 8 Health and sanitation

8.1 Keeping clean 78
8.2 Pests and parasites 80
Practice exam questions 82

Section B: The home and workplace

Unit 9 Temperature control and ventilation

9.1 How is energy transferred? 84
9.2 How is energy transferred in fluids? 86
9.3 Thermostats and thermometers 88
9.4 Evaporation and cooling 90
9.5 Humidity and ventilation 92

Unit 10 Conservation of energy

10.1 Energy 94
10.2 Energy on the move and momentum 96

Unit 11 Electricity and lighting

11.1 Electricity 98
11.2 Fuses and cables (flexes) 100
11.3 Energy consumption 102
11.4 Efficient lighting 104
11.5 Be prepared in an emergency 106
11.6 Safety first 108

Unit 12 Machines and movement

12.1 Simple machines 110
12.2 Using machines 112

Unit 13 Metals and non-metals

13.1 Metals and non-metals 114
13.2 Reactions of metals 116
13.3 Alloys at work 120
13.4 Taking care of iron or steel 122

Unit 14 Acids, bases and mixtures

14.1 Household chemicals 124
14.2 Solutions, suspensions and colloids 126
14.3 Hard and soft water 128
14.4 Household cleaning products 130
Practice exam questions 132

Contents

Section C: Earth's place in the Universe

Unit 15 The Universe and our Solar System

15.1 Our place in the Universe   134
15.2 The Solar System   136
15.3 The Earth, Moon and Sun   138

Unit 16 The terrestrial environment

16.1 Soils   140
16.2 The importance of soil   142
16.3 Natural cycles   144
16.4 Air masses   146
16.5 Air in motion   148
16.6 Tides and tidal waves   150
16.7 Volcanoes and earthquakes   152

Unit 17 Water and the aquatic environment

17.1 Water and life   156
17.2 Purifying water for drinking   158
17.3 Flotation   160
17.4 Water pollution   162
17.5 Fishing   164
17.6 Navigation and safety on the water   166

Unit 18 Fossil fuels and alternative sources of energy

18.1 Fossil fuels   168
18.2 Alternative sources of energy   170
18.3 Solar energy   172

Unit 19 Forces

19.1 Principles of forces   174
19.2 Gravity and stability   176
19.3 Turning forces   178
19.4 Circular motion and satellites   180
     Practice exam questions   182

     Index   184

 Access your support website for additional content and activities here:
www.oxfordsecondary.com/9780198413820

Introduction

This Study Guide has been developed exclusively with the Caribbean Examinations Council (CXC®) to be used as an additional resource by candidates, both in and out of school, following the Caribbean Secondary Education Certificate (CSEC®) programme.

It has been prepared by a team with expertise in the CSEC® syllabus, teaching and examination. The contents are designed to support learning by providing tools to help you achieve your best in Integrated Science and the features included make it easier for you to master the key concepts and requirements of the syllabus. *Do remember to refer to your syllabus for full guidance on the course requirements and examination format!*

This Study Guide is supported by a website which includes electronic activities to assist you in developing good examination techniques:

- **On Your Marks** activities provide sample examination-style short answer and essay type questions, with example candidate answers and feedback from an examiner to show where answers could be improved. These activities will build your understanding, skill level and confidence in answering examination questions.
- **Test Yourself** activities are specifically designed to provide experience of multiple-choice examination questions and helpful feedback will refer you to sections inside the Study Guide so that you can revise problem areas.

This unique combination of focused syllabus content and interactive examination practice will provide you with invaluable support to help you reach your full potential in CSEC® Integrated Science.

1 Matter

1.1 States of matter

Everything on Earth, including its atmosphere, is made up of matter. Matter is anything that has mass and volume. Look at the things around you and the substances that they are made from. You will find wood, metal, plastic, glass, water, air ... the list is almost endless.

There are millions of different substances catalogued by scientists. In general, they can be classified as solids, liquids or gases – known as the three **states of matter**.

Properties of each state of matter

Solids all have a fixed shape and volume. They cannot be compressed.

Liquids have a fixed volume, but they can flow and change their shape. A substance in the liquid state will occupy slightly more space than an equal mass in its solid state (but water and ice are exceptions).

Gases have no fixed shape or volume. They can be compressed easily.

Particle theory

To explain the properties of solids, liquids and gases, we use the particle theory (also known as the kinetic theory of matter).

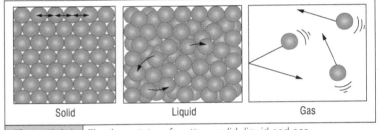

| Solid | Liquid | Gas |

Figure 1.1.1 The three states of matter – solid, liquid and gas

It is based on the fact that all matter is made up of tiny particles and describes:

- the movement of the particles, and
- the average distance between particles

within each state of matter.

Look at the diagrams to the left that represent the three states of matter.

	General properties	Average distance between particles	Arrangement of particles	Movement of particles
Solid	Fixed shape; incompressible	Particles are touching	Regular pattern	Vibrate on the spot
Liquid	No fixed shape; can flow; very difficult to compress	Most particles are touching	Irregular, random	Slip and slide over and around each other
Gas	No fixed shape; spreads out to fill its container; easily compressed	Large distances	Irregular, random	Can move very quickly. In a random manner, between collisions

Each particle in a solid is touching its nearest neighbours and they remain in this fixed arrangement. They cannot move around, but they do vibrate constantly.

The particles in a liquid are also very close together but they can move past each other. This results in a constantly changing, random arrangement of particles.

The particles in a gas have much more space, on average, between them. They can move around at high speeds and in any direction. This means the particles have a random arrangement. The hotter the gas is, the faster the particles move.

Changing state

A solid turns into a liquid at its melting point. This is the same temperature at which the liquid freezes or solidifies back into the solid. The hotter a solid is, the faster its particles vibrate. Eventually, the vibrations will be so strong that the particles begin to break free from their neighbours. At this point the solid starts to melt and become a liquid.

A liquid turns into a gas at its boiling point. The gas condenses back into the liquid at the same temperature. The hotter a liquid is, the faster its particles move around. As the temperature rises, more and more particles gain enough energy to escape from the surface of the liquid. Its rate of evaporation increases. Eventually, the liquid boils and bubbles of gas rise and escape from within the liquid.

Each change of state is reversible. They are examples of physical changes. No new substances are formed in changes of state. Substances with higher melting points and boiling points have stronger forces of attraction between their particles.

Note that if a solid is heated and changes directly to a gas without melting, i.e. it does not pass through the liquid phase, the change of state is called **sublimation**. Also, some people classify a fourth state of matter called plasma. It can be thought of as clouds of 'sub-atomic' particles, i.e. the stuff that makes up the particles in solids, liquids and gases. These are common in outer space.

Figure 1.1.2 | Boiling water in a kettle is an everyday 'change of state'

SUMMARY QUESTIONS

1 Name the following changes:
   a liquid → solid   b gas → liquid   c solid → liquid
   d liquid → gas   e solid → gas (in a single step).

2 Explain why substances have different melting points in terms of their particles.

3 Describe the changes that occur to the particles as a gas is cooled down to a temperature below its freezing point.

4 Evaporation is the change of state that occurs when a liquid changes to a gas below its boiling point. You can investigate the factors that affect the rate of evaporation using a wet paper towel on a high resolution electric balance. Plan an investigation into one factor that might affect the rate of evaporation of water from the paper towel, writing a brief method.

KEY POINTS

1 The three states of matter are solids, liquids and gases.

2 The particles in a solid are packed closely together, fixed in their positions and vibrate.

3 The particles in a liquid are also close together, but can slip and slide over each other in a random motion.

4 The particles in a gas have, on average, lots of space between them and zoom around randomly.

All living things are made up of cells. Cells enable all the processes of life and so are essential for all living things on Earth. Cells are too small to see with the naked eye.

You need a microscope to study the *structure* of cells.

Animal cells

There are many different types of cells in the human body, but they have certain features in common.

Look at the diagram of a typical unspecialised animal cell below.

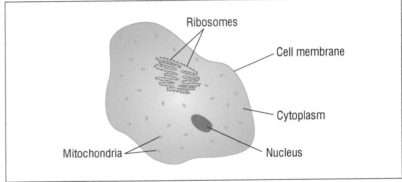

Figure 1.2.1 | A simplified typical animal cell

Functions of the cell parts

Each part of a cell has its own particular functions. The parts all coordinate to ensure a cell works properly.

Nucleus – This is the 'control centre' of the cell. It controls all the activities in the cell and contains the genetic material that controls how the cell develops. This genetic information is carried on **chromosomes**, which contain **DNA** (deoxyribonucleic acid).

Cell membrane – This is the outer part of the cell. It forms a barrier around the cell. It allows simple substances to pass in or out of the cell.

Cytoplasm – This is the jelly-like liquid inside the cell. Most of the chemical reactions we need to keep us alive happen in solution. For example, our cells get the energy they need from respiration taking place here (see Mitochondria below).

Mitochondria – These are found in the cytoplasm and are the sites where respiration takes place.

Ribosomes – Proteins are made here.

Plant cells

Plant cells have all the components of animal cells, but also contain more features.

Look at the diagram of a typical unspecialised plant cell opposite.

Functions of the cell parts

Every plant cell has a cell wall. These surround the cell contents (together with the cell membrane) with a more rigid boundary made of cellulose. This gives the cell support and shape.

Many plants cells also have:

Chloroplasts – These are the green parts (or organelles) in plant cells where photosynthesis takes place. A pigment called chlorophyll gives chloroplasts their green colour. This absorbs light energy when plants make their own food during photosynthesis.

A **vacuole** – The large central part of the plant cell that is full of cell sap (liquid). This helps to support the plant.

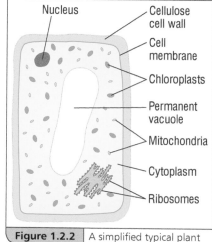

Figure 1.2.2 | A simplified typical plant cell

Labels: Nucleus, Cellulose cell wall, Cell membrane, Chloroplasts, Permanent vacuole, Mitochondria, Cytoplasm, Ribosomes

KEY POINTS

1 A typical unspecialised animal cell contains a nucleus, cell membrane, cytoplasm and mitochondria.

2 A typical unspecialised plant cell also contains a cell wall, chloroplasts and a vacuole in green parts of the plant.

3 Each component of a cell has functions that are interlinked so the cells work properly.

4 Chromosomes carry genetic information in the form of DNA.

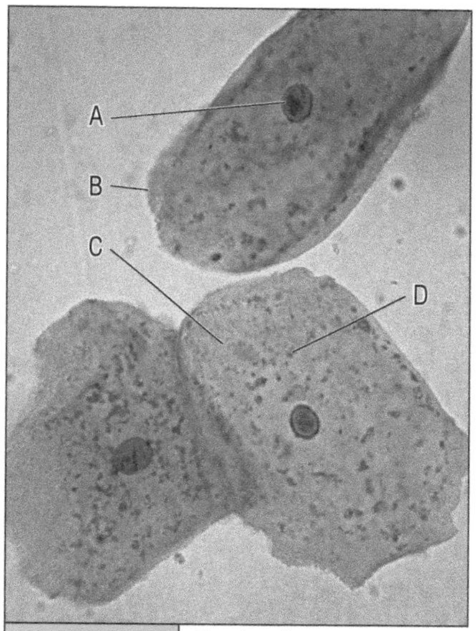

Figure 1.2.3 | Cheek cells

SUMMARY QUESTIONS

1 Draw a labelled diagram of a typical unspecialised animal cell and plant cell.

2 What are the differences between a typical unspecialised plant cell and animal cell?

3 What is the function of:
   a the nucleus
   b chloroplasts
   c mitochondria
   d the cell membrane
   e chromosomes?

4 Look at Figures 1.2.3 and 1.2.4 and identify the labels.

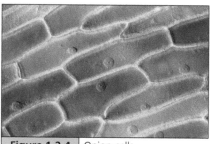

Figure 1.2.4 | Onion cells

Diffusion and osmosis

To function properly, cells need to move certain substances into and out of the cell. Examples of these substances are glucose, water and oxygen. **Diffusion** and **osmosis** are two processes by which this takes place.

Diffusion

All substances are made of particles. In gases and liquids these particles move around randomly. Diffusion takes place when particles (molecules or charged particles called ions) are not distributed evenly. The random motion of the particles means that eventually the particles will be evenly spread. Overall, the particles move from where they are in a high concentration to where they are in a low concentration. Look at Figure 1.3.1 below.

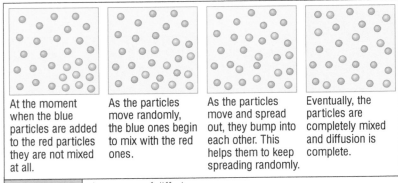

| At the moment when the blue particles are added to the red particles they are not mixed at all. | As the particles move randomly, the blue ones begin to mix with the red ones. | As the particles move and spread out, they bump into each other. This helps them to keep spreading randomly. | Eventually, the particles are completely mixed and diffusion is complete. |

Figure 1.3.1 The process of diffusion

In the process of diffusion we say that the particles move down a **concentration gradient**. They move from an area of high concentration to an area of low concentration. For example, dissolved glucose molecules will move across cell membranes from your gut (where there will be a high concentration of glucose in solution after a meal) into your blood (where the concentration of glucose is lower).

The bigger the difference in concentration between two regions, the *steeper* the concentration gradient. We find that diffusion takes place more quickly when there is a steeper concentration gradient.

Osmosis

Osmosis is a special case of diffusion. Osmosis involves the movement of water through a partially permeable membrane, such as the cell membrane. 'Partially permeable' means that only certain substances can pass through the membrane. Small molecules, such as the solvent water, can pass through, but large molecules cannot.

But which way do the water molecules move in osmosis? The direction is determined by the concentration of water on either side of the partially permeable membrane. We can think of a dilute solution as having a 'high concentration of water'. Then, we can think of water molecules moving from a region where their concentration is high (in a dilute solution) to where their concentration is low (to a more concentrated solution). Look at Figure 1.3.2 below.

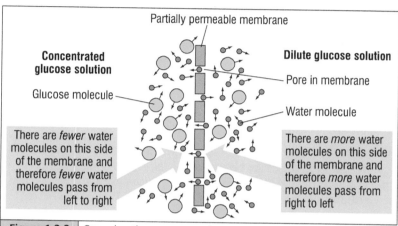

Figure 1.3.2 Osmosis – the movement of water across a partially permeable membrane

We can study osmosis in experiments using partially permeable bags as model cells.

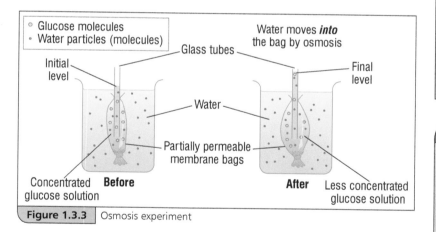

Figure 1.3.3 Osmosis experiment

In this experiment you start with a concentrated glucose solution inside the sealed partially permeable bag. The bag is put in a beaker of water. If left, the bag will swell up. This happens because water moves across the partially permeable membrane into the concentrated glucose solution. Remember that water moves from a region where it is in high concentration (in this case pure water) to where water is at a lower concentration (in the concentrated glucose solution).

SUMMARY QUESTIONS

1 Define the terms a diffusion and b osmosis.

2 Using the substances glucose and water, explain the difference between diffusion and osmosis.

3 Draw a labelled diagram of an osmosis experiment, similar to the one shown in Figure 1.3.3. Start with pure water inside the partially permeable bag and concentrated glucose solution in the beaker.

Active transport

What is active transport?

You have seen how substances can move into and out of cells and between cells, through partially permeable membranes. The processes of diffusion and osmosis make this happen. Both take place *down* a concentration gradient on either side of the membrane. In diffusion, particles of a dissolved substance move from an area of high concentration to an area of low concentration. In osmosis, it is water particles (molecules) that move through the partially permeable membrane from a high concentration of water (in a more dilute solution) to an area of low concentration of water (a more concentrated solution).

However, there are times when it benefits an organism to move substances into, out of, or between cells *against a concentration gradient*. In other words, they move substances from an area of low concentration to an area of high concentration. They achieve this by a process called **active transport**. Cells that move substances by active transport have special molecules (called transport proteins – see Figure 1.4.1 below) in their membranes. These help to move particles of the dissolved substance against a concentration gradient through the cell membrane.

Active transport needs energy to take place, whereas the processes of diffusion and osmosis do not require energy. The cell uses respiration to provide the energy needed. You can find out more about respiration in 5.3 on page 58.

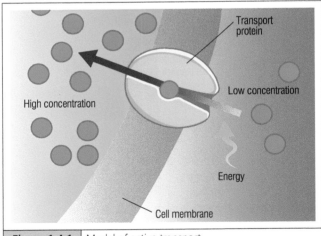

Figure 1.4.1 | Model of active transport

Where is active transport needed?

Here are some examples of situations where an organism needs to move particles against a concentration gradient. The particles are either:

- molecules, such as glucose needed for respiration to release energy, or
- ions, which are charged particles, such as the mineral ions.

The particles might move:

- into the root hair cells on the roots of a plant. The concentration of mineral ions in soil is very much lower than in the root hair cells, so the ions will not enter the cells by diffusion. To get the mineral ions needed by plants for healthy growth, active transport has to take place. The energy needed for the process comes from respiration in the root cells.
- into the bloodstream, out from cells in the kidneys – when blood sugar levels are low a few hours after a meal, the excess glucose absorbed from the blood passes back out of the cells in the kidney tubules by active transport (see 6.1 on page 64).
- into and out of cells to keep the balance of sodium ions and potassium ions at the right levels.
- from a solution of digested food into the cells lining the small intestine – glucose moves against a concentration gradient.

KEY POINTS

1 Substances can be moved against concentration gradients by active transport.

2 The process needs energy from respiration to work.

3 Active transport takes place in the intestines, kidneys and in plants in the root hairs.

SUMMARY QUESTIONS

1 Describe the process of active transport.

2 How is active transport different from the processes of diffusion and osmosis in a cell?

3 Give three examples of active transport that takes place in the human body.

2 Reproduction and growth

2.1   Reproduction

LEARNING OUTCOMES

- Describe the process of simple cell division.
- Describe the process of asexual reproduction in plants.
- Describe the process of asexual reproduction in animals.
- Compare asexual and sexual reproduction.

All living things produce offspring in a process called reproduction. There are two types of reproduction – asexual and sexual.

Asexual reproduction

In asexual reproduction only one parent is needed. The parent organism has cells that can divide in two, multiplying to give identical organisms called clones. See Figure 2.1.1 showing simple cell division.

Single-celled organisms, such as bacteria, reproduce like this. However, more complex organisms can also generate their own offspring.

Yeast (a fungus) and hydra (a water animal) use a process called budding. In this, a cell bulges from the side of the dividing cell in the parent as it fills with cytoplasm. The nucleus of the original cell is copied and is transferred into the newly forming cell. The new cell then breaks off and forms a new organism which is a clone of the parent.

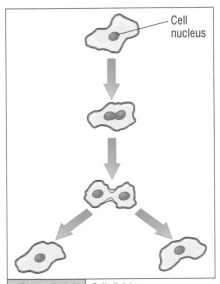

Figure 2.1.1   Cell division

Cell nucleus

Figure 2.1.2   Asexual reproduction in yeast cells is called budding. What type of organism is yeast?

In plants, such as strawberries, reproduction takes place through runners that grow from the parent plant. The runners grow out along the ground, and produce new roots which form shoots and grow into a new plant. The runner then dies and the cloned plant becomes independent of the parent plant.

Flowering plants can also grow storage organs (see Figure 2.1.4). These can be:

- bulbs – layered, swollen, underground stem, for example onions, garlic, lilies
- corms – short, solid, enlarged stem bases, for example dasheen, eddo, crocus, gladiolus
- rhizomes – swollen, horizontal-growing stems, for example iris, ginger
- tubers – swollen root, for example sweet potato, yam.

If the plant dies the storage organ can use its store of energy to grow into a new plant.

We can also take cuttings, which grow into clones of the original plant. For example, we can cut a stem, then plant it in rooting compost (a mixture containing the right nutrients for plant growth).

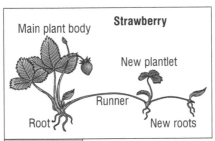

Figure 2.1.3   Some plants reproduce asexually by growing runners

Main plant body

Strawberry

New plantlet

Runner

New roots

Root

Tissue culture is a more modern form of taking cuttings. It uses a few plant cells in a special plant hormone mixture to grow a large mass of cells. Then each cell is put in a growing mixture to produce huge numbers of identical plants.

Grafting is another technique that plant growers use, usually with trees. This makes a new tree by grafting a cutting from one tree into a notch cut into a different tree. If the two plants are bound together they will grow into one new plant.

We can also clone animals now. In this way, a farmer can choose an animal with favourable characteristics to clone. What would be a favourable characteristic of a goat reared in a mountainous terrain?

Sexual reproduction

Cloning is done by taking egg cells from an excellent female specimen. These are fertilised by sperm from a prize male. This part of the process is **sexual reproduction** as there are two parents, each one donating genetic information to their offspring.

The fertilised cell is allowed to grow into a ball of cells (either in the animal or in a science lab). Then the embryo formed has individual cells removed. These are allowed to divide and grow into new identical embryos. This is asexual reproduction. These embryos are transplanted into other female animals to complete the pregnancy. The cloned animals will all be the same because the genetic information carried in their nuclei is identical. They will all have the desired characteristics.

Comparing asexual and sexual reproduction

This table shows some of the advantages and disadvantages of each method of reproduction.

Type of reproduction	Advantages	Disadvantages
Asexual	No need to find a partner as only one parent is needed. Many offspring produced very quickly in the right conditions. Large numbers produced in one place mean they can compete for resources more effectively than other species present in smaller numbers.	Lack of genetic variation – so if a parent is susceptible to a disease all the clones will get the same disease, which puts a species in danger of extinction. New offspring may live very close to the parent, for example in plants where bits break off and grow into new plants, so conditions might deteriorate.
Sexual	Variation will be ensured in a species. Over time the advantageous characteristics will come through in offspring as the species evolves to cope with changes in its environment.	Two parents are needed so time and energy is spent finding a partner. The process of reproduction from fertilisation to birth is much longer.

Figure 2.1.4 Storage organs that can grow into new plants

Labels: Terminal bud which produces new plant; Outer dry leaf; Inner fleshy leaves; Lateral bud which produces new **bulb**; Roots; Swollen stem containing food; New shoot; Bud which produces new **rhizome**; Remainder of previous rhizome; Root; Lateral bud which will produce new **corm**; Bud from which new shoot grows; Corm

KEY POINTS

1 Asexual reproduction takes place when one parent has cells that divide to form a new individual. The offspring are genetically identical. There is no variation from the parent.

2 Sexual reproduction, where two parents share genetic information to produce offspring, gives variety in a species. This helps them evolve and become better adapted to their environment over time.

SUMMARY QUESTIONS

1 Name three ways in which an organism can reproduce asexually.

2 Explain how farmers can clone their best cow.

3 Why does a cutting grow into a plant that looks the same as the parent plant?

4 List two advantages and two disadvantages of asexual reproduction.

Sexual reproduction needs male and female sex cells, called gametes, to meet and fuse together. This is called **fertilisation**. This type of reproduction takes place in most plants and animals.

Sexual reproduction in plants

Flowering plants have male and female parts. The male organs (stamens) make pollen, containing the male sex cells. The female parts (carpels) make the ova (eggs) inside an ovule. Look at Figure 2.2.1.

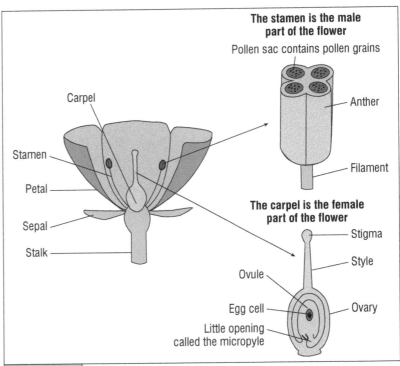

| Figure 2.2.1 | The structure of a flowering plant |

Pollination

The pollen, usually from another plant of the same species, lands on the sticky stigma. It can get there in two ways — transfer by insect and by the wind. In plants with brightly coloured petals, the pollen is likely to be transferred by insects. Insects, such as bees, are attracted by the colours and feed on the sweet-smelling, sugary nectar inside the centre of the flower. As they feed, pollen sticks to their legs and is transferred to the stigma of a neighbouring flower when the bee passes on to feed on more nectar.

Other flowering plants, such as grasses, do not need insects for pollination to take place. They grow long, feathery stamens with lots of light pollen grains that can be blown to the stigmas of other plants by the wind.

| Figure 2.2.2 | This Maraval Lily from Trinidad is an insect-pollinated plant |

Fertilisation

Once the pollen has reached the stigma, the male sex cell, or gamete, has to reach the female gamete inside the ovule. The pollen grain grows a tube down the style into the ovary. The male gamete passes down the tube and on into an ovule. There the male and female gametes join as fertilisation takes place.

The fertilised cell starts the process of division to produce a seed and the ovary turns into a fruit. Think of a tomato – you can see the seeds bedded inside the fleshy fruit that was once the ovary in a tomato plant.

Sexual reproduction in humans

Male and female humans have different sexual organs, as shown in Figure 2.2.4.

Figure 2.2.3 Grasses have long, feathery stamens

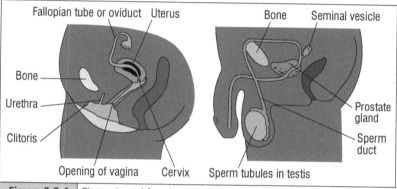

Figure 2.2.4 The male and female reproductive systems

The male gametes (sperm) are produced in the testes and stored there. Then they are released down the sperm duct and out of the penis during ejaculation. For fertilisation to take place the sperm have to meet the female gamete, the ovum (egg). This happens in sexual intercourse where the penis becomes erect and is inserted into the woman's vagina. Millions of sperm are in the ejaculated fluid. The sperm have flagella (tails), which they use to move through the cervix and into the uterus where one sperm meets the ovum. The sperm penetrates the outer layer of the ovum and fertilisation takes place.

Menstrual cycle, pregnancy and birth

- Describe the menstrual cycle and state the hormones involved.
- Explain the menopause and its effects on the body.
- State and explain the process involved in pregnancy.
- Describe the stages of labour and birth.

The menstrual cycle

Menstruation is the discharge of blood and tissue through the vagina. The discharge comes from the lining of the uterus and happens at approximately four-week intervals. Menstruation starts at puberty and lasts until the menopause (see below).

A woman's menstrual cycle is controlled by the release of **hormones**.

1 FSH (follicle stimulating hormone) released by the pituitary gland starts the monthly cycle. As its name suggests, this hormone stimulates an egg to mature in a follicle within the ovary.

2 Oestrogen is then released by the ovary. Its levels rise and cause the lining of the uterus to thicken. This is in preparation for a fertilised egg to start a pregnancy.

3 LH (luteinising hormone) is produced by the pituitary gland as the oestrogen levels fall. LH stimulates the release of the egg from the ovary into the fallopian tube. This is called **ovulation** and occurs at about day 14 of the cycle. The egg is ready to be fertilised.

4 Progesterone is then released about a week later. This causes further thickening of the lining of the uterus. However, if a fertilised egg does not implant itself there, progesterone levels fall and the lining breaks down. It is discharged through the vagina; a process lasting between two and five days. This is menstruation, known as a woman's 'period'. The falling levels of progesterone stimulate FSH production and the cycle starts again.

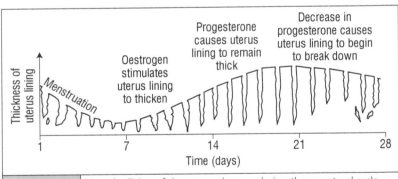

Figure 2.3.1 How the lining of the uterus changes during the menstrual cycle

The menopause

The menopause refers to the end of menstruation. Some time between the ages of 45 and 55, women stop having periods. Low oestrogen levels cause the ovaries to cease functioning. This may cause short-term symptoms such as hot flushes, irritability, dry skin and muscle aches.

LINK

For more information on sexual intercourse and fertilisation, see 2.2 'Sexual reproduction'.

Pregnancy

Pregnancy is the time between fertilisation and birth. This period of time is called the gestational period. It usually lasts for 39 weeks or 9 months in humans.

During pregnancy, the fertilised egg travels down the fallopian tube and implants itself into the lining of the uterus. The embryo grows in the uterus, attached to the mother via the placenta and umbilical cord, and develops into a foetus. The foetus is protected in the uterus by a bag of amniotic fluid. The fluid cushions the foetus if the mother gets bumped.

The mother's blood provides nutrients and removes waste products from the blood of the embryo/foetus. That is why it is important that a mother eats a good diet and avoids smoking, drugs and alcohol during pregnancy. The baby of a drug addict is born addicted to the drug and experiences nasty withdrawal symptoms.

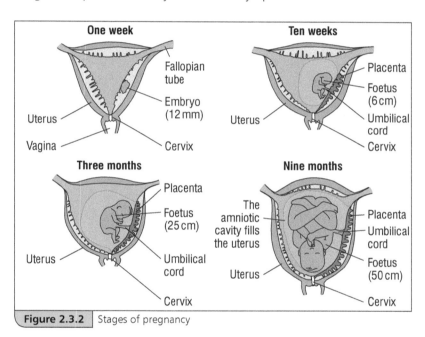

Figure 2.3.2 Stages of pregnancy

The stages of labour and birth

Labour occurs spontaneously at about 9 months and is usually completed in 24 hours.

- During the first stage of labour the muscles of the uterus start to contract. This is caused by the hormone **oxytocin**, released by the pituitary gland. This may also cause the membrane, or amnion, around the baby to break releasing the amniotic fluid. The cervix becomes thinner and widens (dilates).
- The second stage of labour commences when the cervix is fully dilated and the baby's head is delivered from the vagina.
- The third stage involves the placenta separating from the wall of the uterus and being delivered as the afterbirth. Once the placenta is delivered, the umbilical cord is clamped and cut, and the baby is given to the mother.

EXAM TIP

Doctors can sample the amniotic fluid to check for genetic abnormalities in the foetus.

KEY POINTS

1 The menstrual cycle is controlled by hormones. Menstruation occurs about every four weeks. It ceases when a woman reaches the menopause.

2 An embryo develops into a foetus in the uterus during pregnancy.

3 The hormone oxytocin starts the process of labour to give birth to a baby.

SUMMARY QUESTIONS

1 a What is menstruation?

 b Approximately how many days does the menstrual cycle take to complete?

 c What happens to an egg during ovulation?

 d Draw a table to show the hormones involved in the menstrual cycle and their effects.

2 a How does the foetus receive its nutrients during pregnancy?

 b How is the foetus protected in the uterus?

 c What role does oxytocin play in pregnancy?

- Discuss natural methods of contraception.
- Discuss barrier methods, hormonal methods and surgical methods.

Contraception

Birth control, or family planning, allows you to plan when to have children. You can also decide on the size of your family and the time interval between each child. Making an informed choice can avoid the risk of an unwanted pregnancy.

Natural methods

Method	Description	Advantages	Disadvantages
Withdrawal (coitus interruptus)	Penis withdrawn from vagina before ejaculation.	No side-effects.	Fluid secreted before ejaculation may contain sperm. No protection against sexually transmitted infections (STIs). Unreliable.
Rhythm methods Mucus (the Billings method) Temperature	More mucus is secreted at time of ovulation. This is usually more viscous, so intercourse is avoided for a few days on either side of this time. Relies on monitoring the menstrual cycle for a rise in temperature that is associated with ovulation. Intercourse needs to be avoided a few days before and after this time.	No side-effects. Method of contraception recommended by Catholic church. Can be used to plan a pregnancy. No chemicals or physical products used.	Not very reliable as ovulation may be difficult to predict – some women have irregular menstrual cycles. Need to abstain from sexual intercourse at fertile times, or use a condom or other method. It takes three or four menstrual cycles to learn effectively. You have to keep daily records of your temperature.

Barrier methods

Method	Description	Advantages	Disadvantages
Male condom	Made from very thin latex (rubber). It is put over the erect penis and stops sperm from entering the vagina.	No medical side-effects. Easy to obtain free from some clinics and sold widely. Can help protect both partners from some STIs including HIV.	Putting it on can interrupt sexual intercourse. May slip off or split if not used properly. May reduce the sensitivity of the penis.

| Diaphragm/cap with spermicide | A flexible latex or silicone dome shaped device, used with spermicide, is put into the vagina to cover the cervix. This stops sperm from entering the uterus and meeting an egg. | Can be put in at any time before sexual intercourse. No serious health risks. Offers some protection against STIs. | Putting it in can interrupt sexual intercourse. More reliable if used with spermicide, but some people can be sensitive to spermicide. Correct size needs to be known and it needs replacing if a woman changes weight, i.e. gain or loss of more than 3 kg. May be damaged during use. |

Hormonal methods

Method	Description	Advantages	Disadvantages
Contraceptive pill (also available as patch, injection or implant)	It contains oestrogen and/or progesterone. It can thicken cervical mucus to prevent sperm reaching the egg; It prevents implantation and ovulation.	Simple to take — one tablet a day; patch changed weekly; injection lasts for 12 weeks.	No protection against STIs. May have temporary side-effects, such as headaches, mood swings or depression. Increased risk of heart disease and high blood pressure. Not reliable if vomiting and diarrhoea occurs after taking or if on a course of antibiotics.

Surgical methods

Method	Description	Advantages	Disadvantages
Female sterilisation (tubal occlusion)	The fallopian tubes are cut, sealed or blocked by an operation. This stops the egg and sperm meeting.	Sterilisation is permanent with no long- or short-term serious side-effects. Once the operation is carried out there is no need to think about contraception.	Not reversible.
Male sterilisation (vasectomy)	The tubes (ducts) that carry sperm from the testicles to the penis are cut, sealed or blocked.	Permanent with no side-effects. Once the operation is carried out there is no need to think about contraception.	Usually irreversible (although the tubes can be repaired in rare cases). Some people think it might increase the risk of testicular cancer.

KEY POINT

Natural methods of contraception consist in avoiding having sex during ovulation; barrier methods do not let the sperm meet the egg; hormone methods can prevent implantation or ovulation; surgical methods prevent eggs from leaving the fallopian tubes or sperm from leaving the penis.

SUMMARY QUESTIONS

1 Describe two ways of permanently preventing conception (fertilisation) taking place.

2 Which method of contraception
   a depends on predicting monthly ovulation
   b relies on tricking the female body with hormones
   c prevents sperm from entering the vagina and protects against STIs?

Breastfeeding

The production of milk in a mother's breasts is called lactation. Colostrum is the milk produced in the first three to four days of lactation. It is a concentrated form of breast-milk. Colostrum contains all the nutrients and protective factors of breast-milk, but in higher concentrations. Babies receive protection against infection and help for their immune system from their first feed of colostrum.

A woman's body begins to make breast-milk after giving birth. Delivery of the placenta (afterbirth) causes a drop in hormones and allows milk production. When the baby suckles at the breast a hormone (oxytocin) is released into the bloodstream. This stimulates the 'let down' or milk ejection reflex. Placing a baby close to its mother after its birth, especially skin to skin, is good practice. It will increase the mother's hormone levels and milk production, as well as speeding up the bonding process.

Advantages of breastfeeding

Breast-milk:

- is at the correct temperature for the baby
- contains antibodies to help the baby fight off any infections
- contains the correct amount of proteins, carbohydrates, vitamins, minerals and fats in a form that is easy to digest
- changes as the baby grows to give it the perfect nutrients for each stage of its development
- is sterile
- does not cost anything
- helps to form a bond between the mother and baby
- reduces the risk of having diarrhoea and vomiting, chest and ear infections, constipation, eczema, as well as being obese and developing Type 2 diabetes
- reduces the risk of sudden infant death syndrome and childhood leukaemia
- reduces the risk of breast and ovarian cancer and of hip fractures in the mother.

Sometimes mothers who do not breastfeed give their babies powdered milk, or formula, from a bottle. The bottles and teats have to be sterilised. The water used to mix with the powder should not be contaminated and the mixture must be made up under sterile conditions. In some places women are not able to do this and there is a risk of babies getting infections from non-sterile formula milk or bottles.

| **Figure 2.5.1** | Breastfeeding has many health benefits for both mother and child |

Pre-natal care

Pre-natal (also called ante-natal) care monitors the woman's health during pregnancy. It also deals with the health and development of her baby.

Smoking, alcohol and drugs

Smoking is one of the most damaging factors to the health of the unborn baby. Carbon monoxide from tobacco smoke restricts the amount of oxygen carried by the red blood cells. Risks include miscarriage, stillbirth, low birth weight babies that fail to thrive and higher risk of foetal abnormalities.

Alcohol is a poison that can damage both the sperm and the ovum before conception, as well as the developing embryo. The alcohol can be passed from the mother's blood across the placenta to the baby. The main risks to the baby are mental retardation, retarded growth and damage to the brain and nervous system.

Both prescribed and recreational drugs can pass through the placenta to the baby's bloodstream. Marijuana interferes with the normal production of male sperm and the effects take three to nine months to wear off. Hard drugs, such as cocaine, heroin and morphine, can damage the chromosomes in the sperm and ovum leading to abnormalities.

Diet

It is important that the mother has a balanced diet during pregnancy so the baby gets all the nutrients it needs for growth and development.

Supplements of folic acid are recommended when trying to get pregnant and for the first 12 weeks of pregnancy. This reduces the risk of having a baby with conditions such as spina bifida.

Diseases in pregnancy and immunisation of the baby

Pathogens, like viruses and bacteria, can pass from mother to baby.

- German measles (rubella) is caused by a virus that can cross the placenta. It causes abnormalities such as deafness and heart defects.
- The HIV virus that causes AIDS may cross the placenta. Therefore, a baby may be born HIV positive if the mother is infected.
- Listeriosis and salmonella are bacterial infections. They can be picked up by eating certain foods. These include mould-ripened cheeses, such as camembert and brie, as well as raw eggs.

During the first year of life, babies are immunised against certain dangerous diseases. These diseases could cause death or lasting damage. Examples are measles, mumps and rubella (MMR), whooping cough, diphtheria, tetanus and polio.

X-rays

X-rays are high-energy electromagnetic waves. They are dangerous in high doses as they can interfere with body cells, causing cancers. They are harmful in any dose to the developing foetus. Therefore, we cannot use them to monitor development of the foetus. Instead hospitals use ultrasound – a safer wave – for scanning.

LINK

For more information on the rhesus factor in pregnancy, see 4.3 'Blood groups'.

LINK

For more information on immunisation (or vaccination), see 4.4 'Immunity'.

KEY POINTS

1. Pre-natal care looks after the needs of mothers and their unborn babies during pregnancy.

2. Post-natal care monitors the mother and baby following the birth in the baby's first year of life.

SUMMARY QUESTIONS

1. a Why is breast-milk beneficial for the development of the newborn baby?

   b Why do some mothers choose to feed their babies on formula milk mixtures?

2. Make a list of diseases that babies can be immunised against.

3. Besides diseases, make a list of other factors that can harm the unborn baby.

Sexually Transmitted Infections (STIs)

- State the major types of STIs (bacterial, viral and fungal).
- List recommended methods to prevent and control the spread of STIs.
- Discuss the use of retrovirals in treatments of HIV/AIDS.

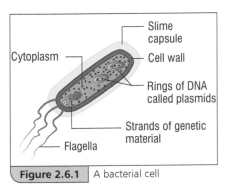

Figure 2.6.1 | A bacterial cell

BACTERIA

Bacteria are single-celled organisms, smaller than animal or plant cells. You need a powerful microscope to see them. Some bacteria have slime capsules and/or flagella. The flagella help bacteria to move around.

Bacteria cause many communicable diseases in animals and plants, and can destroy food stores. However, some bacteria are very useful, for example in making cheese or yogurt, treating sewage and making medicines. Everyone needs the 'good bacteria' found in our guts to remain healthy.

Sexually transmitted infections (STIs) are passed from one person to another during sexual activity. An STI can be caused by viruses, bacteria or parasites, such as fungus.

- Some infections are caused by bacteria such as chlamydia, gonorrhoea and syphilis. These are usually curable.
- However, infections caused by viruses such as HPV, genital herpes, hepatitis B and HIV cannot be cured.

Bacterial infections

STI	Symptoms of disease caused	Treatment
Chlamydia	Women often show no signs; perhaps a slight vaginal discharge; lower abdominal and back pain; nausea; fever.	Treated by antibiotics; if left untreated, it can cause infertility.
Gonorrhoea	First symptoms appear between 2–7 days after infection in a woman; most women show no signs; some have thick cloudy or bloody vaginal discharge and frequent urination. Men have thick yellow-green discharge from penis; sores develop on the penis and pain on urinating.	Treated with antibiotics, although some strains are resistant.
Syphilis	Painless sores on the genitals that can last 3–6 weeks then disappear; swollen glands; skin rashes.	Curable with antibiotics; if left untreated, it can lead to blindness and paralysis.

EXAM TIP

A sexually transmitted infection (STI) is the pathogen that causes the symptoms of a sexually transmitted disease (STD).

Viral infections

STI	Symptoms of disease caused	Treatment
Human Papilloma Virus (HPV)	Mostly without symptoms. A few strains cause visible warts that occur on vagina, penis, urethra or cervix.	No cure, but most infection is cleared by the body in 1–2 years.
Genital herpes	Small painful ulcers on the genitals.	No cure, but can be treated with anti-viral medicines to alleviate symptoms.
Hepatitis B	Viral infection of the liver with symptoms of jaundice – tiredness, nausea and weight loss.	No cure, but can be treated with anti-viral medication.
AIDS (Acquired Immune Deficiency Syndrome) caused by HIV (Human Immunodeficiency Virus).	Early symptoms of AIDS are very much like flu, swollen glands, raised temperature; later symptoms might include weight loss, pneumonia, types of cancer and a decrease in brain function. Not all people develop AIDS; some remain HIV positive, but without symptoms.	No cure, but treatments include anti-viral drugs, some of which prevent the virus multiplying inside the body's cells.

Fungal infection

Candida (also known as thrush) is a fungal infection. It is present in small amounts in healthy people, but may multiply in warm, dark and moist places, such as the vagina. It is not really a sexually transmitted infection, but it can be passed to another person during sex. Using a condom or abstinence will protect against this.

Its symptoms are itching and soreness of the vagina and genitals, plus a thick white or creamy vaginal discharge. It also causes discomfort or pain during sex. It is treated using anti-fungal drugs.

VIRUSES

Viruses are even smaller than bacteria. They cause disease in all living things, including plants. They get into cells, living and reproducing inside them. This damages and destroys the infected cells. Unlike bacteria, they cannot be treated with antibiotics.

FUNGI

Fungi can be single-celled or multicellular organisms. They include moulds, yeasts and mushrooms. They cause many plant diseases, but are useful in brewing and bread-making, which uses yeast. Like candida (see opposite), athlete's foot is also a fungal infection. They are treated with anti-fungal creams.

KEY POINTS

1 Sexually transmitted infections are passed between partners having unprotected sex.

2 Bacterial infections are treated with antibiotics, but there is no cure for viral infections yet.

3 Abstinence or using a condom protects against STIs.

SUMMARY QUESTIONS

1 Draw a table with three headings to show examples of bacterial and viral STIs.

2 What is candida, what are its symptoms and how can it be treated?

3 Why would somebody who ignored their symptoms of syphilis mistakenly think their problem had been solved after a couple of months? Why would this be a very serious mistake?

Growth in plants, humans and population

Germination and growth in plants

Germination is the process that occurs when a seed begins to develop into a new plant. A seed is a food store, so that the new plant can grow and develop until it has produced its own leaves. Then it can begin to photosynthesise.

To germinate and grow into a plant, the seed needs:

- energy
- oxygen
- warmth
- water.

A radicle (root) begins to grow downwards into the soil. Then a plumule (shoot) begins to grow upwards towards the light. It produces green leaves, so it can begin the process of photosynthesis. Oxygen is obtained from the air between particles of soil and is used for respiration.

Temperature is important as if it is too high or too low germination will not take place. Water in the soil helps the surface of the seed to soften and makes it easier for the radicle and plumule to grow out of the seed.

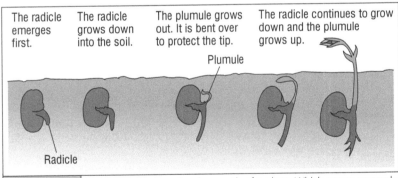

The radicle emerges first.

The radicle grows down into the soil.

The plumule grows out. It is bent over to protect the tip.

The radicle continues to grow down and the plumule grows up.

Plumule

Radicle

Figure 2.7.1 The germination and early growth of a plant. Which grows upwards – a radicle or a plumule?

The rate of plant growth can be seen by its growth curve shown in Figure 2.7.2. It follows the same pattern as most organisms. The plant cells begin dividing, but there are not many cells to start with. Then, as the number of cells increases, the rate of growth increases. There are more cells dividing so the number of cells multiplies quickly. But growth then slows down, either because of genetic factors (the plant has reached its maximum height) or environmental factors that limit growth. The growth ceases when the number of cells dividing equals the number of cells dying.

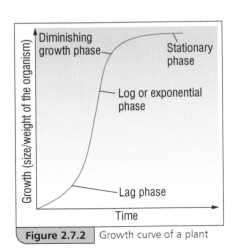

Diminishing growth phase

Stationary phase

Log or exponential phase

Lag phase

Growth (size/weight of the organism)

Time

Figure 2.7.2 Growth curve of a plant

Growth in humans

From birth, babies grow and develop quickly and by the age of one can usually sit up, feed themselves and some may be walking. By the age of two they will be starting to communicate by talking. This development continues steadily until puberty which occurs between 10 and 14.

Then there is another growth spurt and the sex organs become active. The start of puberty can vary from person to person, but girls usually develop earlier than boys. The changes that take place are controlled by hormones.

As well as physical changes these hormones can also make adolescents have mood changes and increased sexual urges.

Following puberty, girls tend to finish growing at about 18 years of age, whereas boys can keep growing slowly until about 21 years of age.

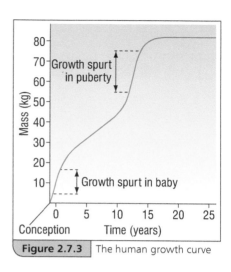

Figure 2.7.3 The human growth curve

Human population growth

The world's human **population** is about 7 billion and is growing. Feeding all these people is extremely difficult and some suffer the effects of famine.

This number of people makes great demands on the Earth's limited resources. Those in developed countries live in societies that use large amounts of energy in their daily lives. Most of this comes from non-renewable fossil fuels. Crude oil, which provides most of our fuels, will run out in a few decades. The Earth's mineral resources, from which we obtain our metals, is also dwindling. The Earth's natural resources cannot support its growing population.

Educating people in developing countries to plan a family that is sustainable is part of the solution. In developed countries there is a problem with too many unwanted teenage pregnancies – again education is needed to reduce the problem. Birth control is the major way to keep our populations manageable.

LINK

For more information on the effects of a shortage of nutrition in the diet, see 3.5 'The importance of a balanced diet'.

SUMMARY QUESTIONS

1 Draw a flow chart to describe how a seed grows into a young plant.

2 a Sketch the growth curve of a normal plant and explain its shape.

  b Do the same as part **a**, but with a human, growth curve.

3 a State two of the Earth's natural resources that will eventually run out.

  b How can the accelerating growth of the Earth's population be slowed down?

KEY POINTS

1 Germinating seeds need energy, oxygen, warmth and water in order to grow into a plant.

2 The growth curve of a plant starts off slowly and gradually speeds up before it slows down again. Eventually the plant grows new cells at the same rate as the old ones die.

3 The human growth curve has two spurts – at the start of a baby's life and at puberty.

4 The world's population is growing at a rate that cannot be sustained. Birth control will be a major part of reducing this population explosion.

3 Food and nutrition
3.1 Photochemical reactions

Some chemical reactions are affected by light. These are called **photochemical reactions**. 'Photo' refers to light; chemical reaction refers to a change in which new substances are produced. For example, in black and white photographs the film contains silver salts, such as silver chloride, which decompose in light.

In this reaction small grains of grey silver metal are formed on the film. You can see this reaction by making a precipitate (an insoluble solid) of white silver chloride using two test tubes. One test tube is put in a dark cupboard and one is left on a window sill next to some light. The one in the light turns a darker colour, whereas the one in the cupboard stays white. This shows that light energy is needed to break down the silver salt.

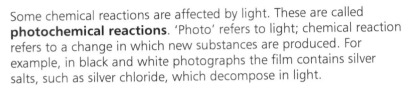

$$\text{silver chloride} \xrightarrow{\text{light energy}} \text{silver + chlorine}$$

The most important of all photochemical reactions is **photosynthesis**. This is the process used by plants to make their own food.

Photosynthesis

Plants use carbon dioxide from the air and water from the ground in photosynthesis. The starting materials, carbon dioxide (CO_2) and water (H_2O), are called the substrates. In a series of reactions in the plant, the substrates are turned into glucose ($C_6H_{12}O_6$) and oxygen (O_2) gas.

Chlorophyll, the green substance in chloroplasts inside plant cells, is needed for photosynthesis to take place. The chlorophyll absorbs light energy from the Sun. This is converted into chemical energy in the products of photosynthesis.

We can summarise photosynthesis by these equations:

$$\text{carbon dioxide + water} \xrightarrow[\text{to 'trap' light energy}]{\text{chlorophyll}} \text{glucose + oxygen}$$

$$6CO_2 + 6H_2O \longrightarrow C_6H_{12}O_6 + 6O_2$$

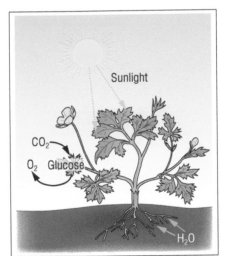

Figure 3.1.1 Summary of photosynthesis

The glucose made is used in the process of respiration to release energy that the plant can use. It is also used to make new substances in the plant. Much of the chemical energy in the glucose made from photosynthesis is stored in the plant as **starch**. Many glucose molecules bond together to make the long-chain molecules of starch.

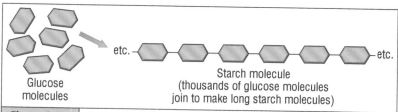

Figure 3.1.2 Glucose units link together to form starch molecules to store chemical energy

Figure 3.1.3 Plants in tropical forests get plenty of sunshine and rain, although those in the shade of the tree canopy need large leaves to collect the sunlight needed for photosynthesis

KEY POINTS

1 During photosynthesis, chlorophyll absorbs light energy which is converted into chemical energy in the products.

2 Photosynthesis can be summarised as:

carbon dioxide + water → glucose + oxygen

3 The glucose made can be turned into starch which stores chemical energy in the plant.

SUMMARY QUESTIONS

1 a Write a word equation to summarise the process of photosynthesis.

b Now write a balanced chemical equation for the same process.

2 Describe the role of chlorophyll in photosynthesis.

3 Compare the type of photochemical reactions we get in black and white photography with those in photosynthesis. How are they similar and how do they differ?

Figure 3.2.1 Planting crops on terraces helps prevent water rushing down a slope and eroding topsoil away

Soil conservation

In certain places, the topsoil (in which plants grow) can be blown away by the wind or washed away by rainwater. The soil can be removed in sheets, like a land-slide, or in channels (small ones are called rills and deeper ones are called gullies). This **soil erosion** is more likely if an area:

- has had all its plants removed, for example by over-grazing – because plant roots bind the soil together
- is on a slope – as water will flow down quickly
- is not sheltered – as the full force of the wind can do maximum damage.

Farmers can conserve their soil, protecting it from erosion, by:

- not removing all plant-life from an area
- creating flatter terraces to grow crops on a sloping site – this is expensive to set up as it requires a lot of labour and large amounts of stone and rock to support the terraces, but it does make farming the flatter land much easier than working on a slope (see Figure 3.2.1)
- planting alternate rows of crops between rows of soil-binding plants, such as grass
- sowing their crops at right angles across the slope of an inclined field – a technique called contour ploughing
- planting in long narrow strips along the contours using crop rotation (called strip planting)
- planting hedges or constructing wind-breaks around fields to shelter soil from the wind.

However, severe weather events such as hurricanes or floods can still quickly erode the soil despite the precautions in place.

Hydroponic farming

Hydroponic farmers grow plants without the use of soil. Instead, the plants are placed in solutions containing carefully controlled amounts of mineral ions (nutrients). This method of growing plants has been known about for centuries, but is now becoming more popular. It is useful where there is limited fertile farmland. As crops grow in ideal conditions in hydroponics, they yield more than crops grown on traditional farms. There is also no need for pesticides, as plants grow indoors. Another advantage is that any mineral ions left in solutions can be re-used once plants are taken to market. They are not released to pollute the environment.

Hydroponics could one day be used to feed cities, housed in multi-storey buildings. This would produce food that does not need to be transported great distances and all from a very small area of land compared to the acres used on traditional farms.

Crop rotation

Intensive farming of the same crop, year after year, in the same field will deplete the soil of nutrients. For example, soils in many Caribbean islands were badly depleted of their plant nutrients by years of monocropping of sugar cane and cotton. Farmers should change the type of crop in the field each year, so the demand on different plant nutrients changes. It is also a good idea in this crop rotation to leave a field fallow every few years. In the fallow year, no crop is grown for harvesting. Instead clover is grown. It is one of a few types of plant that can use nitrogen gas from the air for growth. Clover has root nodules that convert nitrogen into the nitrate ions plants need to make essential proteins.

At the end of the season the clover is ploughed into the field and tops up the nitrogen levels without the farmer needing to add much nitrogen fertiliser.

Greenhouse farming

Commercial greenhouses (or glasshouses) are the best way for farmers to control the conditions in which their plants grow. They can optimise the levels of light and carbon dioxide, as well as controlling temperature and providing the ideal amounts of water and nutrients (mineral ions).

However, greenhouse farming is an expensive way to grow crops so it is mainly used for specialist crops that can be sold at a high price. Large-scale crops, such as maize or sugar cane, would not be cost-effective for farmers.

Figure 3.2.2 A commercial glasshouse ensures that crops can be grown out of season

KEY POINTS

1 Soil erosion is caused by wind and rainwater, but farmers have ways of reducing the loss of topsoil.

2 Crop rotation is a way to conserve plant nutrients in the soil.

3 Greenhouse farming can provide ideal conditions for plant growth but it is expensive.

EXAM TIP

What makes a soil fertile will vary from crop to crop, as will the optimum pH for growing a crop.

SUMMARY QUESTIONS

1 a What do we mean by soil erosion?

   b List the ways in which farmers can reduce the risk of soil erosion.

2 A farmer owns four fields and can sell three different crops for a reasonable price at the end of each growing season. How could the farmer plan his planting to reduce the amount spent on fertilisers each year? Explain your answer.

3 A market gardener can get a good price for her asparagus, but in some years bad weather has spoilt her crop. How might she solve the problem and what should she consider before making her decision?

LINK

For more information about the pH of different soils, see 16.2 'The importance of soil'.

LINK

For more information about photosynthesis, see 3.1 'Photochemical reactions'.

Food chains

All the energy for life on Earth comes originally from the Sun. This energy is passed from organism to organism along food chains. A food chain shows the energy flow as the different organisms feed on each other.

Each **food chain** will start with a green plant or algae as these are able to 'capture' the Sun's energy. As plants or algae photosynthesise they use the Sun's energy in the reaction that makes their food, glucose.

$$\text{carbon dioxide} + \text{water} \xrightarrow{\text{light energy}} \text{glucose} + \text{oxygen}$$

The plant or algae at the start of a food chain is called a **producer**. All the organisms above the producer in the food chain are called consumers.

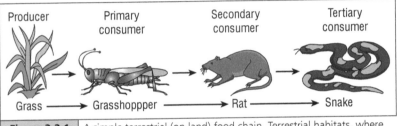

| Producer | Primary consumer | Secondary consumer | Tertiary consumer |

Grass → Grasshoppper → Rat → Snake

Figure 3.3.1 A simple terrestrial (on land) food chain. Terrestrial habitats, where food chains are found, include forests, hedgerows, fields and deserts.

In Figure 3.3.1 the producer is grass. A herbivore (plant-eater), in this case a grasshopper, eats the grass. The grasshopper is the primary consumer in the food chain. Then the grasshopper is eaten by a rat, the secondary consumer. Rats are examples of omnivores because they will eat animals or plants. The rat is then eaten by a snake, the tertiary consumer in this food chain. The snake is a carnivore (meat-eater). Energy from each organism is passed along the chain in the direction of the arrows.

This is an example of a terrestrial food chain as it takes place on land. Food chains are also found in aquatic environments such as seas, rivers, creeks and ponds. For example, this is a food chain from a lake:

algae → water snail → crayfish → crane

The lake forms the habitat where the organisms live. It is part of a wider ecosystem, which includes all the biological and physical aspects of an area.

Each stage in a food chain is called a **trophic level**. As energy is transferred up a food chain, energy is wasted between each trophic level. This is because not all the energy taken in is transferred to useful energy. Some is contained in animals' waste products. **Decomposers** will feed on these waste products. Some energy is used to keep endothermic animals warm and in moving around. So the energy passed on to the next trophic level is less than was taken in. The energy is eventually transferred to the surroundings as heat energy.

Food webs

In reality food chains do not exist in isolation. Animals seldom eat just one type of organism. In order to survive they eat a variety of plants and/or animals.

The interlinking of the linear food chains to describe the more complex feeding relationships produces a **food web**. Look at Figure 3.3.2.

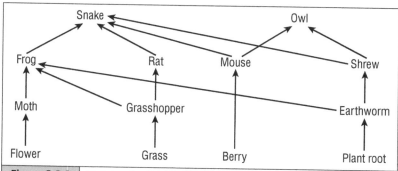

| **Figure 3.3.2** | An example of a simplified terrestrial food web. All the organisms in a food web, plus the habitat they live in, make up an ecosystem. |

The organisms in the food web form the community that live in a particular habitat. The number of any one species in the community is called its population. Any large changes in the population of a species in the food web will affect the other species in the community. For example, if a pesticide kills many of the grasshoppers in a particular habitat, then the population of rats could decrease. Decreasing the rats will mean one of the food sources of the snake is affected. They might need to eat more mice and shrews, which will affect the food stocks of the owls. With fewer shrews the earthworm population could rise, and so on.

Such changes might result in migration of a species to another habitat or a change in feeding habits in order to survive.

SUMMARY QUESTIONS

1 Here is a food chain:

flower → moth → frog → snake

a Name the secondary consumer in the food chain.

b Give an example of a carnivore and a herbivore from the food chain.

c Name the producer in the food chain.

d Describe the flow of energy in the food chain.

2 If a disease wiped out the population of snakes in the food chain in Question 1, what would be the possible consequences for the other organisms in the habitat?

KEY POINTS

1 Feeding relationships in a particular habitat can be described by food chains.

2 Food chains can be combined to form food webs.

3 Energy flows along the food chain, but is reduced at each level.

4 Changes in the population of a species in a food web have knock-on effects for the other species.

Food groups and nutrition

Figure 3.4.1 The six Caribbean food groups

A balanced diet

There is a saying, 'You are what you eat'. It is important that we are aware of the health implications of our diet. In order to stay healthy we need to eat a **balanced diet**. A balanced diet contains all the essential food nutrients we need, in the correct amounts.

Look at the poster from the Pan American Health Organisation in Figure 3.4.1. It shows how typical Caribbean foods can be classified. It also gives the recommended proportions of each needed for a balanced diet.

We can also classify foods according to the nutrition they provide. In this case we would have the following nutrients.

Carbohydrates
These are sugars and starch. They provide the energy our cells need for all the essential processes of life. Sweet foods are rich in sugar and we get starch from rice, pasta, bread, yams and cassava.

Proteins
These are needed for growth and the repair of cells. Meat, fish, eggs, milk, nuts and beans are good sources of protein.

Fats/oils
These are stores of energy and help to keep your body warm. Fats and oils are used to fry foods. They are contained in margarine, butter and anything made using these, such as cakes, pastries and biscuits.

Vitamins
There are 13 types of vitamin which help the body perform vital functions. They regulate the body's metabolism. Although we only need small amounts of the different types, without them the body will start to suffer. For example, vitamin D helps the body to absorb calcium ions. These are needed for healthy teeth and bones. Without vitamin D children develop a **deficiency disease** called rickets where the legs become 'bowed' outwards.

Fruit and green vegetables are rich in vitamins. For example, citrus fruit supplies us with vitamin C. Without vitamin C we would get the deficiency disease scurvy.

Minerals
Like vitamins, minerals help the body build essential materials and help vital chemical reactions take place. They are absorbed in the body as ions. Ions are charged particles, such as the calcium ions for teeth and bones just mentioned. We need about 15 different minerals to stay healthy.

Other essential nutrients in a balanced diet are:

Water
About two-thirds of your body is water. Most of the reactions in your body happen in solutions made with water. It also helps to cool your body when you sweat.

Fibre

This isn't really a nutrient as it is not absorbed into the body. However, it does play an important role in moving solid waste through and out of your body.

Food tests

Most foods contain mixtures of different nutrients, but some are well-known sources of one particular type. For example, rice, bread and pasta are good sources of carbohydrates in the form of starch. Boiled rice contains about 23% carbohydrate, but also has a little protein (2.2%) and only 0.1% fat.

We can identify the major nutrients in food using some simple food tests.

Starch

Starch will turn brown iodine solution to a blue-black colour.

Reducing sugars

Sugars, such as glucose, are also carbohydrates. Sucrose is the sugar you put in tea and coffee. We can test for the sugars called reducing sugars, of which glucose is one, using Benedict's solution. This is a blue solution. When we heat a solution containing a reducing sugar, the solution turns orange or red. You get a positive test with glucose and fructose (but not with sucrose unless it is broken down by acid first).

Proteins

If a food contains protein it will turn blue Biuret solution violet. Look at Figure 3.4.2.

Fats and oils

Add the food to a little ethanol in a test tube and shake it. Pour the liquid off into a second test tube, leaving any solid behind. Add the same amount of water to the liquid in the test tube and shake again. A white suspension in the liquid shows the presence of fat. Alternatively, place the food on a piece of brown paper and see if it leaves a translucent mark.

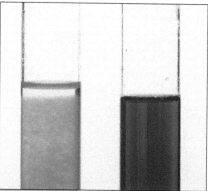

Figure 3.4.2 Biuret solution turns from blue to violet in the presence of a soluble protein

KEY POINTS

1 There are six Caribbean food groups: staples; legumes; foods from animals; fruits; vegetables; fats/oils.

2 The nutrients we get from food are: carbohydrates; proteins; fats/oils; vitamins; minerals. Water and fibre are also essential for a balanced diet.

3 A balanced diet has all the essential food nutrients, in the correct amounts.

4 Positive food tests include: Benedict's solution turns orange/red when heated with a reducing sugar; Biuret solution turns violet with protein; fats leave a translucent mark on brown paper (or filter paper).

SUMMARY QUESTIONS

1 What are the components of a balanced diet?

2 a What do you understand by the term 'deficiency disease'?

  b Identify two deficiency diseases and state the nutrient(s) lacking.

3 How would you test a sample of powdered milk to determine its nutrient composition?

The importance of a balanced diet

People who eat an 'unbalanced' diet over a significant time will become malnourished. There are various types of malnutrition, from the deficiency diseases mentioned in 3.4 (rickets, scurvy) to obesity (excess energy intake) and Protein Energy Malnutrition (insufficient protein and energy intake).

Obesity

There is some concern in the Caribbean (and in many other parts of the world) about the modern-day diet. A growing number of people are becoming obese (very overweight, with a Body Mass Index of over 30).

Nutritionists and dieticians advise us what we should eat and in what quantities. Too much fried food is not good for you and should be avoided. Your body stores fat under your skin and around the organs of your body. Fatty deposits can line the inside of your arteries, increasing the risk of:

- type 2 diabetes
- heart disease
- high blood pressure.

All of these are potentially life-threatening conditions if left untreated. Eating too much saturated animal fat is the main cause of these conditions. On one Caribbean island, figures show that half of the islanders will suffer from hypertension (high blood pressure) by the age of 45 years.

How much energy do we need?

In order to lose weight, people must transfer more energy from their cells than is taken in when they eat. But how much energy a person needs each day varies. It depends on your age, whether you are male or female and how much physical activity you do, for example in your job or in your leisure time (such as sports). Look at the table below.

Person	Energy requirements each day (kJ/day)
Pregnant woman	10 000
Teenage boy	12 500
Man doing manual work	15 000
Young girl	8500
Inactive man over 50 years old	8500
Inactive woman over 50 years old	6750

People require less energy as they get older because their metabolic rate slows down and they tend to be less active. Young people need more energy for the reactions in their body to make new proteins for growth. They usually transfer lots of energy as they play. However, there is concern that video and computer games result in young people doing less physical activity in their spare time than in the past. This and over-eating mean that childhood obesity is becoming more common. This can go on to cause early-onset diabetes in young adults.

Protein Energy Malnutrition (PEM)

Starvation causes Protein Energy Malnutrition (PEM). Lack of food will result in conditions known as kwashiorkor and marasmus. Children suffering from kwashiorkor have a swollen abdomen, with retarded growth and muscle wastage. Without enough energy being taken in, the body starts to break down protein for energy. Marasmus is similar, but children look very drawn around the face and do not have the distended abdomen.

Food additives

Many foods have substances added to improve:

- appearance, for example colourings
- shelf life, for example preservatives
- texture, for example emulsifiers
- taste, for example flavourings and flavour enhancers.

You can see these **food additives** listed on the contents label on cans and packaging.

Some people are worried about the effects of adding artificial chemicals to our food. However, all additives are tested for safety before use with consumers.

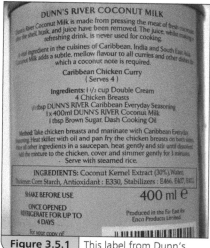

Figure 3.5.1 This label from Dunn's River Coconut milk shows some of the additives used routinely in some parts of the food industry

SUMMARY QUESTIONS

1 What are the health problems caused by obesity?

2 Put the following in order of daily energy requirements, starting with most energy:

a bed-ridden 70-year-old; a sprinter in training; a 9-year-old girl; a pregnant woman.

3 Name two conditions caused by PEM.

4 a Why does the food industry use additives in products?

   b Make a list of 10 food additives from the labels of some common processed foods.

   c Draw a table of the advantages and disadvantages of using food additives. Use the internet to find out health issues associated with certain food additives. Why could the information on some websites be biased?

KEY POINTS

1 Over-eating and under-eating cause malnutrition.

2 Over-eating high-energy foods, such as carbohydrates and fats, leads to obesity. This causes an increased risk of heart attacks, strokes and diabetes.

3 The energy needed by different people depends on gender, occupation and age.

4 Starvation causes PEM.

5 Food additives can improve the colour, texture, taste and shelf life of foods. However, some might cause conditions such as hyperactivity in children.

Digestion

- State the difference between mechanical and chemical digestion.
- Describe the role of enzymes in chemical digestion.
- Identify the parts of the digestive system and explain their functions.
- Explain the words absorption, assimilation and egestion.

We need to digest our food to make use of its essential nutrients. In many foods the nutrients are present as large, insoluble molecules. These include starch, protein and fats. In **digestion** the large, insoluble molecules are converted into small, soluble molecules. The small molecules can then pass through the gut wall into the blood to be transported around your body.

Figure 3.6.1 shows the digestive system.

Mechanical digestion

This is the physical process of breaking up pieces of food into smaller bits. There are no chemical reactions involved so no new substances are made. The molecules remain intact. This process starts with your teeth cutting and grinding food into small bits as you bite and then chew it. The process continues as the food is squeezed by muscles as it passes down the tube (oesophagus) that leads from your mouth to your stomach.

The process of muscular contractions that passes food through the digestive system is called **peristalsis**.

Chemical digestion

Chemical digestion is the process that actually breaks down the large molecules into smaller ones. **Enzymes** in our digestive juices carry out this function. Enzymes are soluble proteins that act as biological catalysts. Different enzymes are needed to break down different types of food molecules.

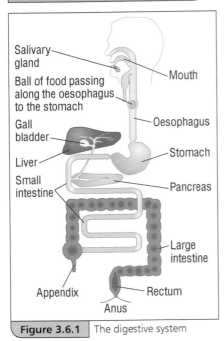

Salivary gland
Ball of food passing along the oesophagus to the stomach
Gall bladder
Liver
Small intestine
Appendix
Mouth
Oesophagus
Stomach
Pancreas
Large intestine
Rectum
Anus

Figure 3.6.1 | The digestive system

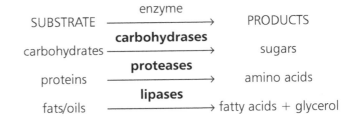

SUBSTRATE $\xrightarrow{\text{enzyme}}$ PRODUCTS

carbohydrates $\xrightarrow{\textbf{carbohydrases}}$ sugars

proteins $\xrightarrow{\textbf{proteases}}$ amino acids

fats/oils $\xrightarrow{\textbf{lipases}}$ fatty acids + glycerol

Varying pH in the digestive system

Enzymes work best in particular pH ranges. The digestive system is adapted to create the best pH for the different enzymes in different parts of the system. For example, in your mouth, saliva has a pH between 6.5 and 7.5 to suit the enzyme called salivary amylase. It breaks down starch (a carbohydrate) into maltose (a sugar).

Further down the digestive system we have food arriving at the stomach that has a pH of about 2.0. Our gastric juices contain hydrochloric acid in which pepsin (a protease) starts the breakdown of protein molecules into smaller chain molecules (called peptides).

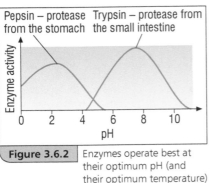

Pepsin – protease from the stomach   Trypsin – protease from the small intestine

Figure 3.6.2 | Enzymes operate best at their optimum pH (and their optimum temperature)

Then in the small intestine the pH is increased by bile and juices from the pancreas and intestines. The bile, which is made by the liver, emulsifies (physically splits up) globules of fats and oils into tiny droplets. The lipases can break down the fats into glycerol and fatty acids. In this higher pH, different proteases help to break down proteins and peptides into amino acids. For example, trypsin works best at pH 7.8 to 8.7.

Absorption and assimilation

The smaller, soluble molecules produced by digestion then pass through the walls of the small intestine by diffusion or active transport. Active transport can move molecules against a concentration gradient.

To make absorption easier, the surface area of the small intestine is very large. Its surface is folded and covered in villi (see Figure 3.6.3). These are like tiny fingers sticking out from the surface. They have capillaries (thin blood vessels) that carry the absorbed food molecules away to the bloodstream.

These molecules arrive at cells where they cross the cell membrane and are assimilated (changed) into substances needed by the body. For example, amino acids are assimilated into proteins to build muscle.

Egestion

The remaining material is passed out of the small intestine into the large intestine (or colon). There, much of the water from the digestive juices is reabsorbed. Otherwise the body would end up dehydrated. The solid waste is called faeces. It passes from the large intestine into the rectum before it leaves the body (is egested) from the anus.

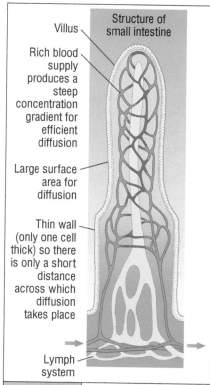

Figure 3.6.3 Villi line the surface of the intestine to absorb the soluble molecules produced in digestion

SUMMARY QUESTIONS

1 Draw a flow chart showing the parts of the digestive system. Include a key that explains the function of each part.

2 Why are the villi important in the process of absorption?

3 a What are the products formed when the following food types are digested?
   i   proteins   ii carbohydrates   iii fats
  b What is the general name given to enzymes that digest?
   i   proteins   ii carbohydrates   iii fats

4 Explain the difference between digestion and egestion.

KEY POINTS

1 Large, insoluble food molecules are broken down during digestion into small soluble molecules.

2 Mechanical digestion breaks pieces of food physically into smaller bits.

3 The smaller bits of food can be more easily chemically digested by enzymes.

4 The enzymes break the molecules into smaller molecules that can pass into the bloodstream by way of villi in the small intestine.

5 Waste material is then egested at the end of the process.

Microorganisms and food preservation

- List the conditions that promote the growth of microorganisms.
- Describe the effects of microorganisms in food.
- Describe different methods of food preservation.

Figure 3.7.1 You can easily see the mould that grows on stale bread. You can help prevent mould by storing bread in a dark place at room temperature and sealing it so no moisture can get to it. Bread can be stored in a freezer

Most microorganisms need the following conditions in order to grow:

- warmth
- moisture
- a neutral pH
- a good food supply, for example sugars, proteins.

Their food supply can be foods meant for human consumption. If untreated foods are contaminated with microorganisms, in favourable growing conditions, the foods will go off. You have probably seen, and smelt, what happens when milk is left out of the fridge too long or when we keep bread too long.

The growth of mould on bread is easy to spot. However, some microorganisms, such as bacteria in meat, can be difficult to see and can be harmful to humans. They are called **pathogens**.

In order to protect our food from microorganisms, people have developed ways of preserving food. Here are some methods used.

Salting

This ancient method can be used with fish and meat. The salt inhibits the growth of bacteria. Water leaves the bacterial cells by osmosis, shrivelling up the bacteria as it gets dehydrated.

Figure 3.7.2 Salted fish are a popular food in the Caribbean

Drying

Microorganisms need water to thrive. So allowing foods to dry out helps to preserve them. The water can be removed by drying in the air, such as sun-dried tomatoes, by warming a food to evaporate off the water or by the more modern method of freeze-drying.

Pickling

The microorganisms that cause harm to humans when digested mainly grow best in nearly neutral pH conditions. Pickling consists in preserving food in vinegar, containing about 10% ethanoic acid. This lowers the pH so that enzymes in the bacteria are de-activated (denatured) in these acidic conditions.

Heating

This is usually used with liquids, such as fruit juices, milk and low-alcohol drinks. The process heats the liquid for a prescribed time then cools it quickly. This kills most of the bacteria and enables the liquid to have a reasonable shelf life. For example, milk can be pasteurised by heating to just above 70°C for about 15 seconds, then cooling it quickly to 4°C.

Refrigeration

The action of enzymes is slowed down at low temperatures, slowing down the reactions that make food spoil. So fridges are set at temperatures around 5°C. If temperatures of 0°C and lower are used (as in a freezer), the water in the food freezes. This means that microorganisms have no liquid water available so they cannot function.

Adding sugar

This works like salting, as water leaves the bacterial cells by osmosis to pass into the syrup, which has a lower concentration of water. This dehydrates the bacteria.

Adding preservatives

Food companies can add substances to inhibit bacterial growth or stop the reaction with oxygen that make the food go off. For example, if you look on food packaging you might see the preservatives benzoic acid, sorbic acid or sulphur dioxide listed. These all create acidic conditions, so bacteria cannot multiply.

LINK

For more information about osmosis, see 1.3 'Diffusion and osmosis'.

KEY POINTS

1 Microorganisms need warm, moist conditions with a neutral pH and a food supply to multiply.

2 Microorganisms spoil food so methods of preserving foods have been developed over time. These rely on killing microorganisms or making sure they do not get the conditions they need to thrive.

SUMMARY QUESTIONS

1 Before the days of refrigeration, how did sailors on long voyages make sure their meat did not go off?

2 List the methods of food preservation and think of a way to classify them into groups. Show your results in a table.

3 Plan an investigation to find out which factors promote the growth of mould on bread.

As you saw in 3.6, the teeth start off the process of mechanical digestion of food. They can cut, tear and grind food into small enough pieces for us to swallow. This physical breakdown of the food also helps the work of enzymes in chemical digestion. That's because the enzymes have a larger surface area to attack and break down the large food molecules.

Figure 3.8.1 below shows the parts that make up a tooth.

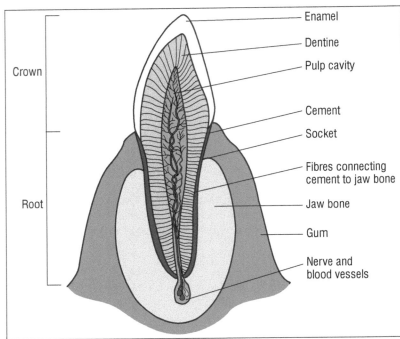

Figure 3.8.1 The general structure of a tooth

To do their job well, humans have different types of teeth. Their teeth have evolved to cope with eating both plants and animals as food.

Children usually have 20 baby teeth that are replaced by 28 to 32 permanent teeth. (Your back four molars may not erupt through your gums.) Look at Figure 3.8.2 opposite to see the types and location of the different types of teeth in your mouth.

Using dental formulae

We can use a dental formula to represent the number and types of teeth found in one half of the upper and lower jaw.

In a child: I 2/2 C 1/1 PM 0/0 M 2/2 = 10 teeth, where I = incisors, C = canines, PM (or P) = premolars and M = molars. The numbers show the number of teeth in the upper quarter/lower quarter. Thus doubling the total in the dental formula gives us the number of teeth in the mouth of a child, i.e. 20.

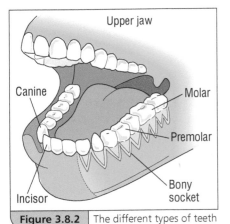

Figure 3.8.2 The different types of teeth

In an adult: I 2/2 C 1/1 PM 2/2 M 3/3 = 16. Thus doubling it gives the number of teeth in the mouth of an adult, i.e. 32 (which includes the wisdom teeth).

The dental formula can also be used to show the teeth in other animals, for example a cat: I 3/3 C 1/1 PM 3/2 M 1/1.

Each of the four types of tooth is shaped to carry out its particular function.

The function of different teeth

Type of tooth	Shape	Its function
Incisor	Broad, flat, chisel shaped	Biting and cutting food
Canine	Pointed	Tearing food
Premolar	Broad flat crown with ridges, two roots	Tearing and grinding food
Molar	Broad flat crown with ridges, three roots	Grinding and crushing food

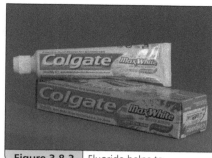

Figure 3.8.3 Fluoride helps to prevent tooth decay by strengthening the enamel that coats your teeth

SUMMARY QUESTIONS

1 Draw a labelled diagram to show the general structure of a tooth.

2 Why are teeth contributors to mechanical digestion and not chemical digestion?

3 Sketch the shape of the visible parts of an incisor, canine, premolar and molar tooth, and relate this to its function in mechanical digestion.

KEY POINTS

1 Adults can have 32 teeth. These are incisors, canines, premolars and molars.

2 The shapes of the different types of teeth are matched to their functions.

4.1 Transport systems in plants

LINK

For more information about photosynthesis, see 3.1 'Photochemical reactions'.

To maintain life, all living things need a way to exchange substances with their environment. They need to take in the essential nutrients and water they need. Then, they transport materials to the cells that need them and also transport waste products back out into the environment.

Transport in plants

Plants need carbon dioxide and water to photosynthesise. They take in carbon dioxide from the air through tiny holes in the surface of their leaves called **stomata**. These are usually in the underside of leaves. Special guard cells control the opening and closing of the stomata.

Plants do not photosynthesise all the time. For example, the guard cells close the stomata at night. Look at Figure 4.1.1 below. The cells in which photosynthesis takes place are usually near the stomata, so the gases haven't got to travel far.

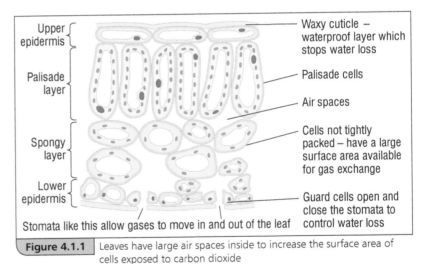

Upper epidermis — Waxy cuticle – waterproof layer which stops water loss

Palisade layer — Palisade cells

Air spaces

Spongy layer — Cells not tightly packed – have a large surface area available for gas exchange

Lower epidermis — Guard cells open and close the stomata to control water loss

Stomata like this allow gases to move in and out of the leaf

Figure 4.1.1 Leaves have large air spaces inside to increase the surface area of cells exposed to carbon dioxide

Plants have two transport systems for moving materials larger distances.

- The **xylem** transports water and mineral ions around the plant.
- The **phloem** transports the glucose made during photosynthesis around the plant.

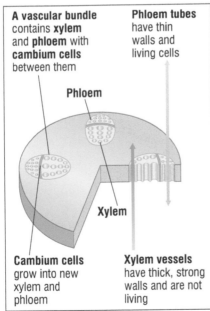

A vascular bundle contains **xylem** and **phloem** with **cambium cells** between them

Phloem tubes have thin walls and living cells

Phloem

Xylem

Cambium cells grow into new xylem and phloem

Xylem vessels have thick, strong walls and are not living

Figure 4.1.2 Transport in a plant – xylem carries the water and mineral ions around and phloem carries the glucose around. Xylem and phloem are vascular bundles of tissue.

Transporting water, mineral ions and glucose

The other substrate needed for photosynthesis is water. This is taken up through the roots. It is transported to the chloroplasts in cells in the green parts of the plant through the xylem. It is drawn up from the roots to replace water lost from the leaves by evaporation. Each root cell is adapted with a long protrusion that gets between soil particles. This maximises the surface area in contact with the very dilute solutions of mineral ions in the soil. Water enters the root cells by osmosis and the mineral ions enter them by active transport against a concentration gradient.

This water evaporates out of the leaves through the stomata. So when the stomata are open to allow carbon dioxide into the leaf, water can also escape from the leaf. As the water escapes, more is drawn up through the xylem to replace it. This loss of water vapour is called **transpiration**.

The glucose made in photosynthesis travels through the phloem tubes to the rest of the cells in the plant. The glucose is needed for respiration in all plant cells or in the growing regions to make new molecules.

Factors affecting transpiration

The rate at which plants lose water in transpiration depends on how favourable the conditions are for photosynthesis and evaporation of water. So transpiration will be fastest when it is:

- hot and not too humid (so water molecules have more energy and can escape more easily into drier air)
- sunny (so stomata are open to maximise photosynthesis)
- windy (so water molecules are removed from around the leaf so the air does not get saturated with water).

LINK

For more information about osmosis, see 1.3 'Diffusion and osmosis'.

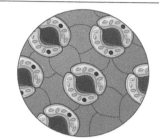

Open stomata

Closed stomata

Figure 4.1.3 | Stomata open to let carbon dioxide into leaves for photosynthesis. At the same time this lets water vapour escape, which can make the plant wilt.

EXAM TIP

Stomata are never completely closed – see Figure 4.1.3.

KEY POINTS

1 Transport systems in living things are needed to exchange materials with the environment and move substances around inside the organism to where they are needed.

2 In plants, the transports systems are xylem (for water and mineral ions) and phloem (for glucose).

3 Plants lose water through transpiration, which supplies the force needed to enable the movement of water up the plant from the roots.

SUMMARY QUESTIONS

1 What is the difference between the functions of xylem and phloem?

2 Explain how the transport of water through a plant is aided by transpiration.

3 Explain the factors that affect the rate of transpiration.

4 How are transport systems different for organisms made of one cell compared with those made of many cells? Why are the differences in the structure of the respiratory systems necessary?

The human circulatory system

The human circulatory system is made up of the heart, the blood and its various blood vessels.

Blood is a mixture made up of plasma, red blood cells, platelets and white blood cells. Figure 4.2.1 shows the composition of blood.

Plasma – this straw-coloured watery liquid makes up most of the blood. It contains the red blood cells and the white blood cells. It also contains small bits of cells called platelets which help in clotting the blood.

Plasma transports the small molecules from digestion such as glucose and amino acids, mineral ions, waste products and various proteins and hormones.

Red blood cells – these 'biconcave discs' transport oxygen from the lungs to cells all round the body. The oxygen bonds temporarily to a **haemoglobin** molecule in the red blood cell and releases the oxygen at tissues.

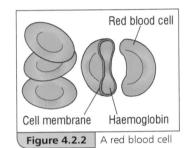

Figure 4.2.2 | A red blood cell

White blood cells – these help to protect us against disease. There are two types of white blood cell – phagocytes, which engulf pathogens, and lymphocytes, which produce antibodies to destroy pathogens. These form part of our immune system.

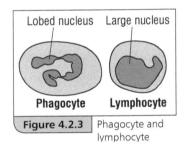

Figure 4.2.3 | Phagocyte and lymphocyte

The blood vessels

There are three types of blood vessel to carry blood around your body.

- Arteries – to carry blood away from your heart
- Veins – to carry blood back to your heart
- Capillaries – to link the arteries and veins.

Figure 4.2.1 | The composition of blood

- 10 cm³
- Plasma – liquid part of blood (55% of blood volume)
- 5 cm³
- White blood cells and platelets
- Red blood cells

Artery	Vein	Capillary
• thick muscular wall, capable of constricting • small lumen • transports blood from the heart (oxygenated except in the pulmonary artery) • blood under high pressure, moving rapidly, in pulses	• thin muscular wall, with no constriction • large lumen • transports blood to the heart (deoxygenated except in the pulmonary vein) • blood flows slowly, under low pressure	• no muscle • large lumen • no constriction • links arteries to veins • blood changes from oxygenated to deoxygenated • flows slowly, under reducing pressure

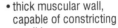

Lumen (opening) — Lumen — Lumen

Figure 4.2.4 | Structure of an artery, vein and capillary

The heart

The heart is a muscular organ that pumps the blood around your body. It is about the size of your fist. Figure 4.2.5 shows its structure.

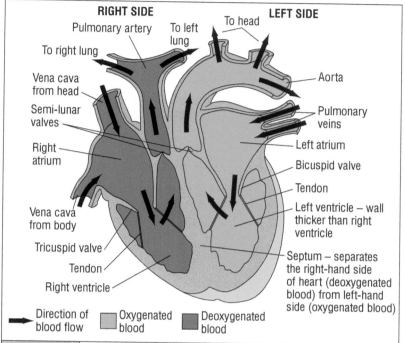

Figure 4.2.5 | The structure of the heart

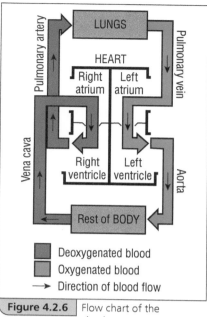

Figure 4.2.6 | Flow chart of the circulatory system

- The heart acts as a double pump. The right-hand side pumps blood away from the heart and the blood returns to the left-hand side.
- Blood comes through veins into the atria chambers at the top of the heart. Oxygenated blood from the lungs arrives into the left atrium. Deoxygenated blood arrives back into the right atrium.
- The atria contract to force the blood down into the ventricles.
- Then the ventricles contract to pump the blood out of the heart down the arteries. The right ventricle sends deoxygenated blood to the lungs to receive more oxygen and get rid of carbon dioxide. The left ventricle sends oxygenated blood to tissues all around the body (this needs stronger muscle than the right ventricle).
- Valves are needed in the heart to make sure blood flows in the right direction and prevent 'backflow'.

KEY POINTS

1 The blood is made up of plasma, red blood cells and white blood cells, with a small amount of platelets.

2 Arteries take blood from the heart; blood returns to the heart through veins; capillaries are the thin blood vessels that link the arteries and veins.

3 The heart pumps blood around the body, acting as a double pump.

SUMMARY QUESTIONS

1 a What makes up most of your blood?

   b Which part of blood helps fight infections?

   c Which part of blood delivers oxygen to cells?

   d What is the role of platelets?

2 Draw a table to summarise the structure and function of the different types of blood vessels.

3 Look at Figure 4.2.5.

   a Which artery takes blood to the lungs?

   b Which atrium does blood from the lungs arrive back into?

   c Which ventricle has the thicker muscle? Why?

   d What separates the two sides of the heart?

   e What stops blood back-flowing in the heart?

Blood groups

LEARNING OUTCOMES

- Name the four blood groups.
- Explain antigens and antibodies.
- Discuss precautions in blood transfusions.
- Explain the rhesus factor (Rh) and blood groups.

Antigens are molecules at the surface of cells that cause an immune response in the body. The response is from **antibodies** in your blood plasma. Antibodies can attach themselves to the antigens, causing the cells to clump together (known as agglutination). The antigens on 'foreign' cells allow cells to be recognised as being from outside your body. Your body's antibodies can recognise their own antigens so do not bind to them.

Antigens and antibodies in different blood groups

Red blood cells can have different antigens on their surface (cell membrane). There are two types of antigen, labelled as A and B. This means there are four types of blood:

- A (with just A antigens)
- B (with just B antigens)
- AB (with both A and B antigens)
- O (with no antigens).

Your blood will make antibodies to attack blood cells that are from a different blood group from your own. We represent the antibodies that attack a particular antigen by its lower case letter. For example, antigen B will be attacked by antibody b. So if you are blood group B, your blood will have a-type antibodies. It will not have b antibodies or it would attack its own blood. The table below shows the antigens and antibodies in each blood group.

Blood group	Antigens present on red blood cells	Antibodies present in plasma
A	A	b
B	B	a
AB	A and B	none
O	none	a and b

Blood transfusions

Only certain types of blood can be given to a person after an accident or during an operation. If the wrong type is given, antibodies will attack the red blood cells causing them to clump together. For example, b antibodies in blood group A would attack the red blood cells with antigen B if blood group B was received.

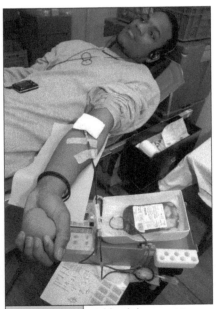

Figure 4.3.1 A blood donor soon replaces the 500 cm³ of blood donated

The table below shows which blood groups are compatible with each other.

		Blood group of the recipient (receiver)			
		A	B	AB	O
Blood group of the donor (giver)	A	yes	no	yes	no
	B	no	yes	yes	no
	AB	no	no	yes	no
	O	yes	yes	yes	yes

For example, we can explain the last column in the table. If you are blood group O, you have antibodies of both a and b. So if you are given blood from groups A, B or AB, red blood cells will stick together and ultimately be broken down. This means you are incompatible with blood groups A, B and AB and only a transfusion of blood group O would work.

Rhesus factor

Another antigen was discovered on red blood cells from research done on rhesus monkeys. The antigen was given the letter D. Humans do not have the d antibodies naturally to attack this.

However, we can make the antibody that will attack rhesus positive blood if exposed to it. So people are now checked to see if their blood is rhesus positive (Rh+) or rhesus negative (Rh−), as well as which blood group they are. Your medical records will show this if you have been tested in case you need a blood transfusion.

The rhesus factor can cause complications in pregnancy. As your blood group is inherited, sometimes a mother can be rhesus negative, while the foetus is rhesus positive from the father.

Near the end of the pregnancy some blood cells can pass into the mother from the foetus. The mother will now make antibody d to attack the 'foreign' red blood cells. These can then pass into the foetus and will attack its red blood cells with antigen D.

The breakdown of some of the first born baby's red blood cells is not usually a problem. However, in subsequent pregnancies, the mother's blood will have more d antibodies that pass into the foetus. The foetus will need blood transfusions while in the womb, otherwise its own red blood cells will be broken down, which would be fatal for the foetus.

To get around this problem, the mother can be injected with d antibodies after her first pregnancy. This destroys all the rhesus blood cells from the foetus. So she will not continue to make her own d antibodies that could attack the next rhesus-positive foetus.

SUMMARY QUESTIONS

1 Name the four blood groups.

2 a Explain why someone with blood group A could not receive a blood transfusion from a donor of blood group B.

  b Explain why blood from donors of blood group O will be easier to match than other blood groups.

  c Which blood group can receive blood donated by an AB donor? Why?

3 Explain how a rhesus-negative pregnant mother and a rhesus-positive father can give rise to problems in their foetus.

Immunity

Preventing disease

Diseases are caused by pathogens (microorganisms such as bacteria or viruses) entering the body. The body's white blood cells are its defence once a pathogen gets into your body.

We have seen in 4.3 that antibodies are produced in the blood. These are made by lymphocytes to help us get rid of 'foreign' cells that enter our bodies. Phagocytes can finish off the job by engulfing the invading cells and breaking them down with enzymes.

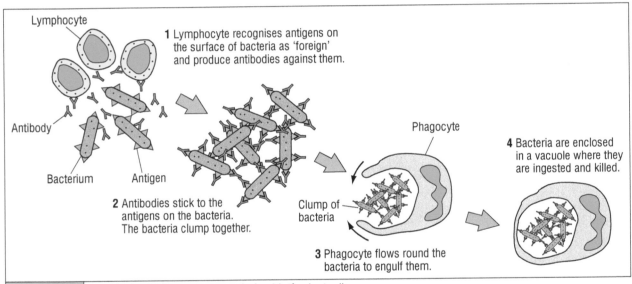

Figure 4.4.1 | How the body's immune system deals with 'foreign' cells

Vaccination

It takes some time for the lymphocytes to generate the antibodies needed to attack a particular pathogen. In this time the pathogen can be multiplying rapidly and you get the symptoms of the disease. So it is best if we can get protection against certain diseases by **vaccination**. This is also known as **immunisation**.

In vaccination, we receive a pathogen's antigens in a vaccine, usually by an injection. This stimulates your white blood cells to produce antibodies against that particular antigen. The antibodies are then ready to deal with that pathogen as soon as it enters your body. The pathogen cannot multiply so you do not get the symptoms of the disease. You have **immunity** against that disease.

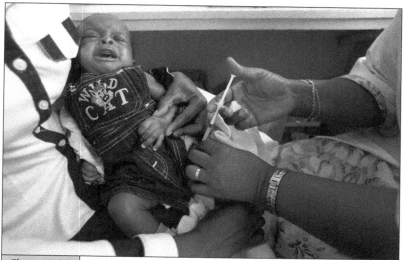

Figure 4.4.2 A baby receives vaccinations against several diseases, such as measles, mumps and rubella, in the first year of its life

Your body can carry on making antibodies once the pathogen has been dealt with. That is why you only get measles once. So a vaccine against measles will not need 'topping up', unlike some others that only work for a certain time. For example, you might have received a booster vaccination for tetanus.

The antigens used in vaccines are often delivered on dead microorganisms that cannot reproduce. Vaccines against typhoid, cholera and whooping cough are made like this. Other pathogens in vaccines may be living, but they have been de-activated in some way so they cannot multiply. These include vaccines against measles, rubella, polio and tuberculosis (TB).

HIV/AIDS

Viruses work by penetrating cells and multiplying with them, destroying the host cell. HIV (Human Immunodeficiency Virus) is a relatively new virus, first diagnosed in 1982. It enters cells that are part of your immune system, called T-helper cells. HIV gets into these cells via an infected individual, usually through unprotected sexual intercourse or by sharing needles to inject drugs.

The virus can lie dormant in the T-helper cells for years before it starts to multiply. At that stage, full-blown AIDS (Acquired Immune Deficiency Syndrome) develops. The infected person becomes open to infection from other pathogens as their immune system is severely damaged by the virus. A secondary disease is usually the cause of death. At present there is no vaccine available against HIV, but research continues, with some positive results reported in 2016. HIV can be successfully treated by combinations of drugs called anti-retroviral therapy. This does not cure AIDS, but stops progression to full-blown AIDS.

KEY POINTS

1 White blood cells defend us against pathogens. Lymphocytes produce antibodies which bind to antigens on the surface of pathogens. The pathogens clump together and are ingested by phagocytes.

2 Vaccination stimulates the production of antibodies against certain diseases.

SUMMARY QUESTIONS

1 Explain the different actions of a lymphocyte and a phagocyte in destroying a pathogen.

2 Describe how vaccination protects us against a disease.

3 a Describe how a person infected with HIV can eventually die of AIDS.

b Carry out some research and write a short information sheet on the latest treatments for people with HIV/AIDS.

High blood pressure and its effects

What causes high blood pressure?

People suffer from high blood pressure (hypertension) when the arteries become narrower. The inside of an artery is usually smooth and wide enough to allow a good flow of blood. However, a diet with too much saturated animal fat, such as butter, milk, red meat and cheese, can affect your arteries. Fatty deposits of cholesterol can build up inside arteries. This makes it more difficult for blood to flow through. Therefore, a higher pressure is needed to pump the same volume of blood around the body at the same rate.

Figure 4.5.1 Blood pressure is usually measured in units called millimetres of mercury (sometimes written as mm Hg). Two numbers are quoted – the systolic pressure of blood leaving the heart, normally between 110 and 140 mm Hg, and the diastolic pressure of blood returning to the heart, normally between 70 and 90 mm Hg.

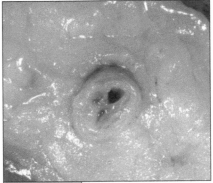

Figure 4.5.2 An artery with the area of its lumen (opening) narrowed by fatty deposits. This is called **atherosclerosis**.

As well as fatty foods, other factors cause high blood pressure. These include:

- alcohol consumption
- smoking
- too much salt in the diet
- diabetes
- stress
- not enough exercise
- obesity
- genetic factors.

Effects of high blood pressure

Over time, high blood pressure increases the risk of:

- heart failure
- heart attack
- stroke
- kidney failure
- diabetes.

When arteries become blocked your heart has to work harder to pump blood around your body. If this carries on over a long time the heart will suffer failure.

Sometimes the narrowing (or hardening) of arteries gets so bad that the blood can no longer flow. If an artery is blocked, oxygen will not get to muscles served by that artery. When this is an artery from the heart, the heart muscle gets no oxygen and dies. This causes the person to suffer a heart attack. It can be fatal. Getting medical treatment early greatly increases the chances of surviving.

Reducing high blood pressure

We cannot do anything about the genetic factors that make some people more susceptible to high blood pressure. However, lifestyle decisions can reduce the risks of high blood pressure in all people.

For example:

- eat a healthy, balanced diet (avoiding too much sugary and fatty food, taking care not to take in more energy from food than you need)
- do not smoke or drink too much alcohol
- take regular exercise.

Figure 4.5.3 Alcoholic drinks are enjoyed by many people, but too much alcohol can cause serious health problems

Why exercise is good for you

Exercising makes you breathe faster and deeper, and your heart beats faster as your muscles need more oxygen. With regular exercise you can build up your heart muscle and increase the size of your heart chambers. So a greater volume of blood is pumped around the body with each beat. That is why trained athletes have a slower pulse rate than unfit people. They are also less likely to be overweight, as they successfully balance their energy intake from food with the energy transferred each day, which includes exercising.

KEY POINTS

1 High blood pressure (hypertension) can cause many ailments and increases the risk of heart attacks.

2 Eating a healthy diet, balancing your energy intake with your energy output and taking regular exercise helps to maintain a normal blood pressure.

SUMMARY QUESTIONS

1 List the factors that cause high blood pressure (hypertension).

2 What are the health issues associated with high blood pressure?

3 Why is taking regular exercise likely to reduce the risk of getting high blood pressure?

Sporting success can bring tremendous fame and fortune to those involved. This tempts some people to go to any lengths to be better than their rivals. Taking prohibited drugs is one way that some try to improve their performance. The ruling bodies of sport have banned performance-enhancing drugs. They monitor competitors in random drug tests. The tests use the latest technology to detect the slightest trace of banned substances.

Performance-enhancing drugs

There are several types of drug that competitors could be using. Here are some examples.

- Steroids – these promote the growth of muscle (mimicking natural hormones such as testosterone) and enable athletes to train harder.
- Hormones – these are naturally found in the body, but are taken artificially by some athletes. For example, athletes in endurance events have taken EPO – a natural hormone that stimulates the production of red blood cells. This enables more oxygen to be carried to your muscles – very useful for marathon runners and long-distance cyclists. This is a form of blood doping. Human growth hormone (HGH) is also abused by those wanting to build muscle quickly.
- Stimulants – these sharpen your senses and quicken your reactions.
- Sedatives – these calm you, slowing down your pulse rate, for example they can stop your hand shaking when taking aim with a gun in shooting competitions.
- Painkillers – these enable you to train and compete by blocking pain.
- Diuretics – these get rid of water from your body and are used in sports where there are weight limits, for example boxing and horse-racing.
- Diet pills – these stop food craving, make you feel full, or stop the body absorbing fat.

Figure 4.6.1 Marion Jones won five medals at the 2000 Olympics (three gold and two bronze). However, she was later disqualified and lost the medals when she admitted taking steroids before the Games. She went to prison for lying in court during an investigation into drug abuse in sport.

As drug testing has improved, cheats have come up with more devious ways of avoiding detection. These include taking other drugs that mask the evidence that the performance-enhancing drug was ever taken.

Another form of blood doping does not involve taking a drug, but is still classed as cheating. An athlete can boost their number of red blood cells by removing some blood from their body before an event and separating out their red blood cells. Then they take an intravenous infusion of these separated red blood cells on the morning of the event. It enhances the performance of the athlete as the increased number of red blood cells delivers more oxygen to the muscles and provides greater endurance and stamina.

Harmful effects of drug misuse

The short-term gains in performance come at a price. The side-effects of the drugs can seriously damage health and even lead to a premature death.

Drug	Harmful effects
Steroids	Liver damage, coronary heart disease, kidney damage, increased aggression
Hormones	EPO – risk of heart failure and strokes HGH – heart disease, diabetes, arthritis
Stimulants	Heart damage
Sedatives	Fatigue, dizziness, poor circulation to hands and feet
Painkillers	Addiction
Diuretics	Dehydration
Diet pills	Hypertension, kidney problems, liver damage

Health and ethical issues

In addition to the drugs already mentioned, there are illegal drugs, such as heroin and cocaine, as well as legal drugs, such as alcohol and nicotine, that can cause health and addiction problems.

Substance abuse and addiction can cause serious health problems. Effects may include:

- depression
- memory loss
- paranoia
- organ damage
- fertility issues or
- cancer.

Drug abuse and misuse cost society a high price for the medical care needed to treat the consequences of addiction.

Figure 4.6.2 To reach the top of your sport takes tremendous commitment and the help of sports scientists who can plan your training and diet

Skeleton, joints and muscles

The human skeleton

All vertebrates (organisms with backbones) have a skeleton. Look at the human skeleton in Figure 4.7.1. Our skeleton has various functions:

- It supports the body.
- It protects the organs inside the body, as well as the blood vessels.
- Its joints help the body to move in different ways, including the role of the ribcage in breathing.

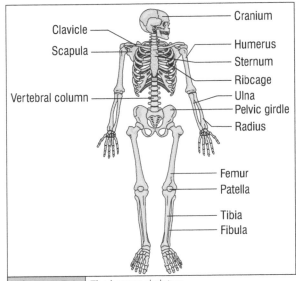

Figure 4.7.1 The human skeleton

Types of joints

Bones are attached to other bones by ligaments and where they can move relative to each other, we find joints (known as synovial joints). At these points in the body, we find cartilage between the bones to stop them grinding together, with synovial fluid to add lubrication to make movement smoother.

There are different types of joint between bones:

Type of joint	Example	Range of movement
Ball-and-socket	Hip, shoulder	Allows a wide range of movement in all directions
Hinge	Knee, elbow	Allows movement in one direction
Pivot	Neck	Rotation and some back and forth and side to side
Fixed	Skull	Nil

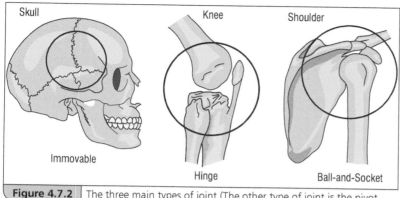

Figure 4.7.2 The three main types of joint (The other type of joint is the pivot joint. There are only three pivot joints in your body: one in your neck, at the base of your skull, and one in each of your elbows.)

Muscles

Muscles provide the forces needed to move bones. They are attached to your bones by tendons. The muscles work by contracting, providing pulling forces on the bones. So in order to move the bones relative to each other they work in pairs, called antagonistic pairs. Look at Figure 4.7.3, which shows how an arm moves about the elbow joint (a hinge joint).

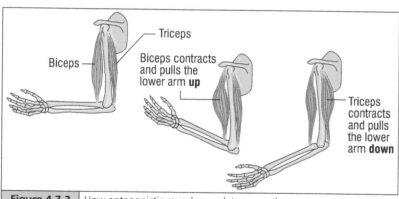

Figure 4.7.3 How antagonistic muscles work to move the arm

5 Respiration and air pollution

5.1 Respiratory surfaces

- State the basic features of a respiratory surface.
- Describe the structure of the alveoli.
- Describe the structures of the lungs in humans and the gills in fish.
- Discuss how fish obtain oxygen from water.

Oxygen is essential for life on Earth. We need oxygen for cells to respire. Respiration is the process by which living things release the energy they need. To get oxygen from the environment and into the blood is the job of the **respiratory system**.

Features of a respiratory surface

In the human body this transfer of oxygen happens when you breathe in air into your lungs. Air contains about 20% oxygen. Look at Figure 5.1.1.

The oxygen enters the blood by diffusion across the cell membranes of the **alveoli** and the tiny capillaries. To ensure diffusion takes place

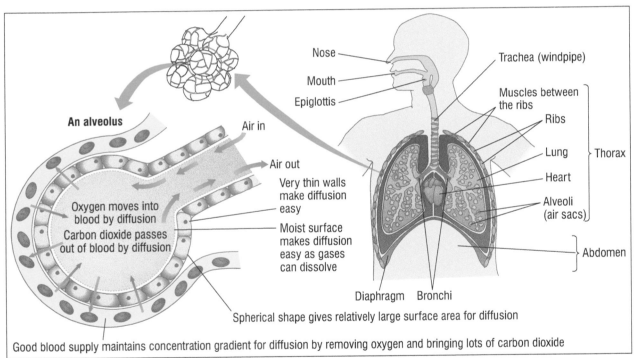

An alveolus

Air in

Air out

Oxygen moves into blood by diffusion

Carbon dioxide passes out of blood by diffusion

Very thin walls make diffusion easy

Moist surface makes diffusion easy as gases can dissolve

Spherical shape gives relatively large surface area for diffusion

Good blood supply maintains concentration gradient for diffusion by removing oxygen and bringing lots of carbon dioxide

Nose

Mouth

Epiglottis

Trachea (windpipe)

Muscles between the ribs

Ribs

Lung

Heart

Alveoli (air sacs)

Thorax

Abdomen

Diaphragm   Bronchi

Figure 5.1.1 The exchange of gases in humans takes place in their lungs at alveoli

You can read more about diffusion in 1.3 'Diffusion and osmosis', and about the lungs in 5.2 'Breathing and gaseous exchange'.

as quickly and efficiently as possible, living things have developed respiratory surfaces that:

- have a large surface area
- are very thin so the distance to diffuse across is as small as possible
- have a good supply of blood
- are always moist.

These will ensure there is a steep concentration gradient.

Gaseous exchange in fish

Fish spend their lives underwater and so they cannot use oxygen gas directly from the air. They have to use oxygen gas dissolved in the water. They have special organs called **gills** to help them to do this. Look at Figure 5.1.2 to see how fish breathe.

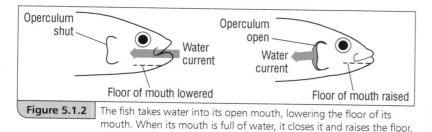

| **Figure 5.1.2** | The fish takes water into its open mouth, lowering the floor of its mouth. When its mouth is full of water, it closes it and raises the floor, pushing water over the gills and out of its body. |

The structure of the gills gives the dissolved oxygen plenty of opportunity to diffuse into the fish's blood. You can see in Figure 5.1.3 that the gills contain stacks of wafer thin layers for the water to pass over and allow diffusion to take place.

Figure 5.1.3 The structure of the gills is adapted to allow diffusion to take place efficiently

Labels in Figure 5.1.3: Rich blood supply; Very thin tissue – short distance for gases to diffuse across; Constant flow of water; Large surface area; Gill stacks

KEY POINTS

The essential features of a respiratory surface for efficient diffusion are:

1 to have a large surface area

2 to be very thin

3 to have a good supply of blood

4 to be moist.

SUMMARY QUESTIONS

1 List the essential features of an effective respiratory surface.

2 Explain why it is important for a respiratory surface to have:
   a a large surface area
   b a good supply of blood.

3 The cell membrane of an alveolus is one cell thick. Why is this important?

4 a Explain how a fish can breathe even though it spends its life underwater.

   b Try to explain why a fish effectively 'suffocates' when it is removed from the water.

Breathing and gaseous exchange

How we breathe in and out

As well as allowing oxygen to move into the blood, the alveoli also let carbon dioxide diffuse out of the blood and into the lungs. Carbon dioxide is a waste product of respiration and must be removed from the body. In order to carry out this gaseous exchange, the body has to breathe in and out continuously. Figure 5.2.1 is a diagram of our respiratory system.

In order to breathe, the diaphragm (tissue and muscle across the bottom of your chest) and intercostal muscles (between the ribs) contract and relax. This changes the volume, and hence the pressure, inside your lungs. Look at Figure 5.2.2 below.

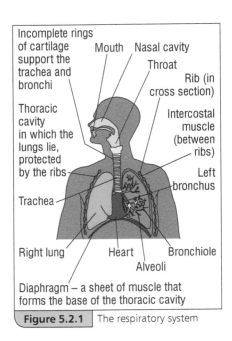

Incomplete rings of cartilage support the trachea and bronchi

Mouth

Nasal cavity

Throat

Rib (in cross section)

Thoracic cavity in which the lungs lie, protected by the ribs

Intercostal muscle (between ribs)

Left bronchus

Trachea

Right lung

Heart

Bronchiole

Alveoli

Diaphragm – a sheet of muscle that forms the base of the thoracic cavity

Figure 5.2.1 | The respiratory system

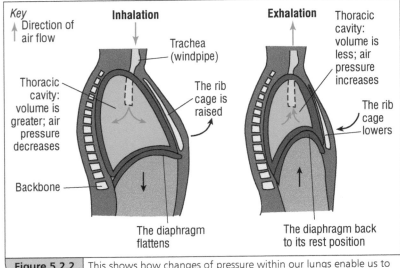

Key
↑ Direction of
↓ air flow

Inhalation

Trachea (windpipe)

The rib cage is raised

Thoracic cavity: volume is greater; air pressure decreases

Backbone

The diaphragm flattens

Exhalation

Thoracic cavity: volume is less; air pressure increases

The rib cage lowers

The diaphragm back to its rest position

Figure 5.2.2 | This shows how changes of pressure within our lungs enable us to inhale and exhale

Inhaling

When the diaphragm contracts it moves downwards. At the same time the external intercostal muscles contract and the internal intercostal muscles relax. This raises your ribcage up and out. These automatic actions increase the volume of your chest cavity, decreasing the pressure of the air inside your lungs. The pressure is lower than the air outside your body, so air is forced to enter your lungs and they inflate.

Exhaling

Then the diaphragm relaxes, rising upwards as the external intercostal muscles relax and the internal intercostals contract. These actions squeeze your chest. This increases the pressure inside them to a value above that of the air outside. This has the effect of forcing air out of your lungs, to equalise the pressure.

Comparing inhaled and exhaled air

We can test the difference in concentration of carbon dioxide in the air we breathe in compared to the air we breathe out, as shown in Figure 5.2.3 opposite.

This experiment shows that exhaled air contains a higher concentration of carbon dioxide than the air we breathe in. That is why the limewater turns cloudy faster when exhaled air is passed through it.

This table compares the composition of inhaled and exhaled air.

Gas	Inhaled air (%)	Exhaled air (%)
Oxygen	21	16
Carbon dioxide	0.04	4
Nitrogen	78	78
Water vapour	Varies	Saturated with water

Exhaled air is also warmer than inhaled air.

Gaseous exchange at the alveoli

Some of the oxygen gas we breathe into our lungs diffuses across the thin cell membranes of the alveoli. Then it diffuses across the thin cell membranes of the capillaries and into the blood. The oxygen is carried by red blood cells and enters the cell. Here it is used to release energy in respiration.

The carbon dioxide made in respiration does the reverse journey. It passes from the respiring cell into the blood where it is carried back to the lungs. There is a concentration gradient between the gas dissolved in blood and that from the air. Therefore, carbon dioxide diffuses out of the blood across the thin cell membranes into the air pocket of the alveoli. From there it is breathed out of the lungs – see Figure 5.2.4.

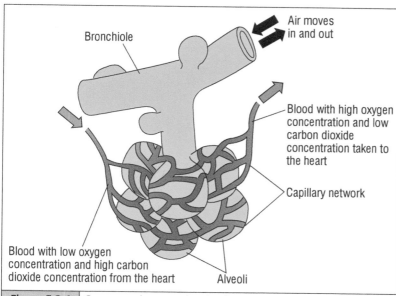

Figure 5.2.4 Gaseous exchange at the alveoli

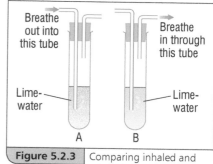

Figure 5.2.3 Comparing inhaled and exhaled air

SUMMARY QUESTIONS

1 How could you use limewater to show that the concentration of carbon dioxide in exhaled air is greater than its concentration in inhaled air?

2 Explain the role of muscles in the mechanism of breathing.

3 In which part of the respiratory system does:

a gaseous exchange take place

b air pass down a cylindrical structure, kept open by rings of cartilage

c air travel through two tubes?

Respiration

LEARNING OUTCOMES

- State what respiration is, including a word equation and a chemical equation to represent the process.
- Explain that respiration takes place both with and without oxygen.
- Compare aerobic and anaerobic respiration.

EXAM TIP

The substrates for respiration are glucose and oxygen, and the products are carbon dioxide and water. We don't call 'energy' a product as it is not a substance.

Note that the equation for respiration is the reverse of the equation for photosynthesis.

Figure 5.3.1 Bread uses the carbon dioxide given off in fermentation to make the dough rise

Respiration is the process by which the cells in living things obtain their energy. This energy is required for all the reactions and processes that cells need to function. It is essential for their metabolism.

There are two types of respiration:

- **aerobic respiration** – which requires oxygen
- **anaerobic respiration** – which does NOT require oxygen.

Aerobic respiration

The process by which cells release some of the chemical energy stored in carbohydrate molecules takes place in their mitochondria. This is not achieved in a single chemical reaction, but in a complex series of reactions. However, we can summarise aerobic respiration by the following equation:

$$\text{glucose} + \text{oxygen} \rightarrow \text{carbon dioxide} + \text{water } (+ \text{ energy})$$
$$\underset{\text{(substrates)}}{C_6H_{12}O_6 + 6O_2} \rightarrow \underset{\text{(products)}}{6CO_2 + 6H_2O} \text{ } (+ \text{ energy})$$

Anaerobic respiration

If there is no oxygen available, cells can still get energy from their carbohydrates by anaerobic respiration. From the same amount of substrate, this process does not release as much energy as aerobic respiration. You need to know about two types of anaerobic respiration, fermentation and production of lactic acid.

Fermentation

In the absence of oxygen, the cells in yeast (a type of fungus) survive by respiring using anaerobic respiration. They release energy from glucose and in the process make ethanol (an alcohol) and carbon dioxide.

$$\underset{\text{(substrate)}}{\text{glucose}} \xrightarrow{\text{enzymes in yeast}} \text{ethanol (alcohol)} + \text{carbon dioxide } (+ \text{ energy})$$
$$\underset{\text{(substrate)}}{C_6H_{12}O_6} \xrightarrow{\hspace{2cm}} \underset{\text{(products)}}{2C_2H_5OH + 2CO_2} \text{ } (+ \text{ energy})$$

This **fermentation** reaction is used in making beer and other alcoholic drinks. To make spirits such as rum or vodka, the alcohol must be distilled to increase its concentration above that in beer or wine. The alcohol can also be used as a biofuel when sugar cane or beet is fermented.

Bakers also use yeast to ferment sugars when making bread. They make use of the carbon dioxide gas given off in the reaction to make the bread dough rise.

Lactic acid production

The other type of anaerobic respiration takes place during exercise, if the muscle cells cannot get enough oxygen for aerobic respiration. In this case, the glucose, in the absence of oxygen, is converted into lactic acid:

glucose ———⟶ lactic acid (+ energy)

This lactic acid builds up in your muscles, causing that uncomfortable 'burning' sensation you get during hard exercise. As in fermentation, the energy released is much less than in aerobic respiration.

Figure 5.3.2 After vigorous exercise lactic acid must be broken down and removed from muscles. To do this we breathe deeply allowing plenty of air to enter our lungs. Our pulse rate stays high to make sure plenty of blood is available for gaseous exchange in the alveoli. We call this 'repaying the oxygen debt'.

SUMMARY QUESTIONS

1 Write the word equations to represent:
   a aerobic respiration
   b anaerobic respiration in yeast cells
   c anaerobic respiration in muscle cells during vigorous exercise.

2 List some useful products made by anaerobic respiration.

3 Explain the data in the table below.

Type of respiration	Energy released per gram of glucose
Aerobic respiration	16.1 kJ
Fermentation by yeast	1.2 kJ
Anaerobic respiration in muscle cells	0.8 kJ

KEY POINTS

1 Respiration releases all the energy required for life processes.

2 Aerobic respiration uses oxygen to release energy from glucose, making carbon dioxide and water in the process.

3 In anaerobic respiration, without oxygen:
   – fermentation with yeast produces ethanol (alcohol) and carbon dioxide
   – during hard exercise, we produce lactic acid in our muscles.

4 Aerobic respiration releases much more energy than anaerobic respiration.

Air pollution

Air pollution is a growing concern around the world. With increasing industrial activity and increasing numbers of vehicles on the roads, emissions into the atmosphere are affecting the natural balance of gases in the air.

Causes of air pollution

Carbon dioxide

The main compounds in fossil fuels are made of hydrogen and carbon (hydrocarbons). When we burn these fuels in a good supply of air, carbon dioxide and water are formed.

$$\text{hydrocarbon} + \text{oxygen} \rightarrow \text{carbon dioxide} + \text{water}$$

Carbon dioxide (CO_2) levels have increased rapidly over the last century. That's because society has become more industrialised and more and more people have cars.

Carbon dioxide is called a **greenhouse gas**. It absorbs energy transferred from the Earth as it cools down and stops the energy escaping out into space, so the average temperature of the Earth has been rising. This is called **global warming**. People are worried that global warming will cause sea levels to rise, flooding low-lying land. It could also affect climates around the world and cause more extreme weather events.

Sulphur dioxide

Whenever we burn a fossil fuel, there is a chance that **sulphur dioxide** (SO_2) gas will be given off. The sulphur is present as impurities in the fossil fuel. The metal extraction industry also produces sulphur dioxide gas, when metal sulphides are roasted in furnaces.

Sulphur dioxide causes breathing problems. It makes asthma worse as it irritates the lining of the lungs. The gas narrows the passages to the alveoli and can trigger an asthma attack. Sulphur dioxide also causes acid rain which affects forests and lakes, together with the plants and animals that live there. It also attacks buildings, especially those made of limestone, and metal structures.

Carbon monoxide

Carbon monoxide (CO) is a toxic gas. It is made when fuels burn in insufficient oxygen. If there is not enough oxygen, some of the carbon in the fuel turns into carbon monoxide instead of carbon dioxide. This happens inside car engines where petrol burns in a limited space.

Carbon monoxide is colourless and odourless so you don't realise when you are breathing it in. This makes the toxic gas particularly dangerous. People can die from faulty gas boilers that burn gas in insufficient air.

Figure 5.4.1 | Carbon monoxide is produced by car engines. Modern cars have catalytic converters fitted in their exhaust systems to remove most of this toxic gas once it warms up. However, they change carbon monoxide to carbon dioxide – which is still an air pollutant.

The carbon monoxide bonds to haemoglobin in your red blood cells. Haemoglobin usually bonds to oxygen and carries it around the blood stream, releasing it at cells where it is needed. So if the haemoglobin molecules are attached to carbon monoxide, they cannot bond to oxygen. With less oxygen, a person starts to feel tired and dizzy, and will eventually lose consciousness. If you are not put in fresh air, you will die.

Lead

Lead (Pb) is an ingredient put in leaded petrol to make older car engines run more smoothly. If a car is running on leaded petrol, the lead is emitted through the exhaust pipe into the air.

Modern cars run on unleaded petrol. That is because lead is a toxic, heavy metal. It affects the development of the brain in children and can cause learning difficulties.

Methane

Methane (CH_4) is another greenhouse gas, like carbon dioxide. It is a more effective absorber of energy than carbon dioxide, but there is not as much of it in the air.

Methane is released from fields used to grow rice, natural marshland and from grazing cattle as a waste product. As the human population rises, more land is being used for growing rice and raising cattle to feed us all. Therefore, methane levels in the atmosphere are increasing.

Respiratory disorders

- We have already seen how sulphur dioxide can trigger asthma attacks. Other respiratory disorders, such as Chronic Obstructive Pulmonary Disease (COPD), are made worse by air pollution.
- Air pollution might also be a factor in the growing number of people suffering from allergies.
- Unburnt hydrocarbons from vehicle exhausts are also a cause for concern. These contain carcinogenic compounds which can cause lung cancer.
- Tiny particles in the air, such as those given off from diesel engines, also irritate the breathing passages and could lead to cancers. Sahara dust and smog also contain some of the particles that are breathed into the lungs.

KEY POINTS

1 Air pollution is caused by carbon dioxide, sulphur dioxide, carbon monoxide, lead and methane released by human activity.

2 Air pollutants can cause various respiratory ailments, such as asthma, allergies and lung cancer.

SUMMARY QUESTIONS

1 Copy and complete the table below.

Air pollutant	Sources	Harmful effects
Carbon dioxide		
Sulphur dioxide		
Carbon monoxide		
Lead		
Methane		

2 Explain why carbon monoxide is a toxic gas.

Figure 5.5.1 Smoking makes your breath smell and discolours your teeth – however, these are minor effects compared with the long-term health problems it causes

Smoking can seriously damage your health. Such warnings are even printed on cigarette packets. Tobacco smoke causes millions of deaths each year – deaths that are often slow and painful. So why would anybody want to smoke? Reasons differ, but many smokers start smoking when they are teenagers, often due to peer pressure. Some people see themselves as 'cool' when they smoke; others think it helps them stay thin.

But whatever the reasons for smoking, the nicotine in smoke is an addictive drug. Once you start smoking regularly, it becomes difficult to stop – even when you know the harm it does.

Harmful substances in tobacco smoke

Carbon monoxide

We have already seen how this toxic gas is made during combustion reactions. It reduces the oxygen-carrying capacity of your red blood cells – one reason why smokers get breathless easily. It can also harm a pregnant woman's foetus, slowing its growth.

Nicotine

This is quickly absorbed into the blood and spread around the body. It makes your pulse race, increasing your blood pressure and the strain on your heart. It is the addictive agent in tobacco smoke.

Tars

These are what cause the characteristic 'smoker's cough' and can go on to cause cancers (by an increased factor of about 25% compared with non-smokers). The tars build up and paralyse the tiny filaments called cilia that naturally remove impurities from your bronchial tubes. So smokers often cough because it is the only way they have of getting rid of the excess mucus that builds up.

Diseases caused by tobacco smoke

Diseases caused by narrowing arteries

The respiratory system is not the only part of the body to be affected by smoking. The blood vessels and heart are also damaged. The arteries of smokers tend to get lined inside with fatty deposits. This makes it more difficult for blood to flow through them. If arteries in the heart are affected it causes heart attacks. If arteries to the brain are affected it can lead to strokes.

Smoking can also lead to amputation of limbs (usually feet and legs) as the blood supply to limbs can eventually be cut off.

Cancers

The cancer-causing chemicals (carcinogens) in tobacco smoke can affect any surface in the respiratory system they come into contact with. Smokers are more likely to get cancers of the mouth, tongue, throat and lungs, as well as the pancreas and bladder.

Breathing diseases

We have mentioned how tars in smoke affect the delicate cilia and cause smokers to cough up excess mucus made in their lungs. Over time this scars and damages the tissues in the bronchus, causing bronchitis. Emphysema and Chronic Obstructive Pulmonary Disease (COPD) are other breathing diseases. Sufferers struggle for breath and tire easily as the respiratory system cannot deliver enough oxygen to the blood. Equally they find it harder to remove carbon dioxide waste from their blood efficiently.

Passive smoking

The dangers that smokers face to their health also apply to others who breathe in their 'second-hand' smoke. When a smoker inhales smoke, not all the harmful substances have been removed, so passive smoking is a real health issue. Consequently, many countries have banned smoking in bars and cafes, and some have a ban in all public places, even those outdoors.

SUMMARY QUESTIONS

1 a Name the addictive substance in tobacco smoke.
  b What immediate effect does this substance have on your heart?
  c What longer-term condition can this substance cause?

2 a Which substances in cigarette smoke cause cancers?
  b List five parts of the body that are more likely to be affected by cancer in a smoker than in a non-smoker.

3 a Name three breathing diseases which can affect smokers.
  b Explain how 'smoker's cough' is caused.

4 The table below shows cigarette consumption and the risk of death by lung cancer.

Number of cigarettes smoked per day	Death rate per year per 100 000 people	Relative risk
0	14	–
1–14	105	8
15–24	208	15
25 and over	355	25

Comment on the trend shown by the data in the table.

KEY POINTS

1 Tobacco smoke contains nicotine (addictive), carbon monoxide (toxic) and tars (carcinogens).

2 Smoking causes many life-threatening illnesses. It increases the risk of death by cancer, COPD, heart attack and stroke.

6 Excretion

6.1 Excretion in humans

LEARNING OUTCOMES

- Distinguish between excretion and egestion.
- Identify excretory organs and their products.
- Describe the structure of the kidneys and the skin.
- Explain osmoregulation.

LINK

For more about the lungs, see 5.2 'Breathing and gaseous exchange'.

LINK

For more about the movement of particles across membranes, see 1.3 'Diffusion and osmosis'.

What is excretion?

There are many chemical reactions going on in your body all the time (metabolism). Some of the products made will be used by your body for various functions. However, the other substances of metabolism are waste products. These are removed from your body in the process of **excretion**.

Excretion should not be confused with **egestion**. Egestion occurs when your body gets rid of undigested material in faeces. This is material that is eaten and travels through the digestive system, but does not get absorbed by the body. It does not take part in the chemical reactions of your metabolism.

The body produces as waste:

- carbon dioxide and water (from respiration)
- urea (made when excess amino acids from proteins are broken down in the liver).

The waste products are transported in the blood to the lungs and the kidneys.

Carbon dioxide is removed from the lungs when we breathe out, along with some water. Urea and water are removed in urine, and water is also removed in sweat from the skin. However, much water is reabsorbed by the kidneys for its many uses.

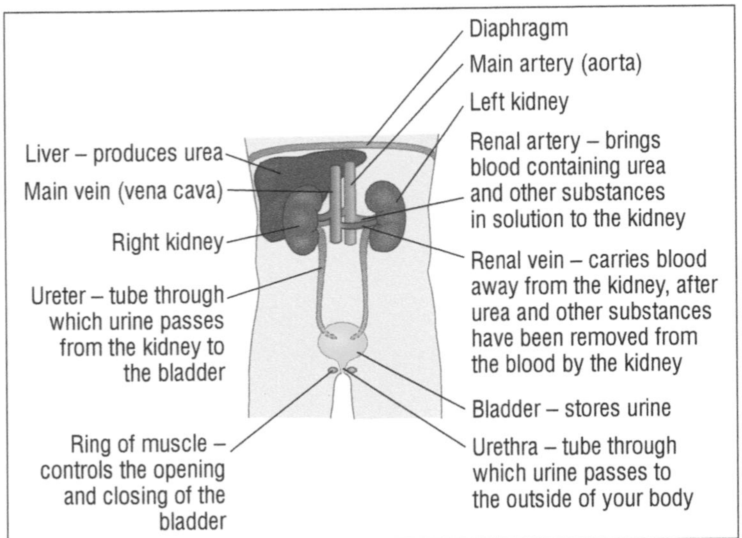

The kidneys

We each have one pair of kidneys. Figure 6.1.1 shows their position and how they are linked to the bladder. Your kidneys help to maintain steady conditions in your body (**homeostasis**). They do this through **osmoregulation**. Osmoregulation is the process in which the body maintains the correct balance of water and ions.

The kidneys remove urea from the blood. This is filtered out through the capillaries in the nephrons. There are about a million nephrons in a kidney. The nephrons are delicate structures where relatively small molecules can diffuse through pores in the capillaries. As well as urea, molecules of glucose, amino acids and mineral ions can all fit through the pores and enter the tubules in the kidney. This is called **ultrafiltration**.

Figure 6.1.1 The kidneys, liver and bladder

Diaphragm
Main artery (aorta)
Left kidney
Renal artery – brings blood containing urea and other substances in solution to the kidney
Renal vein – carries blood away from the kidney, after urea and other substances have been removed from the blood by the kidney
Bladder – stores urine
Urethra – tube through which urine passes to the outside of your body

Liver – produces urea
Main vein (vena cava)
Right kidney
Ureter – tube through which urine passes from the kidney to the bladder
Ring of muscle – controls the opening and closing of the bladder

Then substances that are useful to the body, such as all the glucose and some mineral ions, are **selectively reabsorbed** by the kidney back into the blood. The waste urea and other substances pass out of the kidney down the ureter as urine. This is stored in the bladder.

A hormone called ADH, released from the pituitary gland, controls the amount of water in your urine. ADH makes the walls of the ducts in the kidneys that collect water more permeable. They let more water back into the bloodstream, so less is lost in your urine. No ADH is released if you have too much water in your body, so excess is removed in urine. This is an example of osmoregulation.

Dialysis

We can survive with just one kidney functioning properly. However, if the kidneys are damaged or diseased in some way, people can have their blood filtered by **dialysis**. In dialysis, blood is pumped out of the body through tubes that pass through the dialysis solution (sometimes called the dialysis fluid). The blood is separated from the dialysis solution by a partially (or selectively) permeable membrane (see Figure 6.1.2). Then diffusion takes place along a concentration gradient.

The concentration of glucose and mineral ions in the dialysis solution is set at normal concentrations found in the blood. Therefore, these useful molecules do not pass out of the blood. However, the dialysis solution contains no urea, so that does diffuse through the membrane and out of the blood. This mimics the ultrafiltration process in the kidneys.

The skin – temperature control

The body loses water as water vapour when we breathe out and also as sweat from our skin. The skin has sweat glands which absorb fluid from capillaries. The water passes through a narrow tube to the surface of the skin when we get too hot. The water evaporates from the surface of the skin, cooling us down.

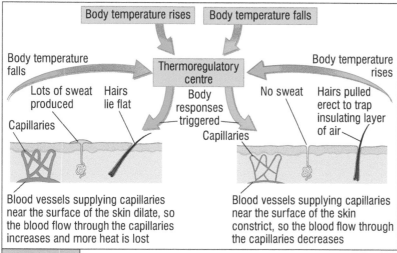

Body temperature rises   Body temperature falls

Body temperature falls

Thermoregulatory centre

Body temperature rises

Lots of sweat produced   Hairs lie flat

Body responses triggered

No sweat   Hairs pulled erect to trap insulating layer of air

Capillaries

Capillaries

Blood vessels supplying capillaries near the surface of the skin dilate, so the blood flow through the capillaries increases and more heat is lost

Blood vessels supplying capillaries near the surface of the skin constrict, so the blood flow through the capillaries decreases

Figure 6.1.2 Water is lost (along with some mineral ions and urea) when we sweat. Why is it more accurate to say 'When the water evaporates from sweat …' rather than 'When sweat evaporates …'?

SUMMARY QUESTIONS

1 What is the difference between excretion and egestion?

2 In the kidneys:
   a What do we mean by:
      i   ultrafiltration
      ii selective absorption?
   b Name a compound containing nitrogen that is filtered out of the blood in the kidneys.
   c Why does the composition of urine differ at different times?

LEARNING OUTCOMES

- Identify waste products of respiration and photosynthesis.
- Describe methods of excreting waste products in plants.

LINK

For more information about photosynthesis and the structure of a leaf, see 3.1 'Photochemical reactions' and 4.1 'Transport systems in plants'.

We have seen that plants make their own food during photosynthesis. In a complex series of chemical reactions, they convert carbon dioxide and water into glucose and oxygen.

carbon dioxide + water → glucose + oxygen

The glucose made is used in respiration in the plant cells where energy is released.

glucose + oxygen → carbon dioxide + water

The glucose is also used to make other compounds that the plant needs. Some of the oxygen made in photosynthesis is used in respiration, but much is released into the atmosphere. Therefore, we can think of oxygen as a metabolic waste product in plants.

The oxygen gas escapes through the stomata in the leaves. How are the openings in stomata controlled by a plant?

The carbon dioxide released from respiration can also be thought of as a waste product – but only at night! Remember that photosynthesis needs energy from light in order to take place. So in daylight, the carbon dioxide produced in respiring cells is used for photosynthesis. It is not excreted from the plant as waste. However, at night no photosynthesis takes place in the dark, but plant cells respire all the time. So at night carbon dioxide is a waste product and it is released through the stomata in the leaves.

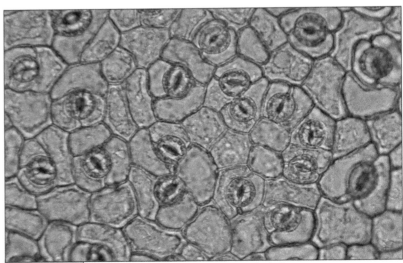

Figure 6.2.1 Plants excrete waste products through their stomata

Water, a waste product of respiration, is released from the plant when the stomata open to let carbon dioxide gas in. If the weather gets very hot, too much water is lost from a plant and it wilts. This is a defence mechanism as the sagging, curled up leaves reduce the surface area exposed to sunlight.

Plants also break down other substances, for example pigments, which produce toxic substances. The plant gets rid of these when the leaves change colour and fall from the plant. This effectively removes any toxic products of metabolism. The following spring new leaves grow again with no toxic compounds present.

Figure 6.2.2 Shedding leaves is one way that plants excrete waste products

Plants can also store waste products, for example in their vacuoles. As well as leaves, other parts die and fall off plants and these can also be used to store waste products. For example, old xylem can be used and trees, such as mangroves, can store waste materials in their bark.

KEY POINTS

1 Oxygen gas is the waste product of photosynthesis in plants.

2 Carbon dioxide is the waste product from respiration.

3 Carbon dioxide, oxygen and water vapour are all released through stomata. The amounts vary according to day/night and temperature.

4 Plants also excrete substances by shedding leaves, and storing them in dead woody parts and bark that will eventually fall off.

SUMMARY QUESTIONS

1 What are the waste products formed by plants during:

a photosynthesis

b respiration?

2 a How are the products of plant respiration removed?

b Why do the amounts of waste product vary in a 24-hour period?

3 How can plants excrete toxic waste products that cannot be released as gases?

7 Sense organs and coordination

7.1 The eye

The eye detects visible light and enables us to see the world around us. Look at its structure in Figure 7.1.1.

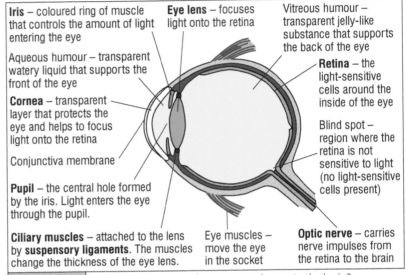

Iris – coloured ring of muscle that controls the amount of light entering the eye

Eye lens – focuses light onto the retina

Vitreous humour – transparent jelly-like substance that supports the back of the eye

Aqueous humour – transparent watery liquid that supports the front of the eye

Cornea – transparent layer that protects the eye and helps to focus light onto the retina

Conjunctiva membrane

Retina – the light-sensitive cells around the inside of the eye

Blind spot – region where the retina is not sensitive to light (no light-sensitive cells present)

Pupil – the central hole formed by the iris. Light enters the eye through the pupil.

Ciliary muscles – attached to the lens by suspensory ligaments. The muscles change the thickness of the eye lens.

Eye muscles – move the eye in the socket

Optic nerve – carries nerve impulses from the retina to the brain

Figure 7.1.1 Structure of the eye. What connects the eye to the brain?

Light enters through the circular gap (the pupil) in the coloured area of the eye (the iris). The iris contains muscles which make the pupil larger in the dark and smaller in bright light.

Other sense organs

Sense organs	Stimulus
Ears	Sound, head position
Nose	Chemicals in air
Tongue	Chemicals in food
Skin	Touch, temperature, pressure, pain

Focusing light in the eye

The light is focused onto the back of the eye, which is called the retina. Here there are sensory cells called rods and cones that turn the light energy into electrical impulses. These are sent down the optic nerve to be interpreted in the brain.

In order to see things clearly the light rays from an object must be focused on the retina. This process of refraction (changing the direction of light rays) starts at the outer surface of the eye – the cornea. Then fine adjustment takes place at the lens behind the iris and pupil. The lens can be made fatter and thinner by circular ciliary muscles which surround the elastic lens. To see near objects the light has to be refracted more so the lens is made fatter. The ciliary muscles contract, releasing tension on the suspensory ligaments. Without being stretched the lens shrinks into a thicker shape (see Figure 7.1.2). The process of focusing light on the retina at the back of the eye is known as accommodation.

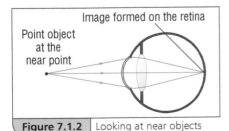

Point object at the near point

Image formed on the retina

Figure 7.1.2 Looking at near objects

To see distant objects, the ciliary muscles relax, pulling the suspensory ligaments tighter and stretching the lens into a thinner shape (see Figure 7.1.3).

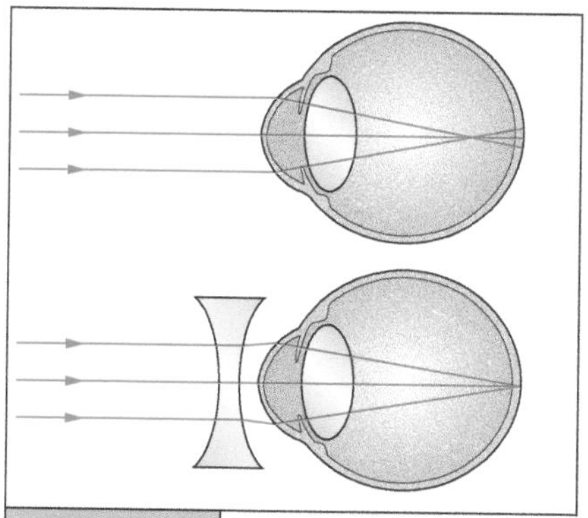

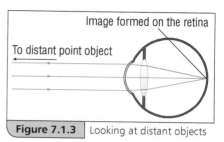

Figure 7.1.3 Looking at distant objects

Defects in the eye

Short-sightedness

Some people are short-sighted. They can see near objects clearly, but cannot focus the light from distant objects. This is because their lens is refracting light too strongly. That makes the rays of parallel light focus in front of the retina. To rectify this, they use corrective lenses in spectacles that bend rays outwards before they enter the eye. Then, if the lenses are the right strength, the light rays focus the light precisely on the retina. Concave lenses are used to bend the light outwards (see Figure 7.1.4). People often wear this type of spectacles when they drive.

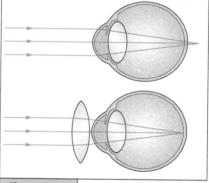

Figure 7.1.4 How a concave lens in spectacles helps people who are short-sighted

Long-sightedness

Other people can see distant objects, but close-up objects are blurred. Their lens cannot bend the light enough to focus the rays on the retina. To rectify this, they wear spectacles or contact lenses with convex lenses. These help to refract the rays more strongly towards each other (see Figure 7.1.5). People often wear this type of glasses for reading.

Astigmatism is a growing problem in Caribbean countries. This is where the cornea, or lens, is not the correct shape. It can result in blurred vision and long- or short-sightedness. It can usually be corrected by using spectacles or contact lenses, but severe cases need surgery.

Figure 7.1.5 How a convex lens in spectacles helps people who are long-sighted

Effects of ultraviolet or bright light

Sunlight contains ultraviolet light which can damage the front part of the eyes, for example the cornea. Very bright light will damage the retina at the back of the eye. Sunglasses with UV protection should be worn in sunshine.

SUMMARY QUESTIONS

1 Draw a table to show the function of the following parts of an eye:
   a iris
   b lens
   c ciliary muscles
   d retina
   e rods and cones
   f optic nerve.
2 Draw diagrams to explain how long- and short-sightedness are rectified.

KEY POINTS

1 The main structures in the eye are the cornea, iris, pupil, lens, suspensory ligaments, ciliary muscles, retina and optic nerve.

2 People who are short-sighted need concave lenses to help them focus light rays on the retina, whereas long-sighted people need convex lenses.

Light and colour

- Describe how white light is separated into its constituent colours.
- Distinguish between primary and secondary colours.
- Discuss the effect of mixing different primary pigments.
- Describe the effects of lighting on the colour of objects.
- Separate different coloured inks by chromatography.
- Distinguish between artificial and natural lighting, and between transparent, translucent and opaque materials.

TRANSMISSION OF LIGHT

Transparent materials let light pass straight through them.

Translucent materials let some light pass through, but it is scattered on the way through, producing a blurred image.

Opaque materials do not let light pass through them.

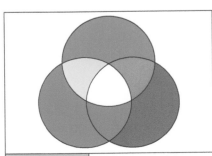

Figure 7.2.2 The primary and secondary colours

The visible spectrum

When a thin beam of white light passes through a glass prism the white light is dispersed into the seven colours of the spectrum. You have probably seen the visible spectrum in a rainbow or when the Sun shines on a puddle with a thin film of oil on top of it. Do you know the colours, in order?

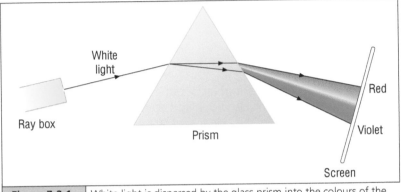

Figure 7.2.1 White light is dispersed by the glass prism into the colours of the spectrum

White light is made up of red, orange, yellow, green, blue, indigo and violet light. By spinning a card wheel with these colours painted on in segments, the wheel should appear white. The different colours have different wavelengths and change direction as they pass from air into the glass. They are diverted in the opposite direction as they pass out of the glass prism back into air. This changing of direction of light travelling from one substance into another is called **refraction**. Red light, with the longest wavelength is refracted least. Violet, with the shortest wavelength in the spectrum, is refracted most.

Primary and secondary colours of light

Red, green and blue are known as the primary colours of the spectrum. If they are combined in the right intensity, they will form white light.

The coloured dots that make up a TV picture are formed from combinations of red, green and blue dots. Indeed our eyes have three types of cone cells to detect red, green and blue light.

Secondary colours are made by mixing two primary colours together.

- Red + green = **yellow**
- Red + blue = **magenta**
- Blue + green = **cyan**

The colour of objects

The colour an object appears depends on which parts of the visible spectrum it absorbs and which it reflects. We see the reflected colours. If all the colours in the visible spectrum are reflected, the object appears white. If they are all absorbed, the object appears black. When we mix pigments together, the colour is the common reflected parts of the spectrum.

The same object can appear different colours using light filters. For example, an object can be red in normal light, but if a filter is used to shine blue light on it, it looks black. That is because the object absorbs the blue end of the spectrum.

Physically separating mixtures of pigments

The technique used to separate mixtures of dyes or pigments is called **chromatography**. The mixture is spotted onto some filter paper (or special absorbent chromatography paper) using a very narrow glass tube called a capillary tube. The paper is left standing in a little solvent in a large beaker.

As the solvent runs up the absorbent paper, the different pigments in the mixture are left behind at different heights. This is because the pigments have different solubilities in the solvent. They also have different forces of attraction with the water bonded into the paper. Those with weak attractions to the water in the paper and high solubilities in the solvent will be carried furthest up the paper.

Natural and artificial lighting

Lighting is very important in any building. Windows, roof-lights and glazed doors all let natural light in. In daytime, if correctly placed, they can let light from the Sun illuminate colours and enable the people inside the building to perform tasks safely.

In places that are not lit up by natural light, reflective surfaces help to bounce light around inside the building. At night, we need to use artificial lighting. The types of light source, their fittings and positioning are essential to the efficient functioning of a building.

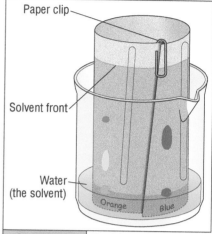

Figure 7.2.3 The ink was spotted on the pencil line drawn near the bottom of the chromatography paper. What colour pigments made up the orange ink?

KEY POINTS

1 White light is dispersed into the colours of the spectrum because the different colours of light are refracted by different amounts.

2 The primary colours of light (red, green and blue) form white when they are mixed together. Two primary colours mixed together form a secondary colour (yellow, magenta or cyan).

3 The colour an object appears depends on the colours it reflects, as well as the colour of the light shining on it.

4 Coloured pigments can be physically separated by chromatography.

SUMMARY QUESTIONS

1 a Name the colours of the spectrum, starting with the shortest wavelength.

 b Explain how white light is dispersed into the colours of the spectrum.

2 What colour is formed when the following colours of light are mixed?

 a red, green and blue

 b red and blue

 c blue and yellow.

3 Write a method for an experiment to see if an orange felt-tipped pen is made from a single pigment or a mixture of pigments.

4 Look at Figure 7.2.3. Explain how the colours were separated.

The ear

LEARNING OUTCOMES

- Identify parts of the ear and state their function.
- Explain how noises (loudness/pitch) affect the ear.
- Describe how hearing loss is caused by damage to the ear.
- Describe how the ear maintains balance.

The ear has two important functions – it detects sound and helps us to maintain our balance. Most of its structure lies within the skull. The external ear is used to collect sounds and direct them to the inner ear. Look at Figure 7.3.1.

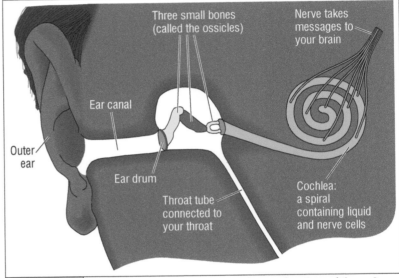

Three small bones (called the ossicles)

Nerve takes messages to your brain

Ear canal

Outer ear

Ear drum

Throat tube connected to your throat

Cochlea: a spiral containing liquid and nerve cells

Figure 7.3.1 The structure of the ear. What are the two functions of the ear?

Sound waves

Sounds are made when objects vibrate. As they vibrate, they cause waves of disturbance in the air molecules. These sound waves spread out from their source, getting weaker the further they travel. The loudness of a sound when it reaches the ear is determined by the strength of the molecular disturbance. This is called the amplitude of the sound wave. The loudness of a sound is measured in units called decibels (dB).

The pitch, or frequency, of a sound wave (for example high or low) is determined by how quickly the source of the sound vibrates. The faster the vibrations are, the higher the pitch of the sound. We measure the frequency of a wave in units called hertz (Hz). The human ear can usually hear sounds with a frequency in the range of about 20 Hz to 20 000 Hz.

How we hear

We hear sounds when the disturbances of the air molecules travel down the ear canal and arrive at the ear drum. The sound waves make the ear drum vibrate. These vibrations are passed on to the three small bones called the ossicles. Their movement causes vibration of the inner ear drum or oval window, which in turn disturbs liquid in the cochlea. This is detected by tiny, sensory hairs in the cochlea. These send an electrical impulse to the brain, which interprets the signals received into the sounds we hear.

Hearing loss

We can lose our hearing if:

- the ear canal becomes blocked with wax
- the ear drum is damaged by excessively loud noises
- the ossicles fuse together and so stop vibrating properly
- cells in the cochlea are damaged (caused by loud noises at a certain frequency – this is why ear protectors are worn by workers in noisy environments and why personal music players should not be turned up too loud).

Maintaining balance

Just above the cochlea we find the semi-circular canals. Look at Figure 7.3.3. The three canals are filled with liquid that have sensory hairs, which detect movement in the liquid. They send their electrical impulses to the brain, which makes the necessary adjustments to muscles to maintain our balance.

Figure 7.3.2 Excessively loud sounds can permanently damage your hearing

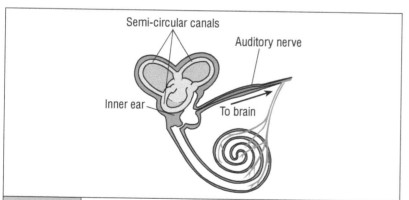

Figure 7.3.3 The semi-circular canals help us maintain our balance. What detects movement in the liquid in the semi-circular canals?

KEY POINTS

1. The ear enables us to hear sounds and maintain our balance.
2. The vibrations of sound waves are passed along the delicate inner structure of the ear.
3. Care must be taken not to damage the sensitive structures in your ears.

SUMMARY QUESTIONS

1 Describe how sounds are made and travel to the ear.

2 Draw a flow diagram to show the sequence of steps when we hear a sound.

3 List the causes of hearing loss.

4 How does the ear help us maintain our balance?

The nervous system

- Name and describe the function of neurones.
- Identify the major parts of the central nervous system and their functions.
- Explain reflex (involuntary) actions.
- State the effects when the central nervous system malfunctions.

Your body has to cope with all sorts of changes in its environment. These changes act as a stimulus to the body to respond in some way. The body detects the changes using its sense organs – eyes, ears, nose, tongue and skin.

Your sense organs contain special cells that detect changes, such as in light, sound, smells, tastes, heat or pressure. These cells are called sensory **neurones**. The neurones are linked in bundles called nerves. There are three types of neurone, shown in Figure 7.4.1.

Voluntary actions

Here is the sequence of events when you decide how to respond to a stimulus.

1 A stimulus detected by a sensory neurone triggers off an electrical impulse that travels along a sensory nerve to the spinal cord.

2 The electrical impulse then travels up the spinal cord to the brain, which coordinates what happens next.

3 The brain sends an electrical impulse back down the spinal cord to the correct nerve which is attached from the spinal cord to a muscle.

4 The electrical impulse leaves the spinal cord via a motor neurone and travels down a motor nerve to the muscle.

5 When the electrical impulse arrives at a muscle, the muscle responds by contracting.

The spinal cord and the brain make up the central nervous system (CNS). The sequence of events for a voluntary action is shown in Figure 7.4.2.

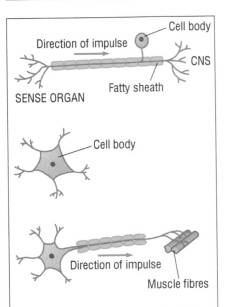

Figure 7.4.1 The three types of neurones – sensory (top), relay (middle), motor (bottom)

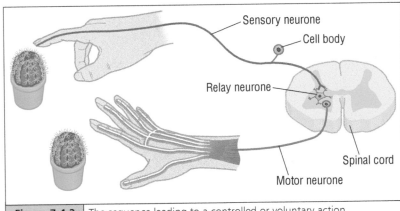

Figure 7.4.2 The sequence leading to a controlled or voluntary action

Reflex (involuntary) actions

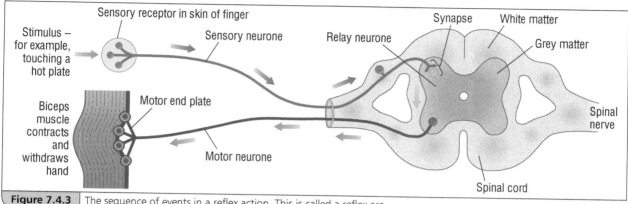

Figure 7.4.3 | The sequence of events in a reflex action. This is called a reflex arc.

Imagine you touch a plate that has been in a very hot oven. You drop the plate automatically before you even feel the pain. This involuntary action is called a reflex action.

You do not need to think about a reflex action. That's because the electrical impulse from the sensory neurones to the motor neurones bypasses the brain. This helps us react more quickly to a stimulus that might cause us harm. The action is quicker as a result of a shorter sequence of events than in a voluntary action where we actively decide what to do. Look at Figure 7.4.3.

The electrical impulse travels between the incoming sensory neurone and the outgoing motor neurone via a relay neurone in the spinal cord. Chemicals are released and received to cross the gaps at either end of the relay neurone so the impulse can bypass the brain.

Other involuntary actions coordinated like this are your breathing, your heart beating and your knee jerking when it is tapped. Can you think of a reflex action in a baby?

Damage to the nervous system

If electrical impulses cannot travel through the central nervous system, you can become paralysed. That is why breaking your back or neck is so potentially dangerous. If the break damages the spinal cord, electrical impulses sent by the brain cannot get to muscles. The higher up the spine the break occurs, the worse the paralysis as more of the muscles can no longer be controlled and actions coordinated.

Other disorders, such as motor neurone disease, affect the upper and lower motor neurones. Degeneration of the motor neurones leads to weakness and wasting of muscles. This causes an increasing loss of mobility in limbs. Eventually there are difficulties with speech, swallowing and breathing – all coordinated by the nervous system.

SUMMARY QUESTIONS

1 Describe the function of:
   a sensory neurones
   b relay neurones
   c motor neurones.

2 Explain the difference between a voluntary and an involuntary action.

3 Explain which break in the spine, severe enough to damage the spinal cord, is more serious – a break near the base of the spine or a break near the top of the spine.

The **endocrine system** and the nervous system act together to coordinate a variety of effects in the body. This table compares the two systems.

	Nervous system	Endocrine system
How 'messages' are sent around the body	Electrical impulses that travel along neurones (which make up nerves)	Hormones (chemicals) that travel through the bloodstream to target organs
Timing and effect	• Rapid response • Almost immediate • Acts in a precise area • Effects are short lasting	• Slower response • Longer term • Can act over a larger area • Effects are longer lasting

The endocrine system is made up of glands, located around the body. Some glands exist as organs themselves or as parts of other organs. Figure 7.5.1 shows where the main glands are found.

The pituitary gland, at the base of the brain, coordinates the effects of most of the other glands. The nearby hypothalamus is the link between the nervous system and the endocrine system.

The endocrine glands release (secrete) chemicals called hormones. They are transported around the body in the blood. The hormone molecules can be thought of as chemical messengers. Some have general effects around the body, but others are targeted at particular organs.

Some hormones are proteins or steroids. For example, growth hormone is a protein and testosterone is a steroid. Testosterone is made in the testes. It stimulates the male characteristics to develop in adolescent boys.

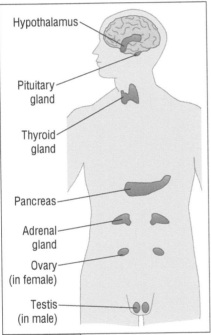

Hypothalamus

Pituitary gland

Thyroid gland

Pancreas

Adrenal gland

Ovary (in female)

Testis (in male)

Figure 7.5.1 The main endocrine glands. How would you describe the position of the pituitary gland?

LINK

For information regarding the abuse of hormones in sports, see 4.6 'Drugs'.

The table below shows some other hormones, the glands that produce them and their effects.

Hormone	Produced by the endocrine gland …	Effect
Adrenaline	Pancreas	Gets the body ready for emergency action, for example raises the pulse rate and dilates blood vessels to muscles, lungs and liver (ensuring muscles have a good supply of glucose and oxygen)
Glucagon	Pancreas	Converts glycogen back into glucose (raises blood sugar level)
Insulin	Pancreas	Converts glucose into glycogen which is stored in the liver (lowers blood sugar level)
Oestrogen	Ovary	Stimulates secondary female characteristics
Thyroxine	Thyroid	Regulates growth

Figure 7.5.2 Taking your first sky dive will get adrenaline surging around your body!

Types of waste

As a society we produce lots of waste as a result of our lifestyles. Here are some examples.

Domestic waste

Think of the rubbish you and your family throw away each week. Most things we buy come packaged in plastic and/or cardboard. Then there is the waste generated in the kitchen. Most of the rubbish we throw into a bin will eventually be taken to a landfill site. These are huge holes where the rubbish is dumped.

Much of the limited space in a landfill site is taken up with plastic waste. Many traditional plastics take a very long time to decompose. They are chemically unreactive – which is one of their useful properties in some applications, but not when disposing of them. Chemists have now developed **biodegradable** plastics that can be broken down by microorganisms in the soil. These biodegradable plastics decompose in landfill sites in a few months.

Figure 8.1.1 | A landfill site on the island of Grenada

Biological waste

We also have to get rid of the waste products our bodies produce. This can be thought of as domestic, biological waste. In towns and cities this sewage is taken in pipes to sewage treatment plants. There the sewage is broken down by microorganisms in tanks that have plenty of air available. The liquid is purified sufficiently to pass back into rivers or the sea. In the countryside, many households have septic tanks from which sewage is collected periodically or they invest in their own small treatment plants.

Industrial waste

Disposing of waste from some industries is more difficult than others. The hotels in the tourist industry produce domestic waste, only on a large scale. However, chemical processing plants can produce toxic or unsightly waste that must be made safe before releasing it into the environment.

| Figure 8.1.2 | These brown lagoons are holding waste iron compounds from the processing of aluminium ore (bauxite) extracted in Jamaica |

Uses of waste

Dumping waste in a landfill site squanders the Earth's limited resources. The landfill sites can also pollute groundwater if any toxic or harmful substances are disposed of illegally in the household rubbish.

It is far better if we can make use of the waste in some way. Here are some uses.

- The solid sludge left after sewage has been treated can be sterilised and used as a fertiliser on fields. This can be used with manure collected by farmers from farm animals.
- Recycling – we can recycle glass, paper, iron/steel and aluminium. This saves resources and energy. Plastics are more difficult to recycle, as there are so many different types, but it is possible when the product packaging is marked with a code to help sort them.
- Biogas can be generated by the action of microorganisms on organic waste. The gas can be burned to generate electricity.

Community and personal hygiene

The taxes people pay to their governments helps to pay for the costs of keeping our environment a clean and healthy place to live in. Regular rubbish collections are organised for the disposal of our household waste. Our sewage is taken away and treated. If this was not done, rubbish and human waste would soon build up and become a breeding ground for all kinds of pests and **parasites**, and the diseases they carry.

SUMMARY QUESTIONS

1 Give an example of the following types of waste:
   a domestic
   b biological
   c industrial.

2 a Rubbish in a landfill site gives off flammable methane gas. What use could be made of the gas?
   b How can a landfill site contaminate drinking water supplies?

3 Predict the consequences if a government was to run out of money and could no longer afford to remove and dispose of waste from homes and businesses for six months.

Pests are organisms that cause us inconvenience at best, and at worst, can cause illness and even death. Mosquitoes are a pest that can be a nuisance, but also spread disease. For example, in 2010 there was an increase, in the disease dengue, which can be fatal. An early rainy season that caused an increase in numbers of mosquitoes was to blame.

Mosquitoes can be controlled by spraying marshy areas with insecticide. However, care must be taken that the chemicals used do not cause harm to the environment or the food chains in the ecosystem.

People who live in mosquito areas are encouraged to never leave any uncovered water in containers outside. Mosquitoes will use the water to lay their eggs in. They should fit screens to doors and windows, and sleep under a mosquito net. These provide a mechanical control barrier to prevent mosquito bites. When outdoors, you can apply anti-mosquito spray to the exposed areas of skin.

Figure 8.2.1 Mosquitoes feed on blood, so they can pass on malaria parasites to humans, and heartworms to dogs, directly into the bloodstream. Parasites live and feed on the host organism they infect.

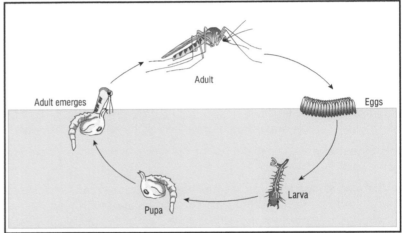

Figure 8.2.2 The life cycle of a mosquito. It varies between four days and a month

EXAM TIP

Do not confuse pests with parasites. Parasites are organisms that feed on their host. For example, worms that live inside animals, including humans.

Numbers of mosquitoes can be controlled by intervening in its life cycle. For example, removing sources of stagnant water stops eggs from developing. You can also introduce biological controls in water, such as mosquito fish that feed on mosquito larvae. Introducing birds, dragonflies and frogs that feed on adult mosquitoes has also been tried.

Cockroaches are another pest. These thrive where they find food, water and shelter. Therefore, keeping a house clean and free from any waste food or water, with any cracks and holes filled in walls, will stop a cockroach infestation. If they find a good food supply and somewhere to hide away, they will cause diseases such as gastro-enteritis, typhus and skin diseases. They also provoke allergic reactions that cause dermatitis, asthma and bronchitis.

Chemical control with insecticides is the usual way to rid an infested building of cockroaches. These are toxic substances and should be applied by professionals. Borax is a traditional, less harmful substance that is effective against cockroaches.

Figure 8.2.3 Cockroaches are found in restaurant kitchens with poor hygiene practices

Pests can also be controlled in agriculture by biological means. The farmer will introduce a predator to feed on the pest. An example is the ladybird that feeds on aphids that destroy plants. Spiders can also be used to decrease the number of flies.

Another species introduced on Caribbean islands is the cane toad. This feeds on pests, such as the white-grub, that attack the sugar cane crop. Cane toads were even introduced into Jamaica to control rats, although this did not seem to work.

Figure 8.2.4 The cane toad is an excellent biological pest control. It will eat almost anything. Unfortunately it can be so effective that it becomes a pest itself!

Figure 8.2.5 Rats are attracted to rubbish and must be controlled, often by chemical means (rat poison) and mechanical means (baited traps). Reducing our waste, reusing or recycling as much as possible will help.

KEY POINTS

1 Pests and parasites breed successfully in dark, damp places where food is readily available.

2 Pests and parasites can be controlled by biological (predatory organisms), chemical (pesticides) or mechanical (barriers or traps) means.

SUMMARY QUESTIONS

1 Mice are seen as pests once they infest a home. Give a:

a biological

b chemical

c mechanical

method that could be used to control them.

2 Explain where you might find cockroaches in a kitchen.

3 Why do mosquitoes pose such a threat to humans?

4 What is the difference between a pest and a parasite?

SECTION A: Multiple-choice questions

1 Which of the following are functions of the human skeleton?

I   Protect the brain and spinal cord

II   Storage of calcium

III   Production of hormones

IV   Manufacture of blood cells

a   I, II and III

b   II, III and IV

c   I and IV only

d   I, II and IV

2 In which part of the kidney does ultrafiltration take place?

a   Glomerulus

b   Trachea

c   Pituitary gland

d   Nephron

3 Which process removes indigestible material from the body?

a   Excretion

b   Digestion

c   Egestion

d   Peristalsis

4 Water vapour is released from plants through:

a   phloem

b   xylem

c   stomata

d   chloroplasts

5 Which of the substances below are produced during aerobic respiration in a cell?

I   Hydrogen

II   Oxygen

III   Water vapour

IV   Carbon dioxide

a   I and II

b   II only

c   I, II and IV

d   III and IV

6 The diagram below shows the reproductive organs of a flowering plant.

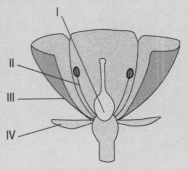

Which label is the stamen?

a   I

b   II

c   III

d   IV

7 Which item listed below will complete the following sentence?

Examples of non-biodegradable waste include plastic, _____ and radioactive waste.

a   banana peels

b   newspaper

c   nylon

d   yard waste

8 Which of the following ways result in food becoming contaminated?

I   Inadequate cooking

II   Poor personal hygiene

III   Chemical and physical contamination

IV   Using clean surfaces in food preparation activity

a   I, II and IV

b   I, III and IV

c   I, II and III

d   II, III and IV

Further practice questions and examples can be found on the accompanying website.

9 a Mrs Clarke is a 45-year-old office worker. She is sitting at her desk most of the day. Her BMI measurement indicates that she is 'obese'.

  i Which two measurements are needed to calculate Mrs Clarke's BMI? *(2)*

  ii Mrs Clarke's mother died at the age of 50 from a heart attack. Describe the change in an artery that can cause a heart attack. *(2)*

  iii Mrs Clarke's doctor carried out tests on her and found increased levels of glucose in her urine. Which medical condition causes this? *(1)*

  iv Which two hormones control the levels of glucose in the blood? *(2)*

  v Which organ produces the two hormones in part **iv**? *(1)*

  vi The doctor tells Mrs Clarke to lose weight. What two pieces of general advice should she follow in terms of her eating and lifestyle? *(2)*

b i The kidney is the major organ of excretion in humans. Name two other excretory organs and state their products. *(4)*

  ii What do you understand by the term 'homeostasis'? *(4)*

  iii The kidney is regarded as a homeostatic organ. Explain fully how it is involved in controlling the water balance of the body. *(7)*

10 a Plants can make their own food by photosynthesis.

  i Name the two substances that plants change chemically to make their food. *(2)*

  ii Name the sugar and the waste product formed in photosynthesis. *(2)*

  iii Which substance is needed to 'trap' the energy from sunlight? *(1)*

b The experiment below is carried out to investigate the effect of changing the intensity of light on the rate of photosynthesis.

  i How do you vary the intensity of light falling on the water-plant using the apparatus shown? *(1)*

  ii The results from the experiment were used to draw the graph below.

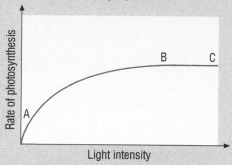

  Explain what is happening between points A and B on the graph. *(2)*

  iii Explain what is happening between points B and C on the graph. *(2)*

  iv Sketch a graph showing the effect of varying the concentration of carbon dioxide on the rate of photosynthesis. *(2)*

  v Sketch a graph showing the effect of varying the temperature between 10°C and 50°C on the rate of photosynthesis. Explain the shape of the line on this graph. *(3)*

> Further practice questions and examples can be found on the accompanying website.

9 Temperature control and ventilation
9.1 How is energy transferred?

Heat energy can be transferred from one place to another in three ways:

- conduction
- convection
- radiation.

In this section we will look at conduction and radiation. Convection is dealt with in 9.2.

Conduction

If you heat a metal spoon at one end, the heat energy is gradually transferred to the other end. This is called **conduction**. We say that the heat energy is conducted through the metal of the spoon.

When a solid is warmed up its particles (atoms, molecules or ions) start to vibrate more vigorously. These increased vibrations are passed on to their neighbouring particles, which in turn get hotter and pass on the vibrations to the particles they are in contact with, etc. Metals also contain free-moving electrons which drift between the particles in their structures. These can transfer the heat energy quickly through a metal. We say that metals are good conductors of heat (or are good **thermal conductors**).

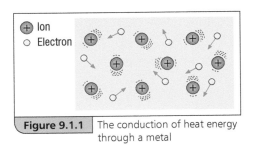

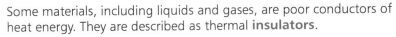

Figure 9.1.1 | The conduction of heat energy through a metal

Some materials, including liquids and gases, are poor conductors of heat energy. They are described as thermal **insulators**.

We can carry out experiments, such as the one shown opposite, to test which materials are good conductors of heat energy. The best conductor will let heat energy travel along it most quickly, melt the Vaseline and the drawing pin will fall off first.

So if you are choosing a material to make a cooking pan, you will decide on a good conductor of heat energy. In addition, the material needs to have a high melting point and should not react readily with steam or hot water. That is why steel, aluminium or copper is usually chosen.

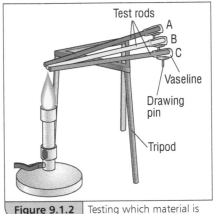

Figure 9.1.2 | Testing which material is the best thermal conductor

Radiation

Radiation is another method of transferring heat energy. It transfers energy in the form of electromagnetic waves, such as infrared radiation. These are given off from any hot object. You can feel the radiated heat energy when you hold your hands in front of a fire.

You might have seen images taken at night using an infrared camera. Instead of responding to light like a normal camera, this detects infrared radiation emitted from objects. The hotter the object, the more infrared radiation it gives off (emits).

The Sun's energy travels through space to reach Earth by radiation. Fortunately for us, radiation does not need a substance to transfer heat energy. That is why it can travel through space, which is a vacuum (contains no particles).

In experiments with shiny silvery cans and dull black cans of water we find that:

- a dull black can of cold water warms up faster in sunlight than a shiny silvery can containing the same volume of cold water
- a dull black can of hot water cools down faster than a shiny silvery can of hot water.

This shows us that:

- dull black surfaces absorb radiation more quickly than shiny silvery surfaces
- dull black surfaces radiate heat energy more quickly than shiny silvery surfaces.

Figure 9.1.3 Police use 'night-vision' cameras to detect suspects as they emit infrared radiation in the dark

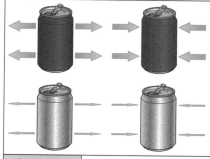

Figure 9.1.4 The differences between dull black and shiny silvery surfaces

SUMMARY QUESTIONS

1 a Which of the following materials is the best conductor of heat energy?

                iron   wood   plastic   glass

  b Explain your answer to part **a** in terms of particles.

2 Describe a fair test you could carry out to show that a black can of water absorbs energy more quickly than a silvery can of water.

3 a Which type of heat energy transfer can take place through a vacuum – conduction or radiation?

  b What evidence have you got for your answer to part **a**?

How is energy transferred in fluids?

- Describe how energy is transferred in liquids and gases (fluids).
- Discuss how convection takes place over the sea and land.
- Explain how convection takes place in a large beaker of water heated by a Bunsen burner.
- Explain how a thermos flask works.

Liquids and gases are sometimes referred to as fluids. The particles (mainly molecules) in a fluid are able to move around. There is more space on average between the particles in a gas than in a liquid and the gas particles can move more freely.

When a fluid is heated its particles move around more quickly. This means that a given number of particles will take up more space.

So as the fluid warms up, it expands and its density decreases. This means that the hot part of the fluid will rise, floating upwards. The heat energy is transferred by the hot particles moving from a warmer place to a cooler place. We call this **convection**.

As the warmer particles rise, cooler ones move sideways to take their place. This in turn makes particles in the fluid move downwards to take their place and a cycle is set up. This is called a convection current.

We can show a convection current in a large beaker of water heated by a Bunsen burner. By adding a coloured crystal we can follow the movement of the fluid, in this case water.

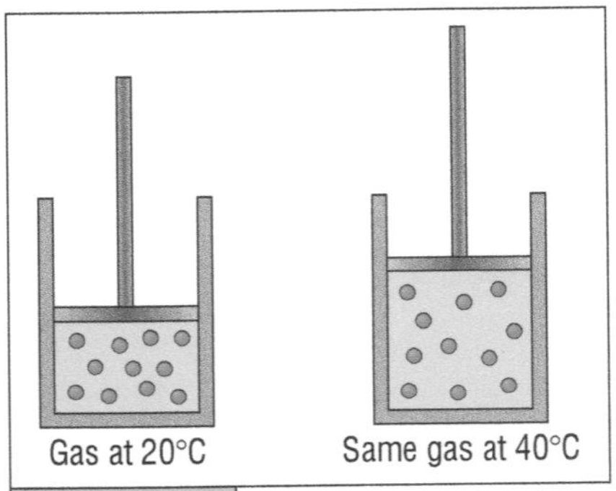

Figure 9.2.1 | A hot fluid occupies a larger volume than when it is cold as its density decreases as its temperature rises

Gas at 20°C Same gas at 40°C

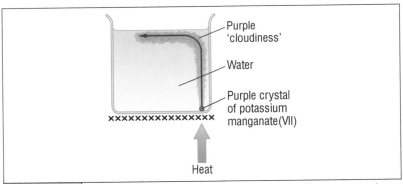

Figure 9.2.2 | Convection current set up in a beaker of water. The hot water above the flame expands, becomes less dense and rises. It is replaced above the flame by colder water and the convection current begins to circulate water around the beaker.

Purple 'cloudiness'
Water
Purple crystal of potassium manganate(VII)
Heat

Land and sea breezes

Have you ever noticed days when the wind direction near the coast changes to the opposite direction in a 24-hour period? The wind will switch from blowing in from the sea in the daytime (a sea breeze) to out to sea at night (a land breeze). We can explain these land and sea breezes by thinking of convection currents in the air. Look at Figure 9.2.3.

In sunlight, the land warms up more quickly than the sea. So the air above the land rises. Cooler air from over the sea rushes inland to take its place. So in daytime we get a breeze coming in off the sea.

EXAM TIP

When a fluid is heated it expands because of the increased movement of its particles – the particles themselves DO NOT expand.

Figure 9.2.3 | Convection currents cause land and sea breezes. Why does hot air rise?

Figure 9.2.4 | Convection currents cause breezes that cool you down on a day at the beach

At night-time, the land cools down more quickly than the sea. So the warmer air above the sea rises. Then the cooler air from over the land rushes out to take its place. This produces a breeze out to sea from the land.

How a thermos (or vacuum) flask works

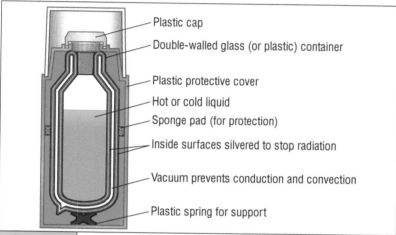

- Plastic cap
- Double-walled glass (or plastic) container
- Plastic protective cover
- Hot or cold liquid
- Sponge pad (for protection)
- Inside surfaces silvered to stop radiation
- Vacuum prevents conduction and convection
- Plastic spring for support

Figure 9.2.5 | A thermos flask helps to keep hot liquids hot or cold liquids cold

SUMMARY QUESTIONS

1 Explain how a convection current is set up in a room heated by a radiator against one wall.

2 Look at the diagram of the experiment in the figure below.

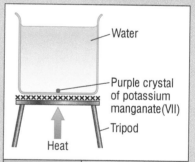

- Water
- Purple crystal of potassium manganate(VII)
- Tripod
- Heat

Figure 9.2.6

Predict what you would see in the beaker as it is heated beneath the coloured crystal.

3 Give two design features of a thermos flask that helps reduce energy transfer from its contents to the surroundings.

Thermostats and thermometers

Thermostats

Using less electricity when operating electrical appliances saves us money. Thermostats are devices that can switch the electric current off automatically once a certain temperature has been reached. The circuit will be switched back on automatically once it cools down below that temperature. So a thermostat can keep appliances at a certain temperature without you having to switch them on and off all the time yourself.

The bimetallic strip

Thermostats contain a bimetallic strip which bends, creating a gap that breaks the circuit when the desired temperature is reached and stops any further heating.

A bimetallic strip is made of two strips of different metals, such as brass and steel. The two strips can be welded together. All metals will expand as they get hot. However, they will differ by how much they expand for a given temperature rise. For example, brass expands more than steel. So when the bimetallic strip is heated, the strip will bend. Look at Figure 9.3.1. Notice how the brass strip is longer than the iron strip.

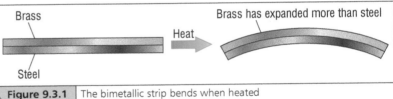

Brass

Steel

Heat

Brass has expanded more than steel

Figure 9.3.1 The bimetallic strip bends when heated

Thermostatically controlled household appliances

Central heating, or air conditioning, is often controlled automatically by thermostats in different rooms. These can feed back to the boiler, or air conditioning unit, when a certain temperature is reached. In this way they can maintain a steady temperature in a building.

In other appliances we can vary the temperature more often using a control knob. For example, when ironing clothes you will need to switch settings between different fabrics. In an iron the control knob will change the distance between the contact point and the bimetallic strip in its electrical circuit. Look at the circuit in Figure 9.3.2.

When ironing synthetic fabrics, the iron should not be allowed to get too hot. Turning the control knob to the right setting will make the gap between the contact point and the bimetallic strip open up at a lower temperature than if the knob is set to 'cotton'.

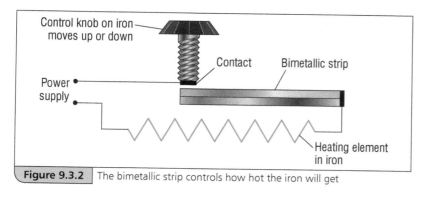

Figure 9.3.2 | The bimetallic strip controls how hot the iron will get

Thermometers

There are several different types of thermometer.

Laboratory thermometer

These are made of glass with a narrow bore and the bulb at the bottom. The bulb and bore have mercury (a liquid metal) in them. There is a vacuum above the thin thread of mercury in the bore. As the temperature increases, the mercury expands and rises up the bore. You read the temperature against the scale, marked in degrees Celsius (°C). They usually have a range from –10°C to 110°C.

Alcohol thermometer

Like the mercury thermometer above, this is a liquid-in-glass thermometer. The alcohol is a colourless liquid so it has red dye added to make reading the thermometer easier. The alcohol boils at 78°C so it can't be used at high temperatures. However, it can be used at lower temperatures than a mercury thermometer.

Clinical thermometer

This is used to take the temperature of the body. They have a narrow range either side of body temperature (37.6°C), from 34°C to 43°C. The bore has a narrow 'kink' (called a constriction). This lets mercury pass up through it, but doesn't let it pass down. So once your temperature is taken, the doctor or nurse can take it out of your mouth and look at the temperature. The thermometer is shaken to return the mercury back to the bulb.

Maximum–minimum thermometer

These are usually used to keep records of the weather, for example, the maximum and minimum temperatures reached in a 24-hour period. They have alcohol on top of mercury in a U-shaped tube. A marker, such as a steel disc, is left at the minimum in one arm of the tube and at the maximum in the other arm. The markers can be re-set using a magnet. Look at Figure 9.3.3.

Digital thermometers

These give a read-out in numbers on a liquid-crystal-display. They are metal probes, such as those used in cooking to insert into meat to see how hot it is inside.

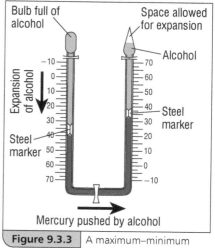

Figure 9.3.3 | A maximum–minimum thermometer

Evaporation and cooling

Evaporation and latent heat of vaporisation

Why do puddles of water on a concrete path exposed to sunlight seem to disappear? Evaporation is the change of state when a liquid turns into its gas (or vapour). Liquids do not have to boil in order to change from a liquid to a gas. Even at room temperature, liquids, such as water, are evaporating.

In any substance, at any temperature, the particles will have a range of energies. A few have low energy, a few have high energy and most have energies somewhere in between. It is the high-energy particles that evaporate off. They have enough energy to escape from the surface of the liquid.

The temperature of a liquid depends on the average energy possessed by its particles. If some of those with the highest energy escape during evaporation, the average energy of the particles remaining will be lowered. Therefore, the liquid's temperature is decreased.

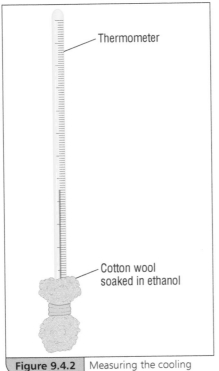

Figure 9.4.2 | Measuring the cooling effect of evaporation

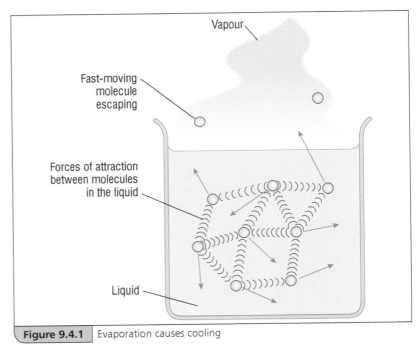

Figure 9.4.1 | Evaporation causes cooling

You can measure the temperature decrease in a practical test like the one shown in Figure 9.4.2 opposite.

The forces of attraction between the particles in the liquid are indicated by its **latent heat of vaporisation**. This is the amount of energy needed to vaporise a kilogram of the liquid without changing its temperature. At its boiling point, you can carry on heating a liquid as it boils away, but its temperature does not rise. That's because the energy supplied is being used to break the attractive forces between the particles in the liquid as they escape as a gas. The weaker the forces of attraction between its particles are, the faster a liquid evaporates.

LINK

To remind yourself about changes of state, see 1.1 'States of matter'.

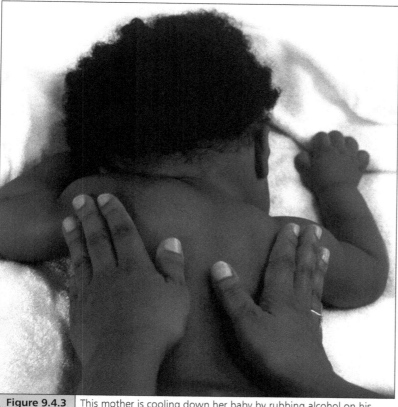

Figure 9.4.3 This mother is cooling down her baby by rubbing alcohol on his back. As the alcohol evaporates it absorbs energy from the baby's body, lowering his temperature.

KEY POINTS

1 Evaporation cools a liquid down as its most energetic particles escape.

2 The higher the latent heat of vaporisation, the stronger the forces of attraction between particles in a liquid.

3 Water evaporating from sweat helps to cool down the body.

Cooling your body down

Our bodies rely on many complex chemical reactions to function properly. All of these reactions make up our metabolism. The speed at which these reactions take place is called our metabolic rate. The faster your metabolic rate, the more heat energy is released and the hotter you get (as when exercising).

Your body cools itself by sweating. Sweat glands near the surface of your skin release sweat. The water in the sweat evaporates, absorbing energy from your body as the water particles escape, cooling you down.

You can lick the back of your hand to feel this cooling effect caused by evaporation. Blowing across the back of your hand speeds up the evaporation and makes your skin feel even colder.

SUMMARY QUESTIONS

1 Describe what happens to the particles in a liquid when it evaporates.

2 Why does sweating help to cool us down?

3 Explain how rubbing on alcohol can help to lower the body temperature of a baby.

Humidity and ventilation

In 9.4 we saw how the forces between the particles in a liquid (as indicated by its latent heat of vaporisation) affect the rate of evaporation.

The other factors that affect the rate of evaporation of a liquid are:

- temperature (the higher the temperature, the faster the liquid evaporates)
- surface area of liquid (the larger the surface area, the faster the liquid evaporates)
- the humidity (water vapour content) of the air above the liquid (the lower the humidity, the faster the liquid evaporates).

Relative humidity

Hot and humid days are often described as 'sticky' days. The relative humidity will be high. This is the amount of water vapour in the air measured as a percentage of the maximum amount of water vapour the air could hold on a particular day.

On these days your clothes tend to stick to your skin because the water in your sweat finds it difficult to evaporate off. Therefore, its cooling effect is limited. So when the relative humidity is high, people can suffer from heat exhaustion. Their bodies can get dehydrated if they do not replace the water lost as sweat. The body will continue to sweat as your core body temperature rises even though not much evaporation takes place.

Evaporation of the water from sweat is slow on a humid day because the air is almost saturated in water vapour. It cannot hold much more. This is why fans help. They blow away the air next to the skin, lowering the humidity long enough for water to evaporate from your skin, absorbing heat energy from your body.

Too much sun

The Sun's rays carry harmful ultraviolet radiation to Earth. If you don't apply suntan lotion of sufficiently high factor or sun-screen or sun-block, you risk getting sunburnt. The ultraviolet radiation will burn your skin, especially pale skin, which will blister and peel. The dark colouring in skin is formed by the body's natural protection, called melanin.

Heatstroke is when your core body temperature rises to dangerous levels. If it rises to about 42°C it can be fatal. The heat we generate in metabolic reactions is usually transferred from our skin as radiated heat energy or as heat energy absorbed by the water in sweat evaporating. But in extremely hot weather or in high humidity, you might not be able to get rid of the heat energy quickly enough.

Victims of heatstroke can feel sick, tired and weak, and might also suffer from dizziness, vomiting, headaches and muscle cramps. When the core body temperature rises too high, people can behave strangely, their pulse will race and breathing will become difficult. In severe cases the person will fall into a coma.

Athletes in endurance events are at risk of heatstroke when they compete in hot or humid weather. They might not be able to dissipate the heat energy from their body quickly enough to maintain a normal body temperature and they can collapse.

The importance of good ventilation

Buildings need to be well-ventilated to keep their occupants comfortable and healthy. If air is not allowed to circulate, and fresh air introduced, the air inside the building will get stale. Humidity will rise if lots of people are inside as they breathe out water vapour that cannot escape. In these conditions, microorganisms can flourish. These can cause respiratory problems and make people feel ill.

Good ventilation can be as easy as opening the correct windows to ensure a good flow of air. You want warm, stale air to leave and be replaced by cool, fresh air. As you know, warm air rises so it is best to have an upper window open as well as one at a lower level. Then convection can take place.

Air-conditioning units use pumps and fans to help introduce cool, fresh air into a building and get rid of, or clean and recycle, stale air.

Humidifiers introduce water vapour into a building if the air gets too dry. Dry air can make people uncomfortable. Humidifiers can help maintain an optimum level of water vapour in the air so people can work comfortably.

In very humid Caribbean territories such as Trinidad and Guyana that are outside of the normal hurricane path, many houses are built with air vents just below the eaves of the roof to allow warm air to leave as it rises. This type of construction, however, is not suitable for other territories affected by hurricanes.

Warmer air leaves room through upper window

Air from outside drawn into room through lower window

Figure 9.5.1 | Windows provide good ventilation

LINK

To remind yourself about convection, see 9.2 'How is energy transferred in fluids?'

SUMMARY QUESTIONS

1 a Design an experiment to show how temperature affects the rate of evaporation of water.

   b Give two other factors that affect the rate of evaporation.

   c Choose which type of day is best for drying clothes on a washing line and explain why.

   A a cool day

   B a hot, humid day

   C a hot, dry day

2 Describe what happens to a person who gets heatstroke.

3 Buildings with poor ventilation can develop 'sick-building syndrome'. Explain why this happens.

KEY POINTS

1 The body sweats more in hot, humid conditions, but high humidity stops the water evaporating off the skin, reducing its cooling effect.

2 Effective ventilation is needed in buildings to make them comfortable to live and work in.

10 Conservation of energy

10.1   Energy

We can't do anything without energy. Energy is needed to produce a change. So energy makes things happen!

There are different forms of energy, which can be converted into each other during changes. However, the amount of energy before the change is the same as the amount of energy after the change. This is called the **conservation of energy**. So when people say that energy is 'lost' that is not really true. Energy gets more and more spread out during energy conversions and is eventually transferred to the environment as heat energy, which is no longer useful energy.

Forms of energy

Energy can be stored or transferred as different forms of energy.

- Chemical energy – the energy stored in chemicals such as fuels and foods. This chemical energy is released during any chemical reaction.
- Kinetic energy (KE) – the energy an object has because of its movement.
- Gravitational potential energy (GPE) – the energy stored by an object because of its position, for example above ground level.
- Elastic (or strain) potential energy – the energy stored in a material under stress, for example in a stretched rubber band or spring.
- Electrical energy – the energy transferred by the movement of electrons in an electric current.
- Heat energy – the energy of an object due to its temperature.

Other common forms of energy are sound and light energy in which energy is transferred as waves.

Energy interconversions

Here are some examples of the ways energy can be transformed from one form to another.

A battery-operated radio
    chemical energy stored in the batteries → electrical energy → sound energy (+ heat energy)

A bungee jumper
    gravitational potential energy → kinetic energy → elastic potential energy → GPE → KE → elastic potential energy → etc. as the person bounces up and down

Figure 10.1.1   A bungee jumper in action – why do they eventually come to rest if the conservation of energy is true?

In a computer

electrical energy → sound + light energy + heat energy

A nuclear power station

nuclear energy → heat energy in steam → kinetic energy of turbines in generator (sometimes called mechanical energy) → electrical energy

In nuclear fission reactions in a power station large atoms are split into smaller atoms. Scientists find that the mass of all the particles after the nuclear reaction is slightly less than the mass before the change. This is not the case in chemical reactions. They conclude that the small amount of missing mass has been converted into energy. In a nuclear reactor in a power station the fission is carefully controlled. However, in a nuclear bomb these reactions are triggered to happen very quickly, producing a massive explosion.

Solar energy is produced on the Sun by nuclear reactions. They are fusion reactions in which small atoms join to make larger atoms.

The unit of energy

Scientists measure energy using the unit called joules, J. It is the energy used when a force of one newton, N, is exerted over a distance of one metre (see 12.2 page 112).

(1000 J = 1 kJ and 1 000 000 J = 1 MJ, where kJ are kilojoules and MJ are megajoules)

Figure 10.1.2 The Doel nuclear power station in Belgium

Energy on the move and momentum

LEARNING OUTCOMES

- Discuss ways in which energy is transported or transferred.
- Explain the principles of momentum.

Moving energy

We have already seen how energy can be transferred from one place to another by conduction, convection and radiation. Waves are another way of transferring energy from place to place. They can be used to transmit messages as light waves through optical fibres. Remember that light forms part of the electromagnetic spectrum of waves. Other electromagnetic waves used to transfer energy in the communications industry are infrared rays, microwaves and radio waves.

We have also seen how energy is moved from place to place by waves in the sea. Sound waves are another way that energy is transferred.

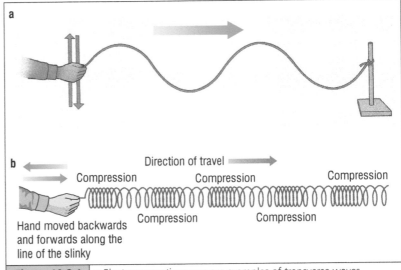

a

b

Direction of travel

Compression   Compression   Compression

Compression   Compression

Hand moved backwards and forwards along the line of the slinky

Figure 10.2.1 **a** Electromagnetic waves are examples of transverse waves
b Sound waves are examples of longitudinal waves

We can also focus energy to concentrate it when we use solar power to generate electricity or for cooking. The use of a curved reflective surface can also re-direct light energy in car headlights where the light emerges as parallel beams.

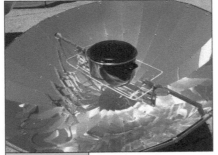

Figure 10.2.2 This solar cooker concentrates solar energy on to the cooking pot

Momentum

Any object that is moving has momentum. The more momentum it has, the harder it is to stop. Objects with a lot of momentum have a large mass and/or a large velocity.

momentum = mass × velocity, written as $p = m \times v$, *where the units are*: momentum in kgm/s; mass in kg; velocity in m/s.

Scientists have found that in any collision the momentum is the same before and after the collision. This is called the conservation of momentum. We can demonstrate this in the suspended metal balls in a 'Newton's cradle' (see Figure 10.2.3).

We can carry out experiments in the lab using trolleys to investigate collisions. We find that when a trolley moving at a certain velocity hits a stationary trolley of the same mass, they move off together, at half the original velocity. This shows that momentum is conserved.

In a car crash, momentum is also conserved so a car hitting a stationary line of cars will transfer its momentum down the line. Momentum, like velocity, has both size and direction, which is important when considering changes in momentum when objects collide.

Figure 10.2.4 Momentum transferred in a car crash (The law of conservation of momentum states that total momentum before collision = total momentum after collision.)

Worked example
An athlete in the hundred metres has a mass of 75 kg and is running at 10 m/s. Calculate the momentum of the sprinter.

momentum = mass × velocity

$$= 75 \text{ kg} \times 10 \text{ m/s}$$

$$= \textbf{750 kgm/s}$$

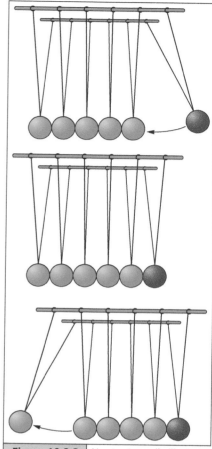

Figure 10.2.3 Newton's cradle illustrates the conservation of momentum

SUMMARY QUESTIONS

1 Give three examples of how energy is transferred from place to place using waves.

2 Describe how a solar cooker works.

3 a What is meant by the 'conservation of momentum'?
  b i Which of these three cars has the greatest momentum when travelling at 20 m/s?
      car A of mass 1000 kg
      car B of mass 1100 kg
      car C of mass 1200 kg
   ii Which car would have the greater momentum – car A travelling at 20 m/s or car B travelling at 40 m/s? Explain your answer.

4 A railway truck travelling down the track at 4 m/s bumps into an identical truck that is stationary. In theory, at what speed should both trucks continue down the track following the collision?

5 Calculate the momentum of a truck of mass 2500 kg moving at a velocity of 15 m/s.

KEY POINTS

1 Energy can be transferred from one place to another by waves. It can also be redirected using reflective surfaces (or lenses in the case of light).

2 Any object that is moving has momentum. The amount of momentum depends on the object's mass and velocity.

3 momentum (p) = mass (m) × velocity (v)

4 Momentum is conserved in a collision.

11 Electricity and lighting

11.1 Electricity

Conductors and insulators

Electricity can only flow if there is a complete pathway, called a circuit, for it to pass around. The electricity itself is made up of moving electrons (the tiny negative particles from inside atoms). Look at the simple electrical circuit in Figure 11.1.1.

We use circuit diagrams to represent circuits. The components in the circuit are each given a symbol.

Materials that let electrons flow through them are called electrical **conductors**.

Materials that do not let electrons pass through them are called electrical **insulators**.

The circuit to test which materials are conductors and which are insulators is shown in Figure 11.1.2.

We find that all metals are good conductors of electricity, whereas most non-metallic materials are insulators. Carbon in the form of graphite is an exception, as it is a non-metal that does contain electrons that are free to move through its structure.

There are some materials, such as silicon, that will conduct electricity slightly (not as well as a metal, but better than an insulator). These are called semi-conductors. They are used to make components for computers.

Series and parallel circuits

Electrical components, such as lamps, can be arranged in series or parallel circuits. In a series circuit the components are connected in line with each other. Look at Figure 11.1.3.

The **current** flows through one lamp then the next. We can measure the current using an ammeter. An ammeter connected into a series circuit in any position gives the same reading. This shows that the current is the same at any point in a series circuit.

If one of the lamps in series is unscrewed or blows, the other lamp goes out too. There is no pathway for the current to make its way back to the other end of the cell. Compare this with the parallel circuit shown in Figure 11.1.4. The current leaving the cell, or battery, is split between the branches of the parallel circuit before rejoining again on the way back to the cell.

In the parallel circuit if one lamp blows, the other stays lit. That's because there is still a complete circuit without the current having to go through the broken branch in the circuit.

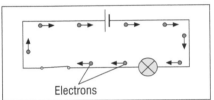

Figure 11.1.1 A simple circuit diagram showing electron flow

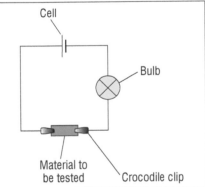

Figure 11.1.2 The material being tested is put across the gap in the circuit to see if the lamp lights up

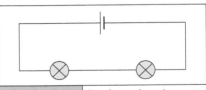

Figure 11.1.3 Two lamps in series

Current, voltage and resistance

Electrical current is the rate of flow of charge around a circuit. It is measured by an ammeter (connected in series). Its units are amps (A).

Electromotive force (e.m.f.) is a measure of the 'pushing power' of a cell or battery. It is measured by a voltmeter (connected in parallel across the cell), in units called volts (V).

The electrons, pushed around by the cell, carry energy transferred from the chemicals in the cell. As they pass through the thin wire in a lamp this electrical energy is transferred to heat and light is released by the lamp. There is a difference in energy before and after each electron passes through the lamp. We call this a potential difference (p.d.), which is also measured in volts.

The **resistance** of a component is a measure of how difficult it is for current to pass through it. We can calculate the resistance, knowing the current and voltage using the equation:

$$\text{resistance, } R = \frac{\text{p.d. across the component, } V}{\text{current through the component, } I}$$

where p.d. is measured in volts (V), current in amps (A) and resistance is in units called ohms, (Ω).

The equation is often rearranged and quoted as $V = I \times R$ and is **known as Ohm's law**. We can say that at constant temperature the current is proportional to the potential difference.

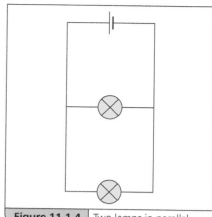

Figure 11.1.4 Two lamps in parallel

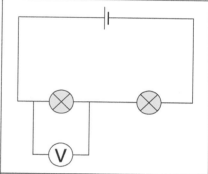

Figure 11.1.5 Measuring the potential difference (p.d.) across a lamp. In parallel circuits, the p.d. across each component is the same. In a series circuit, the p.d. of the battery is shared between the components.

Worked example

A current of 0.05 A, supplied by a 3 V battery, passes through a resistance wire. What is the resistance of the wire?

$$I = 0.05\,\text{A}, V = 3\,\text{V}$$

so

$$R = \frac{3}{0.05}$$
$$= 60\,\Omega \text{ (ohms)}$$

SUMMARY QUESTIONS

1 a Draw a circuit diagram with one cell and three lamps connected in parallel.

  b What would happen if the middle lamp blew and went out? Explain your answer.

2 A wire is connected to a 1.5 V cell and has a 0.2 A current passing through it. What is the resistance of the wire?

3 An electrical circuit has a resistance of 20 ohms and a current of 0.05 A. What voltage is applied in this circuit?

Fuses and cables (flexes)

- Explain how a fuse works as a safety device.
- Use the formula $I = W \div V$ to calculate current, and rearrange it to calculate wattage.
- State the correct colour codes for wires in a 3-pin plug.

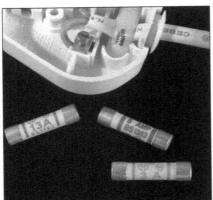

Figure 11.2.1 Fuses have different ratings depending on the power needed to work the appliance. This type of fuse is used inside plugs.

The fuse as a safety device

Electrical appliances are very useful, but if too much current flows into them they can overheat and cause fires. This is why we use fuses. A **fuse** contains a thin wire that melts and snaps if too much current passes through it.

The correct fuse rating (for example, 3 A, 5 A or 13 A) is calculated from the wattage (power is measured in watts (W)) of the appliance and the mains voltage. To calculate the current needed to run the appliance, we use the equation:

$$I \text{ (current)} = \frac{W \text{ (power)}}{V \text{ (mains voltage)}}$$

Then we choose a fuse that will allow this current to pass through, but will 'blow' (melt and snap) if more than that current surges into the appliance.

Worked example

a If you have an appliance that has a power rating of 250 W on an island with a 110 V mains supply, what current will the appliance use?

b Using your answer to a, what fuse should be used with this appliance?

a $I \text{ (current)} = \dfrac{250 \text{ W}}{110 \text{ V}}$

$\phantom{a \ I \text{ (current)} } = \textbf{2.3 A}$

b Therefore, you would need to use a **3 A fuse**.

The equation I (current) $= W$ (power) $\div V$ (mains voltage) can be rearranged to calculate the power of an appliance in watts (W), given the current and voltage supplied:

$$\text{power (in watts)} = I \text{ (in amps)} \times V \text{ (in volts)}$$

Plugs

Appliances with metal cases will be attached to their plugs by three wires:

- the live wire (brown)
- the neutral wire (blue)
- the earth wire (yellow and green).

These are all encased in an outer plastic cable. The wires themselves are made of copper metal. Look at Figure 11.2.2 to see the correct wiring of a 3-pin plug.

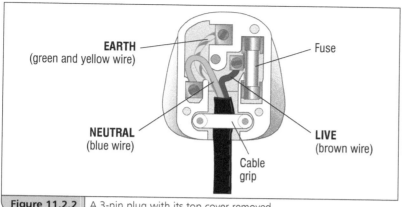

Figure 11.2.2 | A 3-pin plug with its top cover removed

The fuse is placed between the live pin of the plug (hidden under the fuse) and the brown live wire that runs to the appliance. The earth wire is needed for metal-cased appliances. The earth pin is attached via the socket circuit to the ground in case the live wire touches the metal casing. Appliances with plastic casing, such as a hairdryer, only need a two-core cable and in their plug there is no connection to the earth pin.

Figure 11.2.3 | This is a cable used to carry mains electricity into homes. It has thick copper wires inside – the thicker the wire, the lower its resistance, so the cable does not heat up as much, which would waste energy. Overhead and underground power cables from power stations have even thicker copper cores.

KEY POINTS

1 Fuses act as safety devices.

2 You can calculate the fuse needed in the plug of an appliance using the equation $I = \dfrac{W}{V}$

3 There are two-core, three-core and thick overhead/underground cables for different uses and appliances.

SUMMARY QUESTIONS

1 a What is the function of fuse wire?

   b Explain how the fuse in a plug works.

2 a The mains voltage on a particular Caribbean island is 220 V. An appliance has a power rating of 500 W. Calculate the size of fuse that should be used in its plug.

   b What could happen if someone used a 15 A fuse in this appliance?

3 An electrical appliance is designed to run on a voltage of 240 V and a current of 0.5 A. What is the power supplied to the appliance?

4 Why do overhead power cables have thick copper cores?

Energy consumption

- Calculate the energy consumed by different household appliances.
- Describe how to read electricity meters.
- Calculate household energy bills.
- Discuss ways to conserve energy.

Most people now rely on electrical appliances to give us the modern conveniences we have come to expect. However, the electrical energy we use has to be paid for. Therefore, the less energy we consume, the lower our electricity bills. It can also benefit the environment as the electrical energy you use is typically generated from fossil fuels.

We can use this equation to calculate our energy consumption when using an appliance:

$$\text{energy consumption} = \text{power} \times \text{time}$$
$$\text{(in joules, J)} \quad \text{(in watts, W)} \quad \text{(in seconds, s)}$$

Worked example

A 60 W light bulb is left on for 5 minutes. How much energy does it use?

First of all change the minutes into seconds to use in the equation above:

$$5\,\text{min} \times 60 = 300\,\text{s}$$
$$\text{Energy consumed} = 60\,\text{W} \times 300\,\text{s}$$
$$= \mathbf{18\,000\,J}$$

The amount of energy a home needs when quoted in joules is very large. Even using kilojoules (where 1 kilojoule, kJ, is 1000 J), it is still a large number on a bill for a three-month period. So electricity boards find it better to use a unit of energy called a kilowatt-hour (kWh).

1 kWh is the energy supplied to a 1 kW (1000 W) appliance for 1 hour.

The kilowatt-hour (kWh) is the unit shown on electricity bills and the unit shown on electricity meters. Your electricity can show an analogue display (where dials rotate for each digit – see Figure 11.3.1) or a digital display (where numbers change and can be read directly – see Figure 11.3.2).

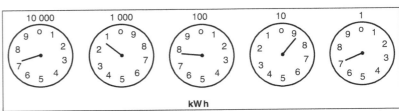

Figure 11.3.1 Reading an analogue electricity meter. This reading is 71 787. The rules for reading an analogue meter are: **a** Read from left to right; **b** If the pointer is between two numbers, record the lower one; **c** If the pointer is directly opposite a number, record that number, and **d** If the pointer is between '9' and '0', record '9' then take one away from the number recorded for the dial on its left

The electricity supplier will read your meter, perhaps every month, or you can read it and send in the reading yourself. They will charge you for the number of kilowatt-hours used, with an additional charge for any units over 100 units consumed per month. The units up to 100 are charged at a variable rate. In the worked example bill from Dominica below, the charge is divided into two rates called Block 1 and Block 2. A fuel surcharge is also applied to the energy consumed for the first 100 units. Some companies also make a standing charge that must be paid even if you use no electricity. There is also Value Added Tax (15% at present) to pay on any units consumed over 100 kWh.

Figure 11.3.2 | A digital electricity meter

Worked example

A consumer used 100 units (kWh) of electricity in a month. 50 units were charged on a Block 1 tariff of 57.8 cents per kWh and the next on Block 2 at 67.0 cents per kWh. The fuel surcharge was 34.3 cents per kWh used. What did the consumer pay for their electricity?

Block 1 charge = 57.8 × 50 = 2890 cents = \$28.90
Block 2 charge = 67.0 × 50 = 3350 cents = \$33.50
Fuel surcharge = 34.3 × 100 = 3430 cents = \$34.30
Total   =   **\$96.70**

Electricity is a major household bill. You can conserve energy and reduce your electricity bills by turning appliances off when not in use, and choosing energy efficient devices when buying new appliances. All electrical goods have efficiency ratings. You can also use energy-saving light bulbs in place of traditional filament bulbs which waste a lot of energy as heat.

SUMMARY QUESTIONS

1 Calculate the energy consumption in joules for:
   a a 500 W electrical heater left on for 10 minutes
   b a 60 W bulb left on for 5 hours.

2 An electricity meter read on 1st October was '1108' units. When it was read a month later it was '1192' units. The cost of the first 50 units was 55 cents per kWh and any units over that, up to 100 units, was 65 cents per kWh. Calculate the cost of the electrical energy consumed during that month.

3 List three ways in which you could reduce the electrical energy you use at home.

KEY POINTS

1 The unit of electrical energy consumed is called the kilowatt-hour (kWh).

2 You can calculate the electricity used in a certain period by reading the electricity meter at the start and end of the period, and subtracting the readings.

3 Your electricity bill is calculated from the units (kWh) used multiplied by the cost per kWh.

4 It is important to conserve energy to reduce bills and help the environment.

More efficient display screens

People are keener than ever to use energy efficient appliances around the home to reduce their energy bills. For example, the screen you use for your TV or computer display is changing from a traditional cathode ray tube (CRT) to a light emitting diode (LED), plasma screen or a liquid crystal display (LCD). In general, the LEDs are the most efficient, and are getting cheaper in price too, although plasma and LCD also offer significant energy savings over the old CRT screens.

More efficient lighting

Traditionally, filament light bulbs have been hung from ceilings and attached to fittings on walls. There is a choice of brightness available in different filament lamps. The bulbs come in 40 W, 60 W and 100 W sizes, with 100 W giving off most light, but also being the most expensive to run.

The main problem with filament lamps is the amount of energy they waste. As much as 95 J of heat energy is produced for every 5 J of light given out. The electricity passes through the thin metal wire filament. There is quite a resistance to the passage of electrons through such a narrow wire and heat energy is released. This heats the tungsten wire up to 'white heat' and this glow is the light we see.

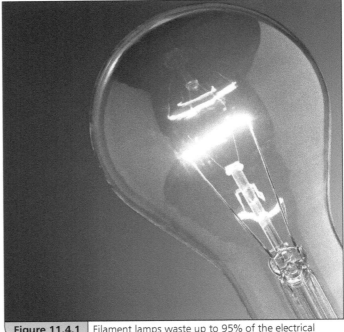

Figure 11.4.1 Filament lamps waste up to 95% of the electrical energy supplied to them by heating up the filament and its surroundings

We are now much more conscious of the environmental impact of wasting energy like this. Therefore new energy-saving light bulbs are becoming more popular with plans to phase out filament lamps. The energy-saving bulbs are derived from fluorescent tube lighting. They use 4 to 6 times less energy than a filament lamp that would give off the same light. Fluorescent tube lighting is given off by the long tubes you see in many shops and public buildings. They do not get as hot as filament lamps.

Fluorescent tubes have electrodes at each end with electrons jumping between them. These pass energy onto the mercury atoms inside the long tube. When the mercury atoms go back to their original energy, they release ultraviolet light. This interacts with the lining of the long tube, which gives off visible light energy. The tube emits light along its whole length. It is not a point-source of light like the filament lamp. This results in very diffuse shadows being formed in fluorescent lighting compared with the sharper shadows in filament lighting. So there are fewer areas of dark shadow in rooms with fluorescent tube lighting.

The new energy-saving light bulbs are called compact fluorescent lamps (CFLs). They are more expensive than filament lamps, but last much longer. They also take a little time to give off their maximum light, whereas a filament lamp lights up fully as soon as you switch it on. The filament tubes also contain mercury, which is a toxic heavy metal. However, these can be recycled and the mercury is collected to use again in new low-energy lighting units. Any disadvantages of the CFLs must be weighed against the energy savings they offer. They only use between a fifth and a quarter of the energy of traditional filament lamps of the same light output. Therefore, they will be the future of lighting along with other new developments.

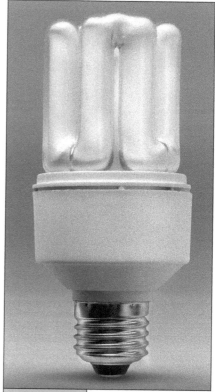

Figure 11.4.2 Fluorescent tube lighting is much more efficient than filament lamps

KEY POINTS

1 Modern LED, LCD and plasma screens are much more energy efficient than older, traditional CRT TVs and computer monitor screens.

2 Filament lamps are very inefficient, wasting 95% of the electrical energy supplied to them as heat energy.

3 Low energy compact fluorescent lighting (CFL) is the environmentally friendly option.

SUMMARY QUESTIONS

1 Which one of the following types of display screen is generally considered the most energy efficient to use?
Plasma; CRT; LED; LCD

2 How does a filament lamp give out light?

3 How does fluorescent tube lighting give off light?

4 Draw a table comparing the benefits and drawbacks of filament lamps compared with fluorescent tube lighting or compact fluorescent lighting.

Be prepared in an emergency

LEARNING OUTCOMES

- Explain the principles of fighting different types of fire.
- Describe first aid methods for different accidents, for example electric shock, burns and cuts.

Figure 11.5.1 Fire-breaks in forests deprive fires of fuel

Fire fighting

For a fire to keep burning it must have three things present:

- fuel
- oxygen
- heat energy.

Without any one of these three things, the fire will go out. This is the basis of fire fighting. For example, a fire starting in a waste paper bin can be put out with water. Spraying water onto the paper fire takes away the heat and the fire goes out. Alternatively, a heat-proof cover could be put across the top of the bin. This extinguishes the fire by cutting off its supply of oxygen.

However, water cannot be used on all fires. In electrical fires and fires involving burning metals or oil, water can make the fire worse. So there are different fire extinguishers to tackle different types of fire.

In fires involving gas, the best way to put out the fire is to remove the fuel by turning off the gas. Carbon dioxide extinguishers are used for electrical fires. The same gas is found inside foam extinguishers used outdoors where the carbon dioxide might otherwise be blown away from the fire. Carbon dioxide deprives a fire of oxygen.

First aid

If an accident happens, it is useful to know how to treat someone in an emergency.

Electric shock

In a case of electric shock, the first thing to do is to cut off the electricity if the patient is still in contact with the supply. If possible, turn off at the mains switch. Phone the emergency services immediately. Do not touch the person if they are still in contact with the faulty equipment as you will also be electrocuted. Follow instructions from the emergency services while you wait for them to arrive. If the current can't be switched off and there is an insulator at hand, they might tell you to push the victim away from the source using the insulator.

In severe cases, the person might stop breathing. Then you should try mouth-to-mouth (or mouth-to-nose) resuscitation. This is also called CPR (cardio-pulmonary resuscitation). First of all loosen any clothing around the neck and chest. Then lay the victim on their back and tilt their head back slightly. Press down on the chest 30 times at a steady rate of just over one compression per second. Make sure their mouth is clear. If it is, pinch their nostrils together and blow into their mouth twice. Your mouth should form a seal around theirs for this to inflate the lungs. Repeat the 30 chest compressions and two rescue breaths until they start breathing again or emergency services arrive. Then place the person in the recovery position (see Figure 11.5.2).

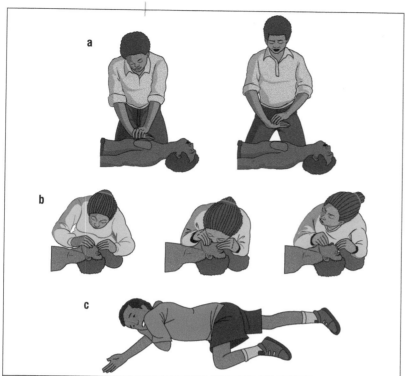

Figure 11.5.2   **a** Carrying out chest compressions
                     b Giving a rescue breath
                     c The recovery position

Burns

In some accidents, including electric shocks, people receive burns. To treat a burn, hold the affected area under cold running water for at least ten minutes. Then cover the burn in cling film (do not use fluffy material). Raise the affected limb to reduce swelling while waiting for medical assistance.

In a science laboratory, there are plenty of risks of injury because you work with glassware, some hazardous chemicals, and sources of heat and electricity. However, every school has rules to follow in a science lab to reduce the risks and make accidents a rare event. Look at your lab rules and think how each one reduces the risk of an accident.

KEY POINTS

1. A fire needs fuel, oxygen and heat energy to keep burning. Removing any one of these can put the fire out.

2. There are different types of fire extinguisher for different types of fire.

3. Basic first aid is useful in case of an accident and can even save a life in a serious case.

SUMMARY QUESTIONS

1 **a** A pan of oil used for deep frying can catch fire if it is allowed to get too hot. It can be put out by placing a damp cloth over the top of the pan. Explain how this method works.

  b Explain how a fire-break works to prevent a bush fire spreading.

2 If there is an accident in the science lab and someone cuts their hand, think of two ways that you could reduce the bleeding from the wound.

3 When you are doing an experiment that needs a Bunsen burner, if it is lit but not being used for heating, how should the burner be left? Explain why.

4 Write a step-by-step guide on how to revive the victim of an accident using mouth-to-mouth resuscitation (CPR), including chest compressions.

Safety first

Types of accidents

You should feel safe in your home, but most admissions to emergency medical departments in hospitals are the result of accidents at home. People have accidents involving:

- electric shocks and fires from faulty or incorrectly used electrical appliances (appliances should be checked regularly and never used if a bare wire or damage to casing is seen – an electrician should repair the faulty equipment)
- fires and inhalation of fumes, such as toxic carbon monoxide, from faulty gas appliances
- sprains and broken bones from falls or maintenance tasks
- cuts from sharp objects, such as kitchen knives.

At the workplace, hazards can be more serious, but workers are trained and should be aware of them. As well as the same hazards listed above, workplace hazards include:

- toxic gases
- flammable substances
- corrosive substances
- excessive noise
- food contamination
- heavy machinery
- lifting heavy objects
- infection by pathogens.

Avoiding accidents

In the workplace, including school laboratories, you will see safety symbols that give advice, such as symbols for wearing eye protection. Here are some safety symbols you might see.

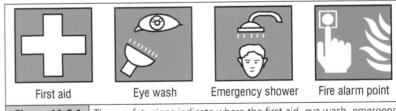

First aid   Eye wash   Emergency shower   Fire alarm point

Figure 11.6.1 These safety signs indicate where the first aid, eye wash, emergency shower and fire alarm point are found in the workplace

Some substances used at home are hazardous. For example, bleach, drain cleaners and oven cleaners. These carry hazard signs on their labels to warn householders of the dangers when using them.

The commonly used hazard symbols found on domestic products or in the workplace are shown in Figure 11.6.2.

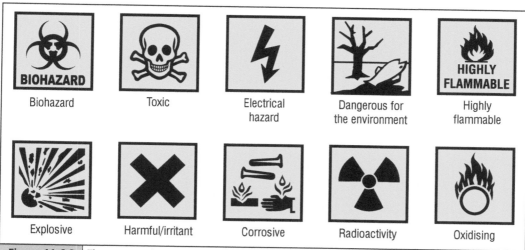

Figure 11.6.2 | The common hazard signs

In the workplace, chemicals can be used that are far more hazardous than those we use at home. Therefore, workers need special protective gear. To remind them that they should be protecting themselves the following symbols are displayed.

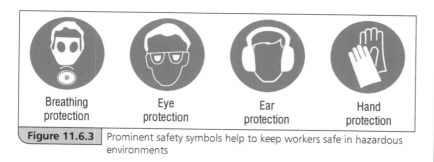

Figure 11.6.3 | Prominent safety symbols help to keep workers safe in hazardous environments

SUMMARY QUESTIONS

1 A person turns on a gas oven but realises there are no matches. They go to get some from another room and return to light the gas. Why is this dangerous?

2 Which toxic gas is given off from a faulty gas boiler that does not mix enough air with the burning gas?

3 Sketch the hazard signs for:
   a harmful   b corrosive   c flammable   d explosive.

4 a Make a list of protective gear that would be useful in the construction industry.

   b Find out what special safety equipment is used by radiographers in hospitals.

Machines are mechanisms that help us do a task more easily. Some simple machines that you will know are levers, pulleys and inclined planes (or slopes). These all make work easier. Other simple machines include gears, which use differently sized cogs.

These machines usually allow you to apply more force to an object than you actually apply. They are examples of force multipliers. For instance, you can use a pulley system when lifting heavy furniture to an upper floor in a house.

Or you can use a spanner to undo a nut on a bolt. A car mechanic will use a longer spanner to free a stubborn wheel-nut. If it still won't move, they can use an even longer hollow steel tube over the spanner.

Examples of different types of lever

A crowbar is a simple example of a lever used to move a heavy object. This is an example of a Class 1 lever where the fulcrum (or pivot point) is nearer to the load than the effort. Look at the example in Figure 12.1.1.

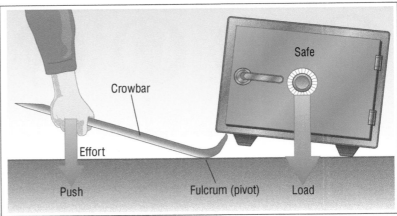

Figure 12.1.1 A crowbar is a force multiplier. It is a Class 1 lever.

By pushing down on the crowbar, the man can use his weight as well as his muscles to move the safe. As in all force multipliers the effort is less than the load. However, the distance the effort force must move is greater than the distance the load moves. This is the payback for using less force in moving the object. Using a claw hammer to remove a nail from a piece of wood is another example of a Class 1 lever.

Many people in the Caribbean, rather than use expensive cranes, still shift small wooden houses and other structures by using a Class 1 lever. This is just a beam of wood wedged under the house or structure and levered from the other end by men. Blocks or a drum may be used as a fulcrum.

A wheelbarrow is a Class 2 lever. In these levers both the load and the effort are on the same side of the fulcrum, with the load nearer to the fulcrum (see Figure 12.1.2).

In a Class 2 lever, the load and effort force are shared out by the fulcrum, so the force needed to lift the object is less than the load force. So a Class 2 lever also acts as a force multiplier. A nut-cracker is another example.

Tweezers are an example of a Class 3 lever. These are like Class 2 levers, but the fulcrum is nearer the effort than the load. In a Class 3 lever the effort is greater than the load, so these levers are used where you want to pick up delicate or small objects (see Figure 12.1.3).

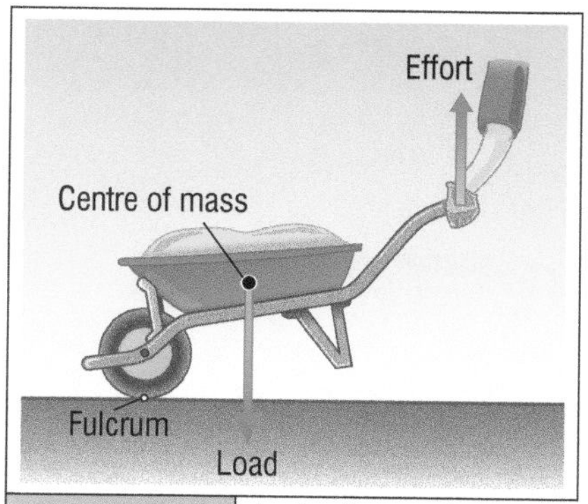

Levers in the body

Bending your arm to lift an apple is an example of using levers. Here the fulcrum is your elbow, the effort is the relatively small contraction in your bicep muscle and the load (apple) is moved a much greater distance than the effort force in your bicep. This is called a distance multiplier rather than a force multiplier.

The inclined plane

It is easier to push a load up a slope to raise it a certain distance than it is to lift the load vertically straight up, but you do have to push it further than lifting it vertically.

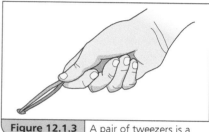

Figure 12.1.2 A wheelbarrow is a Class 2 lever

Figure 12.1.3 A pair of tweezers is a Class 3 lever

KEY POINTS

1 We use simple machines such as levers, pulleys, gears, ramps and wheels every day.

2 Simple machines can make moving large loads easier.

3 There are three classes of lever dependent on the relative positioning of the effort, load and fulcrum.

SUMMARY QUESTIONS

1 Define the words, **a** effort, **b** load and **c** fulcrum.

2 Describe how a Class 1 lever works. Use the example of prizing off the lid from a can of paint using a screwdriver, drawing a diagram and labelling the effort, load and fulcrum.

3 What do we mean when we say that Class 1 and Class 2 levers are force multipliers?

4 Use an inclined plane to show that there is always a trade-off between the energy saved using a slope and the distance you have to move the load.

Doing work

Whenever we move an object, we are doing work. In the process of doing work we are transferring energy from one form to another. For example, if you lift a box from the floor onto a table it requires you to do work.

To do the work on the box you need to transfer chemical energy from the food you have eaten into kinetic energy as the box moves. On the table the box has gravitational potential energy which is stored as it is above ground level.

The heavier the box the more work you have to do to lift it. The higher the table, the more work too. We can show this in an equation:

work done (or energy converted) = force × distance
(in joules, J)   (in newtons, N)   (in metres, m)

So it takes 1 joule of energy to move a force of 1 newton through 1 metre (in the direction of the force).

Worked example

A worker pulls a 20 kg crate across a yard 5 m wide.

How much work was done?

The crate has a mass of 20 kg. To change that into its weight in newtons, we multiply the mass by 10. So the 20 kg mass has a weight of 200 N.

Now substitute the values into the equation:

work done (in J) = force (in N) × distance (in m)
= 200 N × 5 m
= **1000 J (or 1 kJ)**

Mechanical advantage

The mechanical advantage of a simple machine, such as a lever or inclined plane, is the factor by which the effort is multiplied by the machine. It is calculated as:

$$\text{mechanical advantage} = \frac{\text{load}}{\text{effort}}$$

Worked example

Consider using a 4 m ramp to raise a load of 150 N by 2 m.

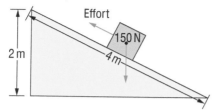

The work done in raising the 150 N by 2 m will be the same whether we use the ramp or lift the load straight up.

Lifting the load vertically:

work done (or energy converted) = force × distance
= 150 N × 2 m
= 300 J

Using the ramp, the work done will also be 300 J.

$$300\,J = \text{effort (in N)} \times 4\,m$$
$$\frac{300}{4} = \text{effort} = 75\,N$$

So the **mechanical advantage** of using the ramp $= \dfrac{\text{load}}{\text{effort}}$

$$= \frac{150}{75} = \mathbf{2}$$

So if you double the distance over which the effort force acts compared to a vertical lift, you halve the force needed to complete the task.

However, mechanical advantage is a theoretical number as in reality energy is wasted in all machines. They are never 100% efficient, so you have to put in more energy than you get out. So more than 75 N would actually be needed to push the load up the ramp in the example above. That is because there is always friction in the moving parts of a machine. This causes the machine parts to heat up and energy is transferred to the surroundings.

To reduce this friction you need to keep machine parts well-lubricated with oil or grease, for example a bicycle chain. A neglected machine, such as a lawn mower left over winter, will rust up. This will cause even more friction between its moving parts and result in more wasted energy.

KEY POINTS

1 Work done (or energy converted) = force × distance moved in direction of the force.

2 Mechanical advantage of a machine $= \dfrac{\text{load}}{\text{effort}}$

3 There is always friction between the moving parts of machines resulting in inefficiency. Lubrication with oil or grease helps to minimise wasted energy.

SUMMARY QUESTIONS

1 a Calculate the energy converted in a machine when:

   i a load of 350 N is raised by 2.5 m

   ii an effort of 100 N is applied through 7.5 m.

   b What would be the mechanical advantage of this machine?

2 Explain why the theoretical mechanical advantage of a machine is never achieved in real life and how we can make machines as efficient as possible.

3 Calculate the work done when a 50 kg rock is raised by 50 cm.

13 Metals and non-metals

13.1 Metals and non-metals

Metals and non-metals

Properties of metals

Many properties of metals are very useful when making a great variety of objects. Figure 13.1.1 shows the general properties of metals.

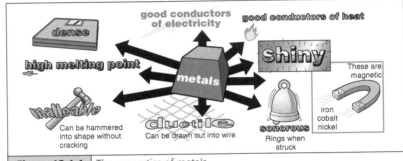

| Figure 13.1.1 | The properties of metals |

The metal copper is a very good conductor of electricity and it can be drawn out into wires (is ductile). Therefore, we use copper for electrical wiring in houses. Why do we use copper for water pipes?

Properties of non-metallic materials

There are many non-metallic substances that we use in our everyday lives. Their properties are very varied. Although metals are all good conductors of electricity, most non-metallic materials are not. So we use non-metallic materials as electrical insulators. We also use them as thermal insulators, especially if gas is trapped inside a foam. Here are some general properties of non-metallic elements.

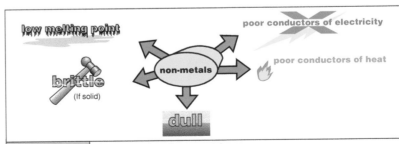

| Figure 13.1.2 | The properties of non-metals |

Wood

Some non-metallic materials occur naturally, while others are synthetic. Wood is a useful naturally occurring material. There are different types of wood, such as soft, low density balsa wood and hard, dense mahogany. Wood is made of long fibres of cellulose. The wood can be split along its grain, as when chopping firewood. However, it is much tougher to cut across its grain.

Plastics

Many different types of plastics have been developed over the last century. Their properties depend on:

- the starting materials
- the conditions used in the reaction to make them
- how the plastic is processed.

Some plastics are flexible and melt or soften at low temperatures. They can be recycled and remoulded to make new objects. Other plastics are hard, rigid and are heat resistant.

Soon we will have to think of new ways to make plastics. That's because crude oil is the main raw material for making most plastics at present. Crude oil is a fossil fuel that is running out, so we will need new raw materials, such as plants, to make our plastics.

Another problem with plastics is their disposal. Most of them are thrown away as rubbish and get taken to landfill tips. However, a useful property of plastics (their lack of reactivity) becomes a disadvantage when we try to get rid of them. Many plastics last for hundreds of years before they are broken down completely by microbes in soil. So they take up valuable space in our landfill sites.

Nowadays scientists are making more plastics that will rot away in the soil when we dump them. These biodegradable plastics can be broken down by microbes more quickly. For instance, scientists can build granules of starch into the plastic that the microbes feed on. There are also some plastics that can be broken down by sunlight.

Some countries burn plastic waste and use the energy given out to generate electricity (saving fossil fuels). However, plastics, such as PVC, produce acidic hydrogen chloride gas when burned. Also, burning plastics that contain nitrogen makes toxic hydrogen cyanide gas.

Recycling some plastics rather than throwing them away can also help solve the problems of disposal. However, recycling plastics needs more sorting than the recycling of iron, aluminium, glass or paper.

An example of plastics in sport

Kevlar is a special plastic, discovered about 40 years ago. It has some very useful properties, such as high tensile strength (difficult to pull apart), low density, high toughness and durability, abrasion and cut resistance, and flame resistance. This has led to its use in making kayaks and oars, tennis racket frames and strings, volleyball nets, fencing suits, fire-proof suits for racing drivers and 'leathers' for motorcycle racers.

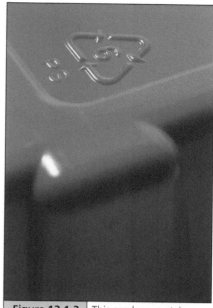

Figure 13.1.3 This produce container is made of polystyrene as shown by its recycling symbol

Reactions of metals

LEARNING OUTCOMES

- Write word equations to show the reactions of metals with oxygen, acid, alkali, water and steam.
- Evaluate the advantages and disadvantages of cooking utensils or canning using aluminium.

Figure 13.2.1 Many metals will react with dilute acids, fizzing as they give off a gas. What is the name of the gas?

The reactivity of metals

Water pipes are often made of copper. Copper is a suitable metal because it can be bent easily so that the copper pipes can be shaped by plumbers. Also, copper metal does not react with water.

We can compare the reactivity of metals by looking at their reactions with other substances. For example, we can compare their reactions with:

- oxygen (the reactive gas in the air)
- water
- dilute acid and alkali.

All these substances are found around the home and in the workplace so metals are likely to come into contact with them.

Not all metals react with dilute acid. Copper, silver, gold and platinum are so unreactive that there is no reaction with dilute acids. However, many metals will react.

If a metal reacts with a dilute acid it gives off hydrogen – a flammable gas. This is the general word equation for the reaction:

$$\text{metal} + \text{acid} \rightarrow \text{a salt} + \text{hydrogen}$$

Different acids will form different salts when the hydrogen in the acid is replaced by a metal.

- Sulphuric acid forms salts called sulphates.
- Hydrochloric acid makes chlorides.
- Nitric acid forms salts called nitrates.

For example, in the reactions between iron and the three acids above:

$$\text{iron} + \text{sulphuric acid} \rightarrow \text{iron sulphate} + \text{hydrogen}$$
$$\text{iron} + \text{hydrochloric acid} \rightarrow \text{iron chloride} + \text{hydrogen}$$
$$\text{iron} + \text{nitric acid} \rightarrow \text{iron nitrate} + \text{hydrogen}$$

By seeing how quickly the hydrogen gas bubbles off the metals, we can put them into an order of reactivity. Look at Table 1, which also contains the reactions of the metals with dilute alkali such as sodium hydroxide solution.

Table 1

Metal (in order of reactivity)	Reaction with dilute acid	Reaction with dilute alkali
Aluminium	Gives off hydrogen gas and a salt is formed (but only if the surface is cleaned first).	Dissolves, giving off hydrogen gas.
Zinc	Gives off hydrogen gas and a salt is formed.	Dissolves, releasing hydrogen gas.
Iron	Gives off hydrogen gas and a salt is produced.	No reaction.
Tin	Only reacts slowly when the acid is warm.	Reacts slowly.
Copper	No reaction.	No reaction.
Silver	No reaction.	No reaction.

Table 2 shows the reactions of the same metals with oxygen and water.

Table 2

Metal (in order of reactivity)	Reaction with oxygen	Reaction with water (or steam)
Aluminium	Rapidly tarnishes in the cold. A thin coating of tough aluminium oxide forms (which protects its surface).	If the oxide coating is removed, it will react with water, giving off hydrogen and releasing a lot of heat.
Zinc	Zinc oxide forms on its surface, slowly in the cold, but more rapidly when heated.	Hydrogen released from steam. Zinc oxide formed.
Iron	Forms an oxide if heated. Rusts in the cold, if water is also present.	Reacts with steam to produce hydrogen. Iron oxide formed.
Tin	Forms an oxide when heated.	No reaction with cold water and only a slight reaction with steam.
Copper	Forms black copper oxide, but must be heated strongly.	No reaction.
Silver	Forms silver oxide (tarnishes).	No reaction.

Metals react with oxygen in the air at different rates, if at all. Gold is so unreactive that it doesn't tarnish. It remains shiny in air. **Tarnishing** is when a metal gets covered by a layer of its oxide on its surface.

Continued

When the metals react with oxygen, they form a metal oxide. For example:

zinc + oxygen → zinc oxide

This is called an **oxidation** reaction. We say that the zinc has been oxidised.

Metals of medium reactivity may react slowly with water, but will react when heated with steam. For example:

zinc + steam → zinc oxide + hydrogen

A closer look at aluminium

Aluminium metal is protected on its surface by a tough layer of aluminium oxide. This oxide layer is impermeable, i.e. it does not let water through to react with the metal. This is why this fairly reactive metal can be used in making drink cans, ladders, patio doors and window frames, without corroding.

Many pots and pans are also made from aluminium. This makes use of aluminium's good thermal conductivity and low density. However, the aluminium oxide layer that forms on the pans and protects the aluminium, can react with both acids and alkalis. So there is a potential hazard when aluminium pans are used under these conditions. For example, you might boil up acidic foods, such as tomatoes, rhubarb, cabbage or soft fruits, in aluminium pans. The protective oxide layer will also be attacked by hot alkaline mixtures. It might also be removed by vigorous scouring when cleaning pans.

Figure 13.2.2 Aluminium is a popular choice in pans because of its high thermal conductivity, low density, corrosion resistance and shiny appearance

Without its oxide layer, aluminium metal can react with liquids and dissolve in the food. There is some evidence that dissolved aluminium in the body is linked to Alzheimer's disease. This brain disease is the most common form of dementia.

So it is not a good idea to store acidic food in uncoated aluminium cookware. That is because over time the dissolved aluminium will build up. However, scientific research differs on the safe limits of dissolved aluminium. Using coated (non-stick) or sealed (anodised) aluminium pans is safe in any conditions. The acid or alkali cannot get through these coatings to react with the bare aluminium metal.

KEY POINTS

1 If a metal reacts with a dilute acid, it produces a salt and gives off hydrogen gas.

2 A metal that reacts with oxygen in the air forms an oxide. Its surface will tarnish as the metal is oxidised.

3 Aluminium is a fairly reactive metal, but is protected against corrosion by the impermeable aluminium oxide layer on its surface.

SUMMARY QUESTIONS

1 Write a word equation to show the reaction between:
 a iron and nitric acid
 b zinc and hydrochloric acid.

2 a Lead is a metal that is more reactive than copper, but is less reactive than tin.

 Use Table 2 to predict what would happen in any reactions between lead and oxygen or cold water. Write a word equation for any reactions you predict would happen.

 b Lead will react with warm dilute hydrochloric acid, but only very slowly. Write a word equation for the reaction.

3 Using the words listed below, identify the missing words a to g.

corrosion density power melting order conductivity cooking

Aluminium is a very useful metal, mainly because it has a low a .... for a metal and it is resistant to b .... so it keeps its silvery appearance. Its lack of reactivity with oxygen and water might seem strange at first sight. After all, aluminium lies above zinc in c .... of reactivity. Aluminium's high d .... point and malleability makes it useful as e .... foil. Its ductility and good electrical f .... means that it is also one of the metals used in overhead g .... cables.

Alloys at work

Cleaning metals

Aluminium pans can be cleaned by boiling some vinegar with water in the pan for about 10 minutes. The acid will react with the protective aluminium oxide layer. However, this means that aluminium is more likely to dissolve into food. The use of abrasive cleaners is not recommended. This will scrape off the oxide layer and will also scratch the relatively soft aluminium, marking the pans.

Other household metals that need cleaning are shown in the table.

Metal	How to clean the tarnished surface of the metal
Iron	Rust can be removed by scouring. You can use steel wool or a scouring powder. However, if an uncoated cooking utensil is scoured, the surface will have to be protected with a thin layer of oil or fat.
Tin	If the very thin layer of tin used to coat objects is scratched by using abrasives, the iron or steel beneath it will rust. Make sure a very fine steel wool is used. This will avoid further damage to the tin coating.
Copper	Make a paste out of lemon juice and salt. Rub it on the copper with a soft cloth then rinse with water and dry.
Brass (alloy of copper and zinc)	Use a metal polish containing: • solvents and detergents to remove the tarnish • mild abrasives to polish the metal • oils to act as a barrier between the exposed metal and air.
Silver	Sprinkle baking soda on a damp cloth and rub the tarnish off, then rinse with water and dry.

Vinegar and lemon juice are weakly acidic. They use chemical reactions to get rid of the basic metal oxide tarnishes. Acids and bases react together in neutralisation reactions.

Neutralisation can be used to remove rust stains from clothing. Rust is hydrated iron oxide. It will react and dissolve in acidic solutions. So try rubbing the stain with lemon juice or white vinegar, mixed with salt to make a paste. This will help dissolve the rust marks. Then the clothes can be rinsed with water.

Abrasives remove anything on the surface of a metal. Metal polishes contain a fine suspension of fine abrasive particles to remove tarnishing. They also contain oils to protect the shiny metal surface which is exposed.

Alloys in the home

Steel is an example of an **alloy** of iron. An alloy is a mixture of a metal with one or more other metals (or non-metals, such as carbon in steel).

We make alloys to improve the properties of metallic elements. Pure metals are relatively easy to stretch and hammer into shapes. However, we can make stronger and harder metals by alloying. The alloy can resist stretching and impact forces more effectively.

Steel is an alloy made mainly of iron with small percentages of carbon (for example, between 0.2% and 1.5%). It sometimes has other metals added to adjust its properties. For example, a very hard and tough steel is made by adding a little tungsten. It can be used to make drills, hammers and other tools. Stainless steel, which does not rust, is made by adding nickel and chromium. It is used to make cutlery and surgical instruments. Various types of steel are used for car bodies, wires, pipes, bicycles, girders and springs.

Brass is an alloy of copper and zinc. It is an attractive golden colour and is much harder than either copper or zinc. These properties make it ideal for door fittings, which need to withstand a lot of wear and tear, and it also looks attractive.

Soft solder is an alloy of lead and tin. It is melted easily to connect components in an electrical circuit. The heat to melt the alloy is supplied by a soldering iron. The molten solder solidifies to make the connections.

Figure 13.3.1 Brass is a shiny, hard alloy of copper and zinc. Which more expensive metal does it look like?

Electroplating

Electroplating is the process whereby a metal object is coated in a thin layer of another metal using electricity. It can be used to protect the metal beneath from corroding; make an object look more attractive/shiny; increase the hardness of the surface or make it more resistant to scratching; save money by using a thin layer of a precious metal instead of using the pure expensive metal.

SUMMARY QUESTIONS

1 a Explain why vinegar is used to clean rust from iron.

b Name another household acid that could be used to get rid of rust.

2 a Why are oils an essential part of a metal polish?

b Which part of a metal polish is used to clean the surface of the metal?

3 a Explain why so-called 'copper' coins are made of an alloy of copper with other metals, such as zinc and tin, and are not made of pure copper metal.

b Why is brass used to make door handles?

c Which metals are used to make soft solder? Explain how it is used in an electrical circuit.

d Give three reasons to electroplate a metal object.

KEY POINTS

1 Tarnishing is an oxidation reaction in which an oxide layer coats the surface of a metal.

2 Metal oxides tend to be basic so will react and dissolve in acids. This is why vinegar and lemon juice are used to clean metals.

3 Alloys are mixtures of metals (and sometimes non-metals, such as the carbon in steel).

4 Alloys can be made with particular uses in mind, such as soft solder which melts at a low temperature.

5 Electroplating uses an electric current to coat a metal in a thin layer of another metal.

Rusting

Iron, often in the form of steel, is the most widely used metal in the construction industry. The tarnishing, or corrosion, of iron is called rusting. The rusting of iron (and steel) costs society millions of dollars each year.

Iron objects rust faster if they are left outdoors in damp conditions. We can investigate rusting in an experiment like the one shown below.

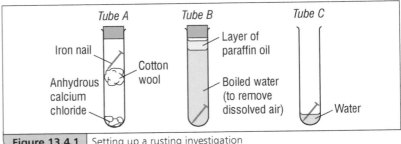

Figure 13.4.1 Setting up a rusting investigation

The test tubes are left for several days.

It is found that iron needs both air (oxygen) and water in order to rust. The iron corrodes to form a layer of hydrated iron oxide that we call rust. The rusting of iron is an example of the oxidation of a metal.

$$\text{iron} + \text{oxygen} + \text{water} \rightarrow \text{hydrated iron oxide}$$
$$\text{(rust)}$$

The rust is a crumbly substance. It flakes off to expose fresh iron to attack so the iron can corrode completely over time (unlike aluminium with its protective oxide layer). So structures containing iron are severely weakened by rusting.

People who live near the coast find that rusting occurs more quickly than in areas inland. Scientists have also found that rusting takes place faster in tropical climates where it is warm and humid, with lots of water vapour in the air. As well as near the sea, areas around industrial plants, such as power stations and metal smelting plants that give off acidic gases, also suffer from the effects of rusting.

From their observations, scientists conclude that rusting is speeded up by:

- high temperatures
- salt (sodium chloride)
- acid.

Preventing rust

We can protect iron and steel from rusting by keeping the metal away from air and water. A barrier on the surface of the iron can be made by:

- covering with oil or grease
- painting
- coating in plastic
- coating in tin
- coating in zinc (or attaching bars of a metal more reactive than iron, for example magnesium).

Tin cans are steel cans that have been coated with a very thin layer of tin. The layer of tin keeps air and water from the steel. It is applied to the steel by **electroplating** (see page 121). However, if the tin gets scratched, the steel beneath will start to rust.

A better way to protect iron or steel is to coat them with a more reactive metal, such as zinc, instead of the less reactive tin. We call this process **galvanising**. Remember that zinc is more reactive than iron. So the air and water will attack the zinc rather than the iron. Bins are often made from galvanised steel because they are likely to get knocked about when they get emptied. But even when the layer of zinc gets damaged, it still protects the exposed steel underneath. This is called sacrificial protection.

Adding nickel and chromium to molten steel forms a rust-proof alloy called stainless steel. However, it is expensive so we still use cheaper, but less effective, methods like painting, for large scale protection.

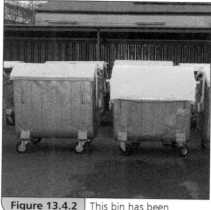

Figure 13.4.2 This bin has been galvanised as protection against rust. Magnesium is used as bars bolted on to iron in extreme conditions, for example in the sea or in underground pipes. Ships have magnesium blocks bolted to their hulls.

14 Acids, bases and mixtures

14.1 Household chemicals

LEARNING OUTCOMES

- List the uses of some common household chemicals.
- Classify household chemicals as acids, bases and salts.
- Explain the use of neutralisation in stain removal.
- Discuss the safe and economic use of household chemicals.

Universal indicator solution
0
1 Hydrochloric acid
2 Lemon juice
3 Orange juice
Vinegar
4
5 Black coffee
6 Rainwater
7 Pure water
8 Baking soda
9 Milk of magnesia
Soap
10
11
12 Washing soda
13
14 Oven cleaner
Sodium hydroxide
Very acidic
Slightly acidic
Neutral
Slightly alkaline
Very alkaline
SOAP
OVEN cleaner

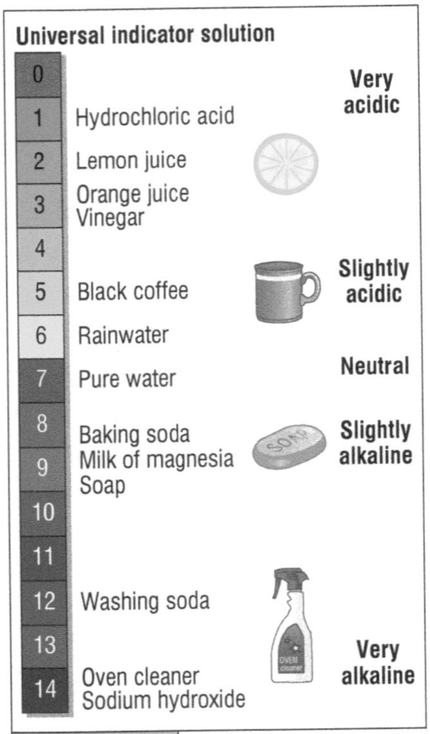

Figure 14.1.1 Some common substances and their pH values. The lower the pH value is, the more acidic the solution. The higher the pH value is, the more alkaline the solution. What do we call a solution that is neither acidic nor alkaline?

We don't always think of the substances we use at home as 'chemicals', but all substances are chemicals. Some common household chemicals would be:

- water (used as a solvent)
- caustic soda (used in cleaning products)
- bleach (used to disinfect areas)
- ethanol (used as a fuel or a solvent)
- methane (used as a fuel)
- bicarbonate of soda (sodium bicarbonate, or baking soda, used in cleaning and cooking)
- salt (used to flavour and preserve food)
- ethanoic (acetic) acid (used in vinegar to flavour and preserve foods).

Compounds and mixtures

All the chemicals listed above are examples of compounds.

Compounds contain two or more different types of atom chemically bonded to each other.

Many household products are not pure compounds, but are mixtures of compounds. In a mixture of compounds, the different compounds present are not chemically bonded to each other. Therefore, mixtures can be separated by physical means, such as filtering, evaporation or distillation.

The composition of a mixture can vary depending on the amounts of each compound mixed together. On the other hand, a compound will always have a fixed proportion of each element in it. For example, pure water will always have twice as many hydrogen atoms as oxygen atoms in it. However, aqueous solutions, made up by dissolving compounds in water, can vary in the ratio of water to compound(s) present. The solution might be concentrated (with a high ratio of compound to water) or dilute (with a high ratio of water to compound).

Acids, bases and salts

As well as classifying household chemicals as mixtures or compounds, we can also sort them into groups of acids, bases or salts.

If the chemicals dissolve in water we can test the solution with Universal Indicator (UI) paper or solution. This is a mixture of indictors that can be a range of colours depending on the acidity or alkalinity of a solution. The colour is matched to a pH value on the pH scale, from pH 0 to 14.

- Acids have a pH value below 7.
- Alkalis have a pH value above 7 (an alkali is a base that is soluble in water).
- A solution with a pH value of 7 is called neutral. Salts made from strong acids and strong bases, such as hydrochloric acid and sodium hydroxide, are neutral.

Acids and bases (or alkalis) react to make a salt and water. The reaction is called **neutralisation**. For example:

hydrochloric acid + sodium hydroxide → sodium chloride + water
     acid   base (alkali)   salt

In this reaction, if just the right amount of acid and alkali are added together, a neutral solution of the salt sodium chloride is formed.

We can use neutralisation reactions to remove stains. For example, if fruit juice is spilt on a shirt you can add bicarbonate of soda to remove the stain. The fruit juice is weakly acidic and the bicarbonate of soda is weakly alkaline. Therefore, neutralisation takes place when they are mixed. Borax is another alkaline substance that can be used to neutralise acidic stains, for example tea or wine stains.

Disinfectants and antiseptics are other chemicals commonly used at home. Both of these kill microorganisms that can cause infections. However, only antiseptics are used on living tissue, as disinfectants are too harsh and will cause injury. Mouthwash is an example of an antiseptic, whereas toilet and bathroom cleaner is an example of a disinfectant.

When using these products it is important to read the instructions on the label. Often they should be diluted down, depending on their use. Not only does dilution make them safer to use, it also saves you money.

LINK

To learn about the dangers associated with the use of household chemicals and see the corresponding warning labels, see 11.6 'Safety first'.

KEY POINTS

1. Household chemicals can be classified as mixtures and compounds or as acids, bases and salts.

2. The pH scale can be used to determine how acidic or alkaline a solution is.

3. pH values below 7 indicate an acid and above 7 an alkali. If the solution tested has a pH of exactly 7 then it is neutral.

4. Neutralisation reactions can be used to remove stains at home.

SUMMARY QUESTIONS

1. Make a table to show five common household chemicals and what they are used for.

2. A group of students did an experiment to follow the pH of an alkaline solution as acid was added, 1 cm³ at a time. Look at the graph showing their results.

   a. How much acid was added to neutralise the alkali? How did you decide?

   b. i. The acid used was hydrochloric acid and the alkali was sodium hydroxide. Write a word equation to show the reaction.

   ii. What do we call this type of reaction?

   iii. Classify each of the chemicals in the word equation as acidic, alkaline or neutral.

3. What is the difference between an antiseptic and a disinfectant?

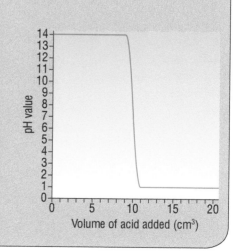

Solutions, suspensions and colloids

LEARNING OUTCOMES

- Classify household chemicals as solutions, colloids and suspensions.
- Explain the action of a solvent in stain removal.
- Discuss the usefulness of aqueous and non-aqueous solvents.

Classifying mixtures

Another way in which we can classify household mixtures that include a liquid is as:

- solutions
- colloids
- suspensions.

These mixtures can all have particles of a solid dispersed throughout a liquid, but the difference lies in the size of those particles. In a true **solution**, such as salt or sugar dissolved in water when cooking, we have a soluble substance dissolved in a solvent. Individual particles (atoms, molecules or ions) of the soluble substance are spread out and mixed completely with the liquid. The particles are too small to be seen, even with powerful microscopes, and pass straight through filter paper. Light passes through the solution so it is transparent.

In **colloids** (sometimes called colloidal solutions) the particles are larger. They are still too small to be seen with normal microscopes, but can be seen using the most powerful ones. These particles are not dissolved in the liquid as in solutions – they are dispersed throughout the liquid.

Light cannot pass straight through the liquid in a colloid. It is translucent rather than transparent. Translucent means that some light passes through the colloid, but you cannot see a clear image from the other side of it.

Like solutions, the particles are small enough to pass through filter paper. However, unlike solutions, the particles cannot pass through membranes.

Other colloids are formed when liquids that do not dissolve in each other are mixed. These mixtures are called emulsions. These include milk, some paint, cosmetics, shaving cream, mayonnaise, salad cream and even disinfectants like Dettol.

We also get colloids in which a liquid is spread throughout a solid. These are called gels. Examples are jelly, cheese and butter.

In **suspensions**, the particles are larger still and are visible to the naked eye. They are opaque as light bounces off the insoluble particles of solid. When filtered, a solid residue will be left on the filter paper. A suspension is made if you stir up chalk dust in water. In the home, metal polish is a suspension of abrasive particles in oils.

How solvents work

A solvent is a liquid that dissolves another substance. Water is often described as the universal solvent. That's because it is so good at dissolving many substances. When a liquid dissolves a solid, its molecules attract the particles (atoms, molecules or ions) that make up the solid. If the attraction is strong enough, the solvent molecules 'pull' the particles of the solid away from its neighbours on the surface. Once separated, the particles of the solid become surrounded by the solvent molecules. They are then free to move around within the solution formed.

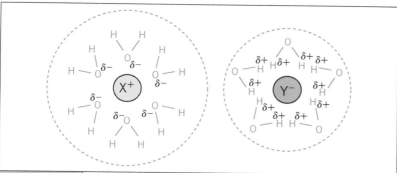

Figure 14.2.1 | Ions (charged particles) surrounded by water molecules in a solution

Water is called a polar solvent. Its molecules have an imbalance of electrical charge within them. One end of the water molecule carries a slight positive charge and the other end is slightly negative. Therefore, it attracts solids that have positive and negative particles (ions) or similar molecules to water itself. So water is good at dissolving salt and similar solids made of ions, as well as sugar and other substances made of molecules with an imbalance of charge.

Other solids and liquids are made of molecules with their charge evenly spread. Water is not good at dissolving substances like this. However, other solvents with similar molecules will dissolve them. So we have non-aqueous solvents, such as turpentine (for dissolving paint from brushes) and acetone (for cleaning off nail polish).

We find that 'like dissolves like'. Solvents dissolve substances with similar particles to their own. Dry cleaning uses non-aqueous solvents, which are good at removing greasy stains from clothes.

Figure 14.2.2 | Nail polish does not dissolve well in water, but it does in acetone, a non-aqueous solvent

KEY POINTS

1 We can classify mixtures as solutions, colloids and suspensions.

2 Solvents dissolve substances made of similar particles to their own.

3 We need water and non-aqueous solvents to dissolve the whole range of different stains we need to remove in cleaning.

SUMMARY QUESTIONS

1 Draw a table to show the properties of solutions, colloids and suspensions.

2 Give some examples of household colloidal mixtures.

3 Explain how water dissolves a solid such as salt (which is made up of positive and negative ions). Include a diagram in your answer.

4 Why is turpentine (a non-aqueous solvent) used to clean gloss paint (which is an oil-based paint) from paint brushes?

Disadvantages of hard water	Advantages of hard water
Difficult to form lather with soap.	Calcium in the water is good for the teeth and bones of children.
Scum forms in a reaction that wastes soap.	Some people prefer the taste.
Scale (a hard crust) forms inside kettles. This wastes energy when you boil your kettle.	Helps to reduce heart disease.
Hot water pipes 'fur up' on the inside. The scale formed can even block up pipes completely.	The coating of scale (sometimes called limescale) inside copper or lead pipes stops poisonous salts dissolving into our water.

EXAM TIP

The hardness of water is often quoted as ppm (parts per million) of calcium ions.

What is the difference between hard and soft water?

Some water is easy to form a lather with when you wash with soap. This is called soft water. However, in some regions, it is difficult to form a lather with soap and a scum forms in the water. This is hard water.

If your water supply has flowed through chalk or limestone (calcium carbonate) it will be hard. Other rocks that contain calcium or magnesium also cause hardness. Gypsum (calcium sulphate) is an example. Calcium sulphate is slightly soluble in water. When a river flows over gypsum, it dissolves some of the rock. Therefore, calcium ions get into the water.

However, the calcium carbonate in limestone and chalk rock is not soluble in water. Water does not dissolve chalk or limestone rock. But rainwater dissolves carbon dioxide – a weakly acidic gas – as it falls through the air:

$$\text{water} + \text{carbon dioxide} \rightarrow \text{carbonic acid (a weak acid)}$$

This weakly acidic solution reacts with and dissolves away the limestone or chalk:

$$\text{calcium carbonate} + \text{carbonic acid} \rightarrow \text{calcium hydrogencarbonate}$$

Calcium hydrogencarbonate is soluble in water. Therefore, the calcium ions get into the water, making it hard. These calcium ions react with ions from soap (sodium stearate) to form the scum seen when washing in hard water. Scum is insoluble calcium stearate. In some Caribbean territories, people still wash in rivers and streams. Scum can then be seen on the water.

Removing hardness from water

If we remove the calcium (or magnesium) ions from the water, we will get rid of the hardness. Hard water from limestone regions, which contains dissolved calcium hydrogencarbonate, is called temporary hard water. When this solution is boiled, the calcium hydrogencarbonate turns back into the insoluble calcium carbonate. Therefore, the dissolved calcium ions are removed from the water.

$$\text{calcium hydrogencarbonate} \xrightarrow{\text{heat}} \underset{\substack{\textbf{scale} \\ \textbf{(or limescale)}}}{\text{calcium carbonate}} + \text{carbon dioxide} + \text{water}$$

So, temporary hard water can be softened by boiling. The calcium carbonate formed is the limescale you get inside kettles and hot-water pipes.

However, not all hard water can be softened by boiling. Other calcium compounds, such as calcium sulphate from gypsum, are not removed by boiling. These form permanent hard water. Permanent hardness can be removed by the following.

1 *Distillation*
To collect the softened water you can distil hard water. But do you think this is a cheap way to get rid of hardness?

2 *Washing soda (sodium carbonate)*
When you add washing soda to hard water, the calcium ions are removed. They react with the carbonate ions from the washing soda. This forms *insoluble* calcium carbonate. Most modern washing powders have their own water softeners added.

3 *Ion-exchange column*
This method is more suitable for large-scale treatment of hard water. A column is filled with a resin which holds plenty of sodium ions. Hard water goes in at the top. On the way down, the calcium ions are swapped for sodium ions. The calcium ions get stuck on the resin. Sodium ions, which don't cause hardness, come out at the bottom in the softened water (see Figure 14.3.1).

Soapy and soapless detergents

Soaps are detergents (or cleaning agents). Traditionally, these soapy detergents are made from animal fats and plant oils. Using soap in areas with hard water causes 'scum' to form. The white bits of 'scum' can stick to clothes when they are being washed.

However, nowadays soapless detergents made from crude oil do not have this problem. Soapless detergents do not make 'scum' in hard water. No detergent is wasted reacting with the hardness, so you save money as well.

About 80% of all detergents made are now soapless detergents. However, soapless detergents are one cause of eutrophication. They often contain phosphates that act as fertilisers for algae if they are discharged into waterways. To make matters worse they are non-biodegradable so they persist in the environment, unlike soapy detergents which can be broken down by microorganisms.

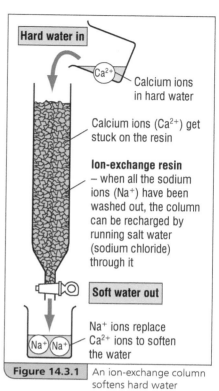

Hard water in

Calcium ions in hard water

Calcium ions (Ca^{2+}) get stuck on the resin

Ion-exchange resin – when all the sodium ions (Na^+) have been washed out, the column can be recharged by running salt water (sodium chloride) through it

Soft water out

Na^+ ions replace Ca^{2+} ions to soften the water

Figure 14.3.1 An ion-exchange column softens hard water

LINK

To find out more about eutrophication, see 17.4 'Water pollution'.

KEY POINTS

1 With hard water, it is difficult to form a lather with soap. A scum is formed as it reacts and wastes the soap.

2 Calcium or magnesium ions dissolved in water cause hardness.

3 Temporary hard water can be softened by boiling. Distillation, washing soda and ion-exchange columns can remove permanent hardness (although distillation would be expensive because of the energy that is needed).

4 Soapless detergents can be used with hard water without forming scum, but they can cause eutrophication in waterways.

SUMMARY QUESTIONS

1 Limestone is insoluble in water. However, water flowing through limestone becomes hard.

   a Explain how calcium ions get into the water.

   b List the advantages and disadvantages of hard water.

   c Explain how adding washing soda removes hardness from water.

2 Give an advantage and a disadvantage of using a soapless detergent in an area with hard water.

Household cleaning products

How detergents work

Detergents are substances that help the cleaning action of water. Water is good at dissolving many things, but it cannot dissolve oil or grease. This is where detergents help. They act as **emulsifiers**. They remove grease and keep it dispersed in water.

The 'head' of a detergent molecule is strongly attracted to water. It is called '**hydrophilic**' which means water-loving. The 'tail' is a long hydrocarbon chain which dissolves in grease. It is called '**hydrophobic**', meaning water-hating — see Figure 14.4.1.

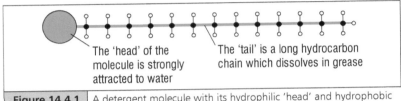

The 'head' of the molecule is strongly attracted to water

The 'tail' is a long hydrocarbon chain which dissolves in grease

Figure 14.4.1 A detergent molecule with its hydrophilic 'head' and hydrophobic 'tail'

The 'tails' of the detergent molecules dissolve into the grease. The charged 'heads' stick out and are pulled towards the polar water molecules. The grease then floats off into the water. The detergent molecules form 'micelles' with the droplets of grease. The micelles repel each other and so remain dispersed throughout the water and they can be rinsed away — see Figure 14.4.2.

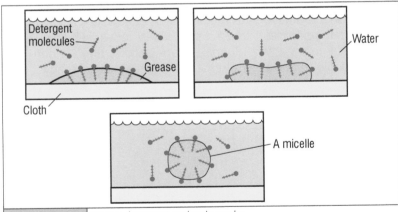

Detergent molecules

Grease

Cloth

Water

A micelle

Figure 14.4.2 How a detergent molecule works

Detergents also help water to soak into clothes when you wash them. They form a thin 'skin' on top of the water. This breaks down the strong forces of attraction between water molecules at the surface, which is called its surface tension. Detergents reduce the water's surface tension. This enables the water to spread out more easily. That's why detergents are called **wetting agents**.

Scouring powders

Scouring powders contain fine abrasive particles mixed with other powders designed to aid cleaning of stubborn stains. The abrasive can be crystals of silica, a very hard compound. This is an irritant to eyes, skin and lungs. Among the other substances, you often find sodium carbonate, an alkali, which will attack greasy stains and chlorinated detergents, such as trichloroisocyanuric acid. These chlorinated compounds make the products harmful to aquatic organisms and may have long-term effects on waterways. They can also cause the corrosion of the surfaces they are scrubbed on to.

Some scouring cleaners also contain sodium hydroxide or bleach. These can irritate mucous membranes, and can cause liver and kidney damage.

| **Figure 14.4.3** | Scouring powders are mechanical cleaners, which physically break down stubborn dirt and stains. However, you must follow the instructions on the label carefully. The hard abrasives can scratch and damage polished surfaces, even those made of steel. |

SUMMARY QUESTIONS

1 a Draw a labelled sketch of a detergent molecule.

  b Explain how detergent molecules act as cleaning agents. Include diagrams in your answer.

2 A scouring powder cleans mainly 'by mechanical means'. What does this mean?

3 Scouring powders can be corrosive and toxic. Which chemicals in the mixture are responsible for these drawbacks to the use of scouring powders? Why are they added?

SECTION B: Multiple-choice questions

1 How is heat energy transferred from the Sun to the Earth?
   a   Conduction
   b   Convection
   c   Evaporation
   d   Radiation

2 We often get a sea breeze on the coast. Which process causes the sea breeze on a sunny day?
   a   Convection
   b   Conduction
   c   Radiation
   d   Reflection

3 Which of the following types of day is MOST likely to cause a person to produce most sweat?
   a   Hot and humid
   b   Hot and dry
   c   Warm and dry
   d   Warm and humid

4 Which one of the following is an electrical safety device?
   a   A variable resistor
   b   A voltmeter
   c   An ammeter
   d   A fuse

5 A potential difference of 2 volts is applied to a circuit with a resistance of 5 ohms. What current flows around the circuit?
   a   10 amps
   b   3 amps
   c   2.5 amps
   d   0.4 amps

6 The following are the pH values of various solutions.
   I   1.2
   II   4.5
   III   7.0
   IV   11.3
   Which solutions are acidic?
   a   I only
   b   I and II
   c   II and IV
   d   I, II, II and IV

7 Which substance can be used to soften hard water?
   a   Common salt (sodium chloride)
   b   Limestone (calcium carbonate)
   c   Vinegar (ethanoic acid)
   d   Washing soda (sodium carbonate)

8 Desalination converts seawater into drinking water. Which process is used to achieve this in a desalination plant (see page 159)?
   a   Chromatography
   b   Filtration
   c   Distillation
   d   Crystallisation

9 A 500 kg object is travelling at a speed of 5 m/s. What is its momentum?
   a   2500 kgm/s
   b   505 kgm/s
   c   495 kgm/s
   d   100 kgm/s

Further practice questions and examples can be found on the accompanying website.

10 The rusting of iron costs society many millions of dollars every year.

The experiment below shows an investigation into the factors that are needed for iron to rust.

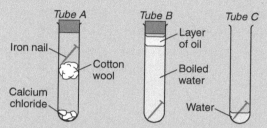

Tube A   Tube B   Tube C

Iron nail

Cotton wool

Layer of oil

Boiled water

Calcium chloride

Water

a Which test tube shows an iron nail in contact with:

  i   only air

  ii   water and air

  iii   only water?   (1)

b Why is the water in Tube B boiled?   (1)

c Explain why the nail in Tube A is suspended on cotton wool above the calcium chloride in the bottom of the tube.   (1)

d What will be the conclusion drawn from this experiment?   (2)

e i   Car owners who live near the coast often complain that their cars have more problems with rust than those in other places.
Which chemical compound causes their cars to rust more quickly?   (1)

  ii   Describe a simple experiment that you could do to show that the substance in part i makes an iron nail rust more quickly.   (2)

f Name the method used to prevent rusting in order to protect:

  i   a bicycle chain

  ii   a food can

  iii   an underground pipe.   (3)

g Steels are alloys of iron.

  i   What is an alloy?   (1)

  ii   Stainless steel is used to make cutlery. Why is it used instead of cheaper types of steel?   (1)

h The hull of a giant oil tanker has blocks of magnesium metal bolted to it. This prevents the ship from rusting. What do we call this type of protection and explain how it works.   (2)

11 a State two differences between an acid and a base.   (2)

b Khara noticed that her skirt has a rust stain after sitting on an old metal bucket.

  i   What is the name of the chemical found in rust?   (1)

  ii   In which one of the following categories does rust fall, a base or an acid?   (1)

  iii   Which type of chemical would be most suitable for the removal of rust stain and suggest a household chemical that may be suitable.   (2)

  iv   Give the name of the chemical reaction that takes place if the rust stain is removed.   (1)

c Some insect stings, such as bee stings, are acidic. Calamine lotion is usually prescribed by doctors to soothe the pain caused by the sting.

  i   Explain why calamine lotion is used on bee stings.   (1)

  ii   Suggest why vinegar may not be suitable to soothe bee stings.   (1)

d Write the general word equation for the chemical reaction between an acid and a base.   (2)

Further practice questions and examples can be found on the accompanying website.

15 The Universe and our Solar System
15.1 Our place in the Universe

LINK

For more information on each planet orbiting the Sun, see 15.2 'The Solar System'.

Our planet, Earth, might seem a big place to us, but it would be just a tiny speck if we could draw a picture of the whole Universe.

The Universe is made up of billions of galaxies. Each single **galaxy** can contain billions of stars. The stars, such as our Sun, can have planets orbiting them and planets can have moons orbiting them in turn.

The Earth has one orbiting moon and orbits one star (which we call the Sun). There are eight planets orbiting the Sun.

The Sun is just one of the billions of stars in the galaxy called the Milky Way. If we could look down on the whole Milky Way, this is what it would look like:

Figure 15.1.1 The shape of the Milky Way, our galaxy

The Milky Way is like a massive disc, spinning as it travels through space, with four arms spiralling out from its centre. The Earth and our Solar System are a tiny part of one of these arms. The Milky Way is so large that it takes light about 100,000 years to travel right across it … and remember that it is just one of billions of other galaxies in the Universe!

Exploring space

Human exploration of space started in the late 1950s with the first manned rocket sent into orbit around the Earth. Since then there have been great technological advances, with the first men landing on the Moon in 1969, followed in 1981 by the first launch of the space shuttle STS-1 (a spacecraft that could land back on Earth on a runway, like an aeroplane). The space shuttle was able to take men to and from a space station that constantly orbits the Earth. Scientists can conduct experiments that can only be carried out in the weightless conditions on the space station.

There have been no manned space flights to other planets, but there have been many unmanned spacecraft sent to other planets and beyond. These 'probes' are loaded with sensors and analytical instruments to send back data to Earth.

In the 2014 Rosetta mission, a probe was actually landed on the surface of a comet. Scientists can collect data from these unmanned flights that would be impossible to gather from Earth.

Figure 15.1.2 Rosetta is the spacecraft that successfully landed on a comet in 2014

Figure 15.1.3 The first space shuttle was launched into space in 1981. The space shuttle was connected to a large rocket to take off, but was able to land and be re-used many times. The last space shuttle mission was in 2011 after 135 shuttle voyages, shared between six different space shuttles.

Figure 15.1.4 Many important discoveries have been made by scientists visiting the International Space Station; launched in 1998, it is still in orbit and in use. However, the high costs of the space programme should be weighed carefully against the benefits of the resulting research.

KEY POINTS

1   The Universe is made up of billions of galaxies.

2   Each galaxy is a collection of millions or billions of stars.

3   The Earth is located in the Solar System.

4   Earth is a planet orbiting one star (the Sun) in the galaxy known as the Milky Way.

5   Human exploration of space is expensive to fund, but has resulted in many new scientific discoveries.

SUMMARY QUESTIONS

1   What is a galaxy?

2   a   Which galaxy is the Earth found in?

   b   Describe the shape of this galaxy.

3   What is the name given to the Sun and its planets, including the Earth?

4   Give one argument for the continuation of the space programme and one argument against it.

The Solar System

- Describe the Solar System.
- Analyse data about the planets in the Solar System.

The Sun is at the centre of the Solar System. The Solar System consists of our Sun plus a very large number of differently-sized objects that orbit around it.

Of the larger objects, there are **eight planets** that orbit the Sun. We can observe the planets with telescopes using reflected light from the Sun.

| Figure 15.2.1 | The eight planets of the Solar System (distances not drawn to scale). Between the orbits of Mars and Jupiter there is a ring of irregular sized objects around the Sun called the 'asteroid belt'. |

The planets

The inner planets

The four planets nearest the Sun are called the 'inner planets'. They are Mercury, Venus, Earth and Mars. These planets all have surfaces made up of solid rock, so they are also known as the 'terrestrial planets'.

Mercury is the nearest planet to the Sun and is the smallest of all eight planets. It has a very high temperature at its surface because of its position close to the Sun.

Venus is similar in size to the Earth. Its atmosphere contains a much higher proportion of carbon dioxide gas than Earth's atmosphere. The carbon dioxide traps energy through a process called the greenhouse effect. This makes Venus the hottest planet even though it is further from the Sun than Mercury.

Earth is the planet we inhabit. It is at just the right distance from the Sun to have temperatures which are between the freezing and boiling points of water. So we have liquid water covering most of the Earth's surface. Liquid water is essential for life as we know it to exist.

Mars is not as big as the Earth. It appears reddish in colour and is known as the 'red planet'. Its colour is caused by the iron(III) oxide in its soil. It is a planet that has had many unmanned probes from Earth on its surface. The robotic probes can collect mineral samples and test them, relaying the results back to Earth.

The outer planets

The four outer planets are nothing like the 'terrestrial' inner planets. They are very much larger than the inner planets and do not have solid surfaces. They are made up of very cold gases, such as hydrogen or helium, and super-cool liquids, such as ammonia (which is a gas at temperatures found on Earth).

Jupiter is the largest planet in the Solar System, with a surface made up of bands of turbulent gases. These cause huge storms. The red spot observable on Jupiter is a storm that has lasted for three hundred years. This largest of the planets has 67 known moons.

Saturn is another 'gas giant' like Jupiter, but it is famous for its 'rings'. The rings are made up of tiny particles of dust and ice that orbit around the planet. Saturn has 62 known moons.

Uranus is a smaller gas giant. It is much colder than Jupiter or Saturn because it is further from the Sun. Its atmosphere is so cold it contains solid ammonia. It looks like a smooth blue sphere.

Neptune is the furthest planet from the Sun and it has the coldest surface of all eight planets. It is very similar to Uranus, but its atmosphere shows evidence of a more turbulent atmosphere, with its white 'clouds' and dark spots caused by storms.

Planetary data

The table below shows some observable data to compare the eight planets of the Solar System. The planets in the Solar System rotate around the Sun in elliptical orbits (like slightly squashed circles). The time it takes a planet to travel one complete orbit around the Sun is the length of the planet's 'year' (see 'Orbital period', measured in Earth years):

Planet	Mercury	Venus	Earth	Mars	Jupiter	Saturn	Uranus	Neptune
Diameter /km	4 878	12 104	12 756	6 787	142 800	120 000	51 118	49 528
Distance from the Sun (compared to Earth)	0.39	0.72	1	1.52	5.20	9.54	19.18	30.06
Surface temperature /°C	180 to 430	465	−89 to 58	−82 to 0	−150	−170	−200	−210
Orbital period / Earth years	0.24	0.62	1	1.88	11.86	29.46	84.01	164.8
Rotational period / Earth days	58.65	243	1	1.03	0.41	0.44	0.72	0.72
Number of moons	0	0	1	2	67	62	27	13

The Earth, Moon and Sun

The planets in the Solar System rotate around the Sun in elliptical orbits and do not fly off into outer space. That is explained by the gravitational forces of attraction that all objects have for each other. The more massive the object, the greater the force of attraction. The nearer the objects are to each other, the greater the attraction. So planet Earth experiences its main attractions from the Sun, because it is so large, and from the Moon, because it is relatively close to the Earth (see 16.6).

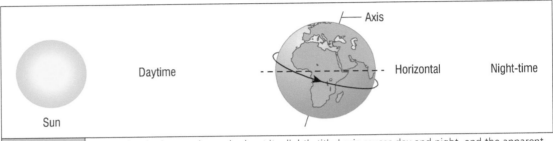

Figure 15.3.1 The Earth spinning continuously about its slightly tilted axis causes day and night, and the apparent motion of the Sun across the sky during the hours of daylight

Day and night

As the Earth orbits the Sun, it is also spinning around continuously. It spins about its axis (see Figure 15.3.1) in an anticlockwise direction. So at any time, the side of the Earth facing the Sun receives sunlight and experiences daytime. The other side of the Earth, facing away from the Sun, is in night-time and no sunlight falls on it. It takes the Earth 24 hours to spin around once on its axis – the length of one Earth 'day'.

Solar eclipse

The Moon orbits the Earth continuously (taking about 28 days for one complete orbit). These movements of the Moon around the Earth, and the Earth around the Sun, mean that occasionally the Earth and Sun line up to cause an **eclipse**. During an eclipse, all or part of the Moon or the Sun are covered by a shadow.

The Moon is about 400 times smaller than the Sun, but it also just happens to be about 400 times closer. The result is that from Earth, they appear to be the same size. And when its orbit around Earth takes the Moon directly between Earth and the Sun, the Moon blocks our view of the Sun in what we call a **solar eclipse** (see Figure 15.3.2).

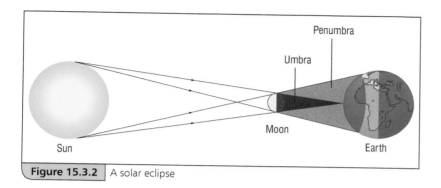

Figure 15.3.2 | A solar eclipse

Because the Sun is not a point source of light, there are areas around the position of total darkness that have reduced light intensity (in the penumbra), experiencing a partial eclipse.

Lunar eclipse

Sometimes the Sun, Earth and Moon line up precisely, with the Earth in the middle (see Figure 15.3.3). The Earth then blocks the light from the Sun, stopping it reaching the Moon. That's a lunar eclipse. During a **lunar eclipse**, parts of the Moon's surface seem to vanish as the Moon passes through the Earth's shadow. When the Moon is completely in the shadow, the surface can only just be seen as it is lit up by light refracted (changed direction) as it passes through the Earth's atmosphere.

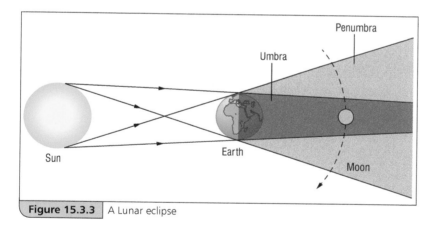

Figure 15.3.3 | A Lunar eclipse

SUMMARY QUESTIONS

1 Define an 'Earth day' in terms of movement of the planet.

2 Explain why at any instant, parts of Earth are experiencing day and in other parts it is night.

3 Explain the difference between a solar eclipse and a lunar eclipse.

Figure 16.1.1 Limestone is chemically weathered by rainwater and over millions of years forms underground caves such as the caves in Curacao

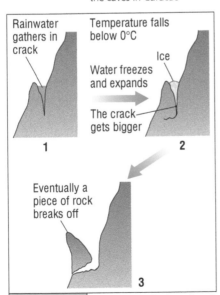

Figure 16.1.2 Physical weathering of rock

All soils contain tiny pieces of rock, often formed from the breakdown of the bedrock beneath it.

Weathering is the breakdown of a rock in nature.

Chemical weathering

Rainwater is slightly acidic and that is not just because of pollution from acid rain.

Carbon dioxide gas in the air dissolves slightly in water, forming a weakly acidic solution. Over time, this acid can attack some of the mineral compounds in rocks.

Limestone rocks, common in the Caribbean, contain the mineral calcite. Its chemical name is calcium carbonate ($CaCO_3$). Acids react with carbonates. They form a salt, plus carbon dioxide and water. So the limestone breaks down into solution. It is weathered by rainwater.

Granite rock is a mixture of three minerals – quartz, feldspar and mica. The acid in rainwater attacks the feldspar and mica minerals. Eventually the granite is weathered into small particles of clay. These are carried away, along with the compounds in solution, by the water. The breakdown of rock by reactions is called **chemical weathering**.

Chemical weathering will take place more quickly if you have more concentrated acid. This could be in areas affected by acid rain or in the ground beneath vegetation. High rainfall and high temperatures will also aid the breakdown of rocks by acidic solutions.

Physical weathering

As well as weathering by reactions with acid, water and oxygen, rocks are also broken down by forces resulting from **physical weathering** processes.

Freeze/thaw

Water expands when it freezes to form ice. This causes physical weathering of rock.

Water collects in cracks in rocks when it rains. If the temperature drops to 0°C or below, the water freezes. As it turns to ice, it expands and opens the crack a little wider. When this has been repeated many times the crack gets big enough to physically break off a rock fragment. Look at Figure 16.1.2.

Temperature changes

As you know, when solid materials get hot they expand. When they cool down they contract. Rocks are mixtures of minerals. During heating and cooling, each of the minerals expands and contracts by different amounts. This sets up stress forces within the rock that eventually causes the surface to crack and peel away. This is called exfoliation (or 'onion-skinning'). If the climate is right, these cracks can also be subject to the forces of freeze/thaw weathering.

It is important to realise that rocks will undergo many types of weathering at the same time. For example, once cracks open up, chemical weathering will also have a greater effect as the rock will have more surface area exposed to attack.

Biological weathering

Rocks can also be broken down by the actions of animals or plants. This is called **biological weathering**. For example, the roots of a tree growing in a crack in a rock can split the rock physically. Burrowing animals also break down rock, as do some microorganisms that feed on minerals in rock.

Types of soil

The characteristics of each type of soil are determined by:

- the size of the rock fragments it contains
- the chemical composition of the rock fragments
- the amount of other organic materials mixed in it. This organic material is called **humus** and originates from living organisms.

Some people classify soils into six main types:

- clay
- sandy
- silt
- peat
- chalky
- loam.

But others simplify this to just three categories of soil:

- clay
- sandy
- loam.

A clay soil contains very tiny pieces of weathered rock. This means that there are few gaps between particles for water to drain through. Therefore, clay soil can get waterlogged in the rainy season. It contains little air, especially when wet, because there is not much space between its small particles. You can recognise clay soil as it is lumpy and sticky when wet, but turns rock-hard and can crack when dried out.

Compare this with a sandy soil, which feels gritty to the touch, and drains water quickly because of its larger grains of rock. This also means that there are more gaps between soil particles for air (which is needed by organisms that live in the soil, for example the roots of plants). The sandy soil does have a disadvantage in that heavy rain can wash away the soluble nutrients from the soil. We say that the nutrients are leached from the soil.

Loam soil has a more equal mixture of small and large grains of rock. This means that it can retain water without getting waterlogged. It also contains more humus than clay or sandy soil.

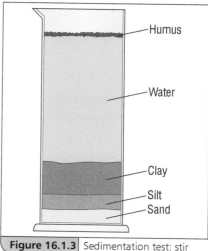

Figure 16.1.3 Sedimentation test: stir two large spatulas of soil in a measuring cylinder of water then leave it to stand overnight

KEY POINTS

1 Rocks can be broken down over time by chemical, physical and/or biological weathering to form the grains that are found in soils.

2 There are three types of soil – clay, sandy and loam.

3 Clay contains the smallest grains and sand contains the largest. Loam contains a more even mixture of grains (as well as more humus).

SUMMARY QUESTIONS

1 Explain how limestone is weathered by rainwater.

2 Explain how rocks can be physically weathered.

3 What else, besides deposited rock fragments, do we find in soil?

4 Draw a table to compare the grain sizes, water retention properties and the amount of air in clay, sandy and loam soils.

- Discuss the general importance of soils.
- The role of earthworms and nematodes in improving soil fertility.
- Explain the chemical and physical properties of soils and the factors that determine them.
- Discuss how the chemical and physical properties of soil determine its fertility.

Soil is vitally important because it is the medium in which plants grow and plants are needed as a food source for living things. Plants use the soil to anchor themselves in a stable position. They also get their nutrients from soluble minerals in the soil, which are absorbed by their roots.

The amount of nutrients in the soil depends to some extent on the population of earthworms and nematodes (tiny worms about 1 mm long) in the soil. Earthworms feed on organic matter, breaking it down and helping nutrients in the organic matter to become available for plants. Likewise with most nematodes. They increase the availability of soluble mineral ions. However, larger nematodes feed on plant roots, so they can damage crops, acting as parasites (see 8.2). Earthworms also break up the structure of the soil by their burrowing activity.

Physical properties of soil

We have looked at some of the physical properties of soils in 16.1.

Permeability is measured by the rate at which water can drain through a soil. This is shown in Figure 16.2.1.

The amount of water held in the soil depends not only on its particle size, but also on the percentage of humus. The more humus, the better the soil can retain water for use by plants. Not only that, the humus also provides most of the nutrients a plant needs. It is where the recycling of organic materials takes place. It is made from dead plant material and animal waste, as well as their decomposing bodies.

We can work out the amount of humus in the soil by this method.

1 Warm a sample of soil to evaporate off any water.

2 Weigh the dry soil.

3 Then heat the dry soil strongly to burn off any humus in the soil. This is best done in a fume-cupboard because of the smell.

4 Re-weigh the sample when cool and calculate the percentage of humus in dry soil.

Chemical properties of soil

The pH of different soils can also vary. For example, soil with a high percentage of its humus as peat is often acidic, i.e. pH below 7. Peat is a partially decomposed plant material which forms a brown spongy layer in the ground. This type of soil contains lots of organic material because it doesn't rot down in the acidic conditions. The bacteria that aid decomposition cannot thrive in the acidic soil. So you might expect a peaty soil to be rich in nutrients because of the plants returning their nutrients to the soil. However, these tend to be 'locked up' in the organic matter as it doesn't decompose readily. Therefore, you need to add fertilisers. Then you have an excellent soil for growing plants because peaty soil holds moisture well.

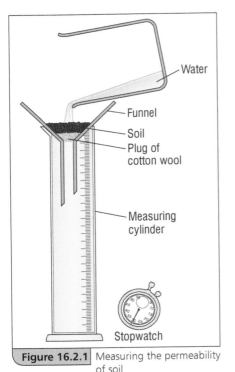

Figure 16.2.1 Measuring the permeability of soil

Water
Funnel
Soil
Plug of cotton wool
Measuring cylinder
Stopwatch

If you have a chalky soil you will find that its pH is 7.5 or above. This is often a stony soil that drains well. It is usually found above beds of chalk or limestone rock. The alkaline nature of the soil means that some essential minerals needed for plant growth, such as manganese and iron, cannot be absorbed. This results in plants that have yellowing leaves (chlorosis) and poor growth. You can rectify this by adding fertilisers containing the missing minerals.

Most plants grow best in soil with a pH value between 6.5 and 7.0. That is because their minerals are most easily absorbed within this range. However, some plants prefer more acidic or alkaline conditions. Look at some examples in the table below.

Plants that grow well in acidic soil	Plants that grow well in alkaline soil
Camellia	Brassicas (cabbage family)
Rhododendron	Lilac tree
Azalea	Madonna lily

Figure 16.2.2 The Bird of Paradise plant grows well in acidic soil

SUMMARY QUESTIONS

1 Which part of a soil determines its fertility?

2 Which rock fragments can make a soil alkaline?

3 Describe how you would determine the percentage of humus in a soil sample.

4 Describe how the presence of earthworms and nematodes can improve the fertility of the soil.

KEY POINTS

1 A soil's physical properties are determined by its particle size, and its water, air and humus content.

2 In general, earthworms and nematodes have a beneficial effect on the fertility of soil.

3 A soil's chemical properties are determined by its pH and mineral content.

The gases nitrogen, oxygen and carbon dioxide are the most important ones in our atmosphere. Their levels are kept roughly constant at 78% nitrogen, 21% oxygen and 0.04% carbon dioxide by the reactions that take place in their cycles.

The nitrogen cycle

The nitrogen in the air cannot be used directly by most plants. They need to take in nitrogen in soluble form, as nitrate ions, through their roots. Turning nitrogen gas into nitrate ions that plants can use is called nitrogen fixation. This is done during thunderstorms by lightning or by nitrifying bacteria in the soil. We also saw that unlike most plants, clover can use nitrogen gas from the air. Clover, along with peas and beans, has nodules on its roots which contain bacteria to fix nitrogen gas.

Nitrogen is important in living things as it is a key element in proteins. It is returned to the air as nitrogen gas when those living things decompose after death by the action of de-nitrifying bacteria.

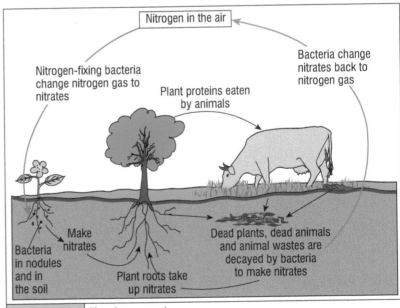

Nitrogen in the air

Nitrogen-fixing bacteria change nitrogen gas to nitrates

Plant proteins eaten by animals

Bacteria change nitrates back to nitrogen gas

Bacteria in nodules and in the soil

Make nitrates

Plant roots take up nitrates

Dead plants, dead animals and animal wastes are decayed by bacteria to make nitrates

Figure 16.3.1 The nitrogen cycle

The oxygen cycle

The key reactions in the oxygen cycle are:

- the removal of oxygen from the atmosphere by living things, using it in respiration to release the energy stored in glucose
- the return of oxygen to the air when plants photosynthesise.

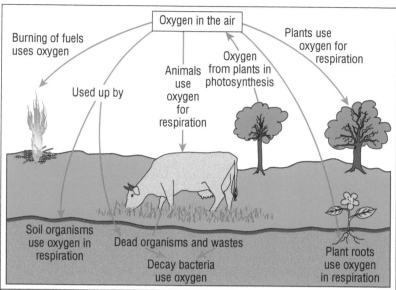

Figure 16.3.2 The oxygen cycle

The carbon cycle

Carbon is an important element as it is present in all organic compounds, which make up all living material. It is not recycled in nature as carbon, the element, but in organic compounds, carbonate rocks and carbon dioxide gas. In the opposite reactions to the oxygen cycle, carbon dioxide is removed from the air in photosynthesis and returned to the air in respiration.

Human activities, such as deforestation, the burning of fossil fuels and intensive farming, are now disrupting these natural cycles.

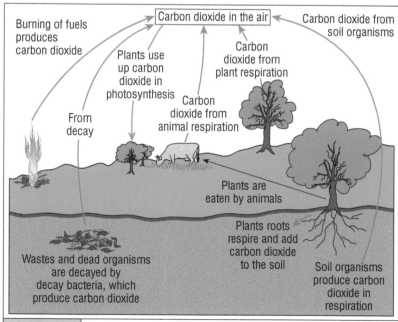

Figure 16.3.3 The carbon cycle

LINK

For more information about another important natural cycle, the water cycle, see 17.1 'Water and life'.

KEY POINTS

1 Nitrifying and de-nitrifying bacteria play important roles in the nitrogen cycle.

2 Photosynthesis and respiration play important roles in the oxygen cycle and the carbon cycle.

3 Human influences can disturb the natural balance of gases in the air and nutrients in the ground.

SUMMARY QUESTIONS

1 In the nitrogen cycle:
  a What part of the cycle do farmers disrupt when they harvest their crops?
  b What do we call the bacteria that fix nitrogen from the air?
  c What do living things use nitrogen to make?

2 Explain a human activity that could interfere with the replacement of oxygen gas back into the atmosphere.

3 Explain which human activity has caused the recent increases in levels of carbon dioxide in our atmosphere so that people are concerned about an enhanced greenhouse effect on the Earth's climate.

Air masses

- Describe what an air mass is.
- Explain how air masses affect the Caribbean.
- Discuss the effects that an air mass can have on an area's weather.

Air masses are huge volumes of air that form around the world. They can be thousands of miles across (see Figure 16.4.1). The temperature across the air mass is similar, as is its pressure, at a given altitude, as well as its humidity (its water vapour content).

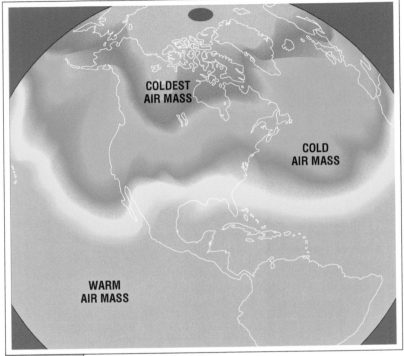

Figure 16.4.1 Air masses

An air mass forms when a large body of air remains roughly in one position over the Earth for a period of time. If it is over a polar region it will form a cold air mass. If that area is over a continent the air mass will not hold much water vapour – the air will be cold and dry. These air masses are called polar continental air masses such as those formed over North America.

On the other hand, an air mass formed over tropical seas will be warm and very humid. We call these tropical maritime air masses, for example those from the Atlantic.

Other air masses can be polar (cold), maritime (moist, relatively humid), tropical (warm) or continental (dry).

Moving air masses

The movement of these huge air masses around the globe dictates our weather. The moving of the air masses means that air from one part of the world circulates to another region. This can have unfortunate consequences. For example, pollutant gases released in one country can end up having a greater effect in another country hundreds or even thousands of miles away.

Air masses can also carry nuclear fallout, as in the accident at the Chernobyl nuclear power plant in 1986. The accident happened in Ukraine (Eastern Europe), but the radioactive pollution was carried right across Europe and fell to earth wherever it rained. Other man-made pollutants to be carried by air masses are waste gases from industry (such as sulphur dioxide, which causes acid rain) and fumes from landfill sites where rubbish is tipped.

The air masses also transport particles of dust around the atmosphere. In the Caribbean, sand from the Sahara desert in Africa is deposited as a fine dust. We also find that after a large volcanic eruption, dust affects sunsets around the world.

LINK

For more information about the effect of moving air masses on the weather, see 16.5 'Air in motion'.

Figure 16.4.2 Much Sahara dust will be deposited in the Atlantic Ocean, but lighter particles are carried further

SUMMARY QUESTIONS

1 Imagine taking measurements across an air mass at 200 m above sea level. What factors would remain roughly constant across the air mass?

2 What is the name given to an air mass that:
   a is cold and dry
   b is warm and humid
   c is warm and dry?

3 Make a list of the possible pollutants transported and deposited by air masses.

KEY POINTS

1 An air mass is a large body of air with similar temperature and pressure at a given height.

2 Examples of air masses are tropical maritime from the Atlantic and polar continental over North America.

3 The energy from an air mass can transport volcanic dust, radioactive fallout and industrial pollution over vast distances.

Local weather fronts

You have probably heard weather reporters on TV talking about 'fronts' on a weather map. These fronts are the boundaries between air masses.

- If a cold air mass is moving towards a warm air mass, the area or plane where the cold air is replaced by the warm air is called a **cold front**.
  Cold air is denser than warm air. So when cold air meets warm air, the cold air burrows under the warms air, forcing it upwards. If the warm air is humid, the water vapour cools as it rises and condenses to form clouds and rain, possibly stormy showers. The sky then clears and there is a sharp change in the direction of a cooler wind. The Caribbean is normally affected by cold fronts from North America during the northern winter.
- If a warm air mass is moving towards a cold air mass, the area, or plane, where the warm air is replaced by the cold air is called a **warm front**.
  When these air masses meet, the warm air mass slides gradually up and over the cold air mass. Clouds will form more slowly than at a cold front and it may well cause it to rain. The weather change is not as violent as at a cold front. A period of warmer weather follows behind the front.
- Occasionally we get a front that does not move much at all and these are called **stationary fronts**.
  This will bring with it a period of weather that remains unchanged.
- If a cold front catches a warm front, we get an **occluded front**.
  In this case the warm front is forced upwards as it gets caught between the rapidly approaching cold front and the cooler air mass in front of the warm front (see Figure 16.5.2). Rain clouds continue to form and bring mature storms that have almost run their course along the occluded front.

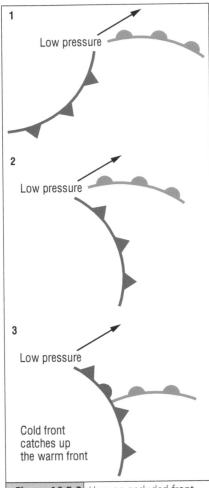

1
Low pressure

2
Low pressure

3
Low pressure

Cold front catches up the warm front

Figure 16.5.2 How an occluded front forms

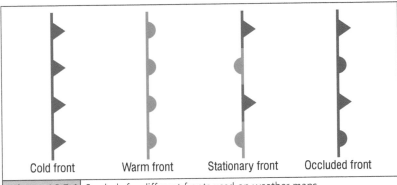

| Cold front | Warm front | Stationary front | Occluded front |

Figure 16.5.1 Symbols for different fronts used on weather maps

How hurricanes form

Hurricanes are areas of very low pressure in the tropics. Low pressure is found where warm air rises at a weather front (where cold air descends we get high pressure). The hurricane originates over the sea (tropical maritime air mass).

Hurricanes produce damagingly strong winds and torrential rain. Along with wind damage and flooding from heavy rain, hurricanes can produce exceptionally high sea levels. This is because of the very low air pressure above the sea, which causes more flooding.

As warm, humid air rises it cools, forming water droplets and releasing energy (latent heat of condensation), which keeps the hurricane growing in strength until it gets over land when its energy dissipates. So damage from a hurricane will be worse near the coast (see Figure 16.5.3)

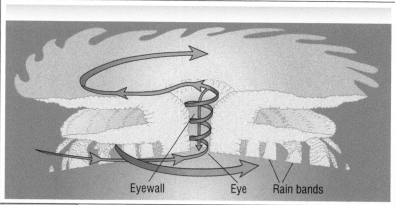

Figure 16.5.3 The structure of a hurricane. Notice the 'eye' at the centre – an area of clear sky where the strong winds die down until it passes over.

Eyewall   Eye   Rain bands

Hurricanes are extreme examples of cyclonic storms. A storm becomes a hurricane when the wind speed exceeds 120 km per hour (about 70 miles per hour).

Hurricane precautions

Meteorologists are constantly improving their powers to predict the paths of hurricanes, but they can be unpredictable.

When the threat of a hurricane has been identified,

- a battery operated radio is needed in preparation for a hurricane as the power may be cut off
- windows should be boarded up and taped and any moveable objects placed indoors
- a source of lighting, such as a torch, will be useful as will a supply of bottled water, some canned food and a camping gas stove
- evacuation to a safe area may be necessary in extreme cases.

Remember that when the wind drops, it might just be the eye of the storm. Your radio will tell you when it is safe again.

**When you see low pressure on a weather map
Don't forget to pack your mac
The wind will be swirling into the skies
But in which direction? Anti-clockwise!**

Figure 16.5.4 This poem works in the Caribbean, but in the southern hemisphere the wind goes round an area of low pressure in a clockwise direction. This swirling of winds is caused by the rotation of the Earth, just like water going down a plughole.

KEY POINTS

1. There are four types of local weather front: cold, warm, stationary and occluded.

2. A cyclonic storm in the Caribbean is a low pressure area with an anti-clockwise circulation of winds.

3. A cyclonic storm becomes a hurricane when the wind speed exceeds 120 km per hour (about 70 miles per hour).

SUMMARY QUESTIONS

1. Draw the weather symbols for:
   a a warm front
   b a cold front
   c an occluded front
   d a stationary front.

2. a How are cyclonic storms formed in the Caribbean?
   b What distinguishes a cyclonic storm from a hurricane?

3. List five things to do in preparation for a hurricane.

Tides

You will have noticed the tides rise and fall regularly around the coastline. Tides are caused by the gravitational forces of attraction between the Earth (and its oceans), the Moon and the Sun. Look at Figure 16.6.1 to see how the Earth and the Moon interact.

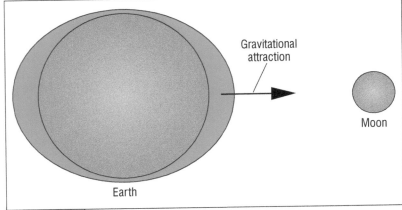

Figure 16.6.1 Effect of the Moon on tides

The rotation of the Earth means that the tide comes in and goes out roughly twice a day. The highest of the high tides (and lowest of the low tides) comes when the Sun and Moon line up with the Earth, either the new moon or full moon. These are called spring tides (see Figure 16.6.2).

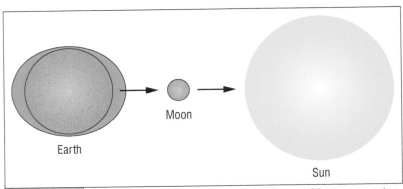

Figure 16.6.2 The combined gravitational pull of the Moon and Sun causes spring tides about every two weeks

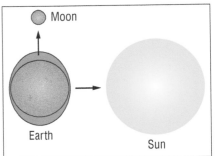

Figure 16.6.3 Neap tides occur in the quarter phases of the Moon when the Moon and Sun's gravitational pull on the Earth oppose each other

When the Moon and Sun are at 90° (right angles) to the Earth we get the lowest of the high tides (and highest of low tides). This is when the Moon is in its quarter phases. These are called neap tides (see Figure 16.6.3).

Tidal waves

These are larger than normal waves caused by the tides that come ashore. They are most likely to occur at spring high tides in a cyclonic storm. If the strong winds are blowing the waves on-shore, coupled with the low pressure above the sea and spring tide, then a tidal surge can happen producing large tidal waves that will flood low-lying land.

Tidal waves can also arise from natural 'funnels' on the coastline, such as a narrow estuary. An exceptionally high tide will cause a tidal surge up the river called a bore tide.

Tsunamis

Tsunamis are a series of large waves that result from the sudden movement of the ocean floor or from a huge landslide. A volcanic eruption beneath the sea can also cause tsunamis and so could, according to scientists, large meteors from space landing in the sea.

The resulting tsunami can be hundreds of miles away from its source. If an earthquake beneath the ocean suddenly lifts a section of the seabed a couple of metres, a wave a couple of metres high will form at the surface and start rippling outwards. When this powerful wave reaches the shallow waters near a coast its energy will cause the height of the wave to increase.

Then when it hits the shore, the tremendous energy of the water in the tsunami smashes and carries almost everything in its path. The objects it carries along make it even more destructive until its energy is dissipated. Then the water retreats back to the sea leaving chaos and death behind.

Figure 16.6.4 The incredible power of a tsunami causes massive destruction. This earthquake, followed quickly by a tsunami, caused thousands of deaths and devastated the north east coast of Japan in 2011.

KEY POINTS

1 The gravitational pull of the Moon and, to a lesser extent, the Sun on the Earth's oceans causes the regular tides on coastlines.

2 Tidal waves cause flooding when conditions coincide to produce large incoming waves.

3 Tsunamis are caused by shocks on the surface or beneath the surface of oceans, such as earthquakes. They can travel over great distances before meeting land and causing devastation.

SUMMARY QUESTIONS

1 a Explain what causes a high tide.

   b Explain how spring tides and neap tides arise.

2 How can a hurricane cause a tidal wave?

3 In what ways do tidal waves and tsunamis differ?

Volcanoes and earthquakes

The Earth's surface is divided into massive slabs of rock called tectonic plates (see Figure 16.7.1). These plates are moving very slowly, at about the rate your fingernails grow. They move because of convection currents deep underground, driven by the heat energy released by radioactive rocks.

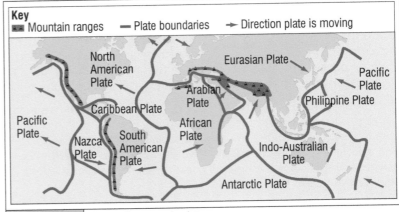

Figure 16.7.1 The Earth's tectonic plates

It is interesting to see the world's earthquake and volcanic activity plotted on the same map (see Figure 16.7.2).

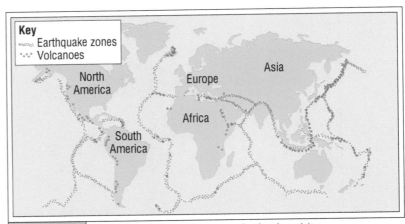

Figure 16.7.2 The Earth's earthquake zones and volcanic activity

Notice how the earthquakes and volcanoes are sited at the boundaries between tectonic plates. The plates sometimes get stuck in positions above the convection currents. The stress builds up at the plates until suddenly the forces are released and the plates slip past each other. This sudden jarring movement causes an earthquake.

Vibrations spread out from the focus to the surface. They are strongest directly above the focus where the slip occurred, at the epicentre, but spread out in all directions. They can be detected thousands of miles away as slight tremors. However, buildings near to the epicentre can be completely flattened.

Figure 16.7.3 In 2010 a devastating earthquake hit Haiti, killing over 100 000 people. The epicentre was near the capital Port-au-Prince where the Caribbean plate moves relative to the North American plate by a couple of centimetres a year.

Measuring the strength of earthquakes

The strength of the vibrations following an earthquake is measured by a seismometer. This is a sensitively balanced instrument. It draws a straight line until it is shaken when the line shows the movement felt. A line traces the size of the vibrations on a **seismograph** (see Figure 16.7.4).

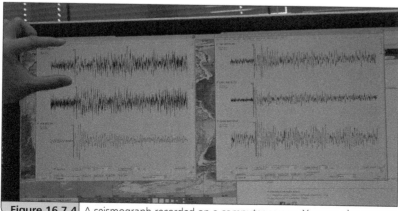

Figure 16.7.4 A seismograph recorded on a computer screen. You can also get pen recorders that produce a paper copy directly from the seismometer.

Continued

The magnitude of vibrations is compared on a scale called the Richter scale. The higher the number, the larger the vibrations detected. The earthquake that struck Japan in 2011 was 9 on the Richter scale and was one of the largest ever recorded. The damage caused in the Haitian earthquake in 2010 resulted from an earthquake of magnitude 7 on the Richter scale (see Figure 16.7.3).

Types of volcano

At tectonic plate boundaries, the friction between the plates causes the rocks to heat up and possibly melt. The molten rock beneath the ground is called magma. The magma is less dense than the surrounding rock so tends to rise towards the surface. When it breaks through to the surface we have a volcanic eruption. The molten rock is called lava.

Lava can be different in different places. It can vary in its temperature, the amount of gas dissolved in it and the mixture of minerals it contains. These factors affect the thickness of the lava. Some lava is thick and gooey like molasses, whereas other lava is much runnier. This alters the shape of a volcano and the type of eruption that takes place (see Figure 16.7.5).

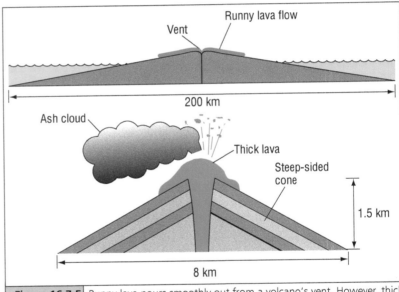

Figure 16.7.5 Runny lava pours smoothly out from a volcano's vent. However, thick lava tends to block up the vent. With thick lava, the pressure builds up inside the volcano until magma bursts out in a violent eruption. The volcano's sides are built up from layers of rock formed from each eruption.

Violent volcanic eruptions destroy the surrounding area covering the landscape in lava, which solidifies back to rock, and in thick ash. Animals lose their habitat and plants cannot photosynthesise because they are burnt or coated in ash. However, over time, the slopes of a volcano weather down to form fertile soils. Therefore, you always find some people willing to risk another eruption in order to farm near volcanoes despite the dangers.

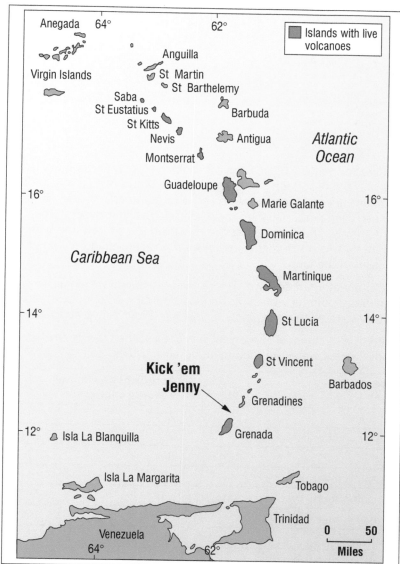

Figure 16.7.6 Here are the Caribbean islands with live volcanoes. Kick 'em Jenny is an underwater volcano off Grenada. It erupts regularly, but is still 180 metres below the surface of the sea.

KEY POINTS

1 Sudden movements of the Earth's tectonic plates cause earthquakes at the boundaries between plates. Volcanoes are also found at these plate boundaries.

2 The strength of an earthquake is shown on a seismograph and is measured on the Richter scale.

3 Runny lava spews smoothly out of volcanic vents, whereas thick lava explodes out violently.

4 Many Caribbean islands are volcanic. This can cause natural disasters, but produces very fertile soils.

SUMMARY QUESTIONS

1 a Where do we find earthquakes and volcanoes around the world?

 b i What instrument do we use to measure the intensity of an earthquake?

 ii What scale is used to measure the size of the vibrations from an earthquake?

2 Explain why some volcanic eruptions are far more dangerous than others.

3 A volcano that has not erupted for a long time is described as dormant. What are the advantages and disadvantages of living near a dormant volcano?

Water and life

Water is one of the most important substances on Earth. It is vital in many of the processes of life. For example, water plays a role in the reactions needed for respiration and photosynthesis. It helps control our body temperature when it evaporates from the sweat on our skin. It is also the solvent that carries substances around the body in blood. It dissolves nutrients in digestion and is used in the exchange of gases in the lungs.

Without water our cells would lose their shape and metabolic reactions would be impossible. In fact, over 60% of our body mass is water. We need to drink plenty of water to avoid dehydration.

Water is also essential in everyday life. Look at the table to see how many litres of water are used in domestic activities.

Use	Approximate volume of water-use (litres)
Shower	27
Power shower	80
Bath	80
Flushing toilet	9
Brushing teeth, washing hands	4
Washing machine	80
Dishwasher	30
Washing dishes by hand	7.5

In a garden, a hosepipe uses about 15 litres of water per minute and a sprinkler uses about 9 litres per minute.

The water cycle

The water cycle shows how water is recycled in nature (see Figure 17.1.1).

Energy from the Sun drives the water cycle as it causes evaporation of water from the sea. Water vapour also enters the air from other sources. For example, water evaporates from the soil, plants (especially trees) lose water vapour through transpiration and animals breathe out water vapour.

As the water vapour rises it cools down and condenses to form clouds made from tiny water droplets. It gets colder again as the clouds are forced to rise higher, for example over high ground or where air masses meet. This causes more water to condense out, as the air becomes saturated, holding its maximum amount of moisture. So the droplets get bigger and heavier. They then fall as rain, hail or snow. This is called precipitation. Eventually the water returns to the sea via rivers, streams and underground waterways. The water cycle ensures there is a constant supply of fresh water, although it is not distributed evenly.

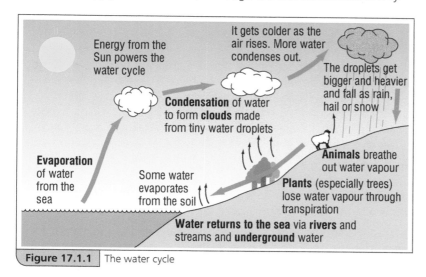

| **Figure 17.1.1** | The water cycle |

Conserving our water supplies

The actual proportions of water used in farming, in industry (including generating electricity) and at home differ from country to country. For example, some African nations can use almost 90% of their water in farming. That's because they need to irrigate their crops as the climate is dry, whereas in European countries, the proportion used in industry and in producing energy is likely to be over 50%. The percentage of water used in industry can be used as a measure of how developed a country is.

The individual usage of water (average per person) also varies widely. A person in the USA is likely to use at least 20 times as much water as a person in Africa each day.

Once we have used water, we can't just dump dirty water directly into rivers and seas. Cleaning up our waste water costs us money. As time passes there will be more and more people competing for the planet's water. So we need to conserve our water and do even more to restore its quality after use. By saving energy, we are also helping to conserve water. That's because power stations use large volumes of water.

Purifying water for drinking

Water's properties

Water is an odourless, colourless liquid. Its melting point (and freezing point) is 0°C and its boiling point is 100°C. It is an excellent solvent, dissolving many salts and also some organic compounds such as sugars and alcohols. It is chemically neutral when pure, being neither acidic nor alkaline. Water does react with more reactive metals and causes the important metal iron to rust (when oxygen is also present).

These properties make it an ideal medium for many chemical reactions to take place in solution. Unfortunately its ability to dissolve things means that water is easily polluted with dissolved substances. This is why we need to purify our drinking water.

The vast majority of aquatic life live in seawater and can tolerate the salt concentrations. Their bodies have quite high concentrations of sodium and chloride ions so no more will diffuse into their cells from the sea. Freshwater creatures cannot live in salty conditions as this would disrupt their exchange of ions across membranes in cells. The sodium and chloride ions diffusing into their cells would be fatal. However some fish, such as salmon, can survive in both seawater and fresh water.

Sources and treatment of water

About 97% of the water on Earth is in the salty oceans. However, we can use fresh water drawn from:

- lakes
- rivers
- aquifers (water held in underground rocks)
- reservoirs (large lakes created for storing water).

These are sources of fresh water, but they still have to be purified to make water fit for drinking.

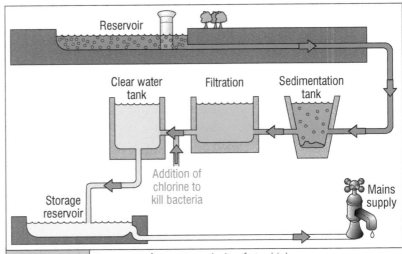

Figure 17.2.1 Treatment of water to make it safe to drink

Water can be stored in a reservoir before being piped to homes and industry. Before it gets there it goes through several stages as shown in Figure 17.2.1.

Larger solid particles are allowed to settle at the bottom of the sedimentation tanks. But there are still smaller colloidal particles of clay dispersed in the water. The tiny particles are electrically charged (negative). They stay spread throughout the water because they repel each other. So water companies add aluminium sulphate to coagulate the clay. The particles are attracted to the highly charged aluminium ions. They form clumps, which get heavy enough to settle on the bottom of the tank.

Then the water is filtered through layers of sand and gravel to make sure all insoluble solids are removed. These filter beds can also contain carbon slurry to get rid of substances that would give the water an odd smell or taste.

Chlorine is added to kill bacteria in the water. This prevents diseases. The water company will add enough chlorine to kill all the bacteria. They remove any excess chlorine by treating the water with **sulphur dioxide**. This reacts with the chlorine, getting rid of its smell and taste. A little chlorine is left in the water to keep it free from bacteria on the journey to your tap.

Other methods to purify water

For many hot countries, getting a reliable supply of fresh water is difficult. With low rainfall, rivers and lakes run dry in hotter months. However, these countries sometimes have large coastlines. They have plenty of sea water, but this salty water is unsuitable for most uses.

Special **desalination** plants (see Figure 17.2.2) can take most of the dissolved salts out of seawater or from brackish water from marshes. In distillation, water is evaporated, then cooled and condensed to separate it from dissolved solids. The process used in some desalination plants is based on distillation.

In a desalination plant, the pressure above the water is reduced. This lowers the boiling point of the seawater. The process is called flash distillation.

Another process called reverse osmosis is getting more popular. This uses a membrane to separate the water and the salts. There is no heating involved so it uses less energy than distillation. However, energy is still needed to pressurise the water.

Modern membranes can remove 98% of dissolved salts from seawater. However, corrosion of pumps and pipes is a problem. Desalination is used in Middle Eastern countries that can use money from their oil to pay the costs. In the Virgin Islands, in the Caribbean Sea, 90% of water used is desalinated as they have no source of fresh water other than any rainwater they can collect.

Figure 17.2.2 A desalination plant uses distillation to obtain pure water from seawater. The process requires large amounts of energy to boil the seawater

Flotation

- State the conditions for flotation in terms of upthrust and density.
- Draw a diagram showing the forces acting on an object as it floats or sinks.
- Explain the importance of the Plimsoll line to boats and ships.

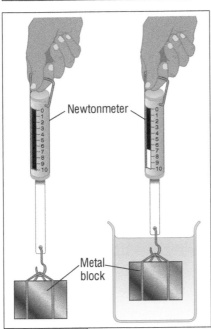

Figure 17.3.1	The upthrust experienced by the block is 3 N, i.e. (10 − 7) N

Some materials float in water and some sink. The property which determines this behaviour is the density of the material.

All objects experience a force upwards when placed in water. You have probably noticed this when you walk out into deeper water in the sea or in a swimming pool. Your body seems to get lighter the deeper you go. When you lie on your back and float, you feel weightless.

This is explained by Archimedes principle. It states that an object immersed in a fluid is buoyed up by a force equal to the weight of fluid displaced by the object.

The force of water (or any other fluid) on an object acts upwards and is called **upthrust**.

You can measure the upthrust using a newtonmeter as shown in Figure 17.3.1.

$$\text{Upthrust} = \frac{\text{weight of}}{\text{object in air}} - \frac{\text{weight of}}{\text{object in water}}$$

When the upthrust is equal to the weight of an object, the object will float. The upthrust, acting upwards, will balance the weight of the object, acting downwards. However, if the weight is greater than the upthrust, the weight pulls the object downwards and the object sinks (see Figure 17.3.2).

The density of water is 1.0 g/cm³. Any material with a density of less than this will float on top of the water. Any material with a density greater than 1.0 g/cm³ will sink. We can calculate a material's density using the equation:

$$\text{density (in g/cm}^3) = \frac{\text{mass (in g)}}{\text{volume (in cm}^3)}$$

(Alternatively, density can be expressed in units of kg/m³.)

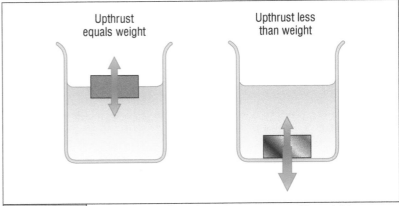

Figure 17.3.2	For an object to float, the upthrust must equal its weight

Finding the volume of a block of material is easy. You just measure the length, the breadth and the width and multiply them together. So if a block of iron has the dimensions 3 cm by 4 cm by 4 cm, its volume is $(3 \times 4 \times 4) = 48\,cm^3$.

If an object has an irregular shape you can find its volume using a measuring cylinder and a displacement can. Look at Figure 17.3.3.

If you then find the mass of the block on a balance in grams (g), you can work out the density in g/cm^3. The iron block has a mass of 384 g. Therefore, its density is mass (384 g) ÷ volume (48 cm³) $= 8\,g/cm^3$.

This means that the block of iron will sink in water. Yet, iron ships weighing thousands of tonnes can float. Here we must not confuse a material with objects made from that material. A ship is shaped so that the majority of it is actually air, and all gases have very low densities. The density of air is $0.0013\,g/cm^3$. So the combined density of the iron and other solid materials in the ship, plus the air inside is less than $1.0\,g/cm^3$.

The upthrust on an object depends on the mass of liquid it displaces. If you fill a ship with too much cargo, the ship will need to sit lower in the water to get the extra upthrust to keep it afloat. But if too much is put aboard, it can get dangerously low in the water and risk sinking. That's why ships have a Plimsoll line on the side – to check that they are carrying a safe load (see Figure 17.3.4).

The same ship can carry a larger load in seawater than in fresh water. That is because the upthrust experienced by an object in seawater is greater than the upthrust in fresh water as seawater has the higher density. So the same mass of cargo will make the ship go lower in fresh water to get the same upthrust as in seawater.

Submarines use their ballast tanks to change their density. The submariners can allow water into the tanks to dive down (increasing their mass and hence their density) or can pump water out of their tanks to rise up to the surface again. Bony fish use a similar principle, using their gas-filled swim bladder.

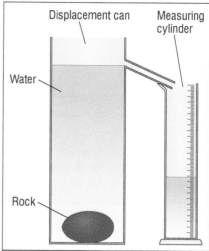

Figure 17.3.3 Fill the displacement can to its spout then lower in the object. The volume of water that spills over into the measuring cylinder tells you the volume of the object.

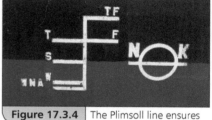

Figure 17.3.4 The Plimsoll line ensures the safety of ships

SUMMARY QUESTIONS

1 Draw a diagram showing the forces acting on a floating object.

2 A volume of 2.5 cm³ of lead metal has a mass of 27.5 g. What is the density of lead?

3 A piece of wood has a density of 1.2 g/cm³. Explain whether the wood will float or sink in water.

4 a Explain how a submarine rises to the surface.

   b Explain the difference in ballast tanks of a submarine when it dives in seawater compared with the same dive in fresh water.

Are you concerned about the pollution of our rivers, lakes and seas? It is not possible to get absolutely pure water in nature because water is so good at dissolving things. This is often useful to us, but also makes it easy to pollute water.

Eutrophication

Sometimes farmers will add too much nitrate fertiliser to their soil or it is added at the wrong time of year. This can cause pollution in rivers and creeks.

Some nitrate fertiliser is washed down through the soil by rain. We say that it is leached out of the soil. The dissolved fertiliser drains from the fields into rivers and other waterways. Phosphates also get into the waterways from fertilisers as well as from detergents. This starts off a chain of events called **eutrophication**.

1 Tiny water plants, called algae, thrive on the nitrate or phosphate compounds in the leached fertilisers.

2 The algae start to cover the surface of the water. This cuts off light to other living things in the river.

3 Plants on the riverbed die, along with some algae, so bacteria decompose them.

4 The bacteria multiply quickly with so much food. They use up much of the oxygen dissolved in the water.

5 This means that fish and other water animals cannot get enough oxygen. Soon they start dying.

Figure 17.4.1 This stretch of water has been affected by eutrophication

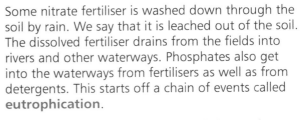

Untreated sewage in waterways also causes eutrophication, but brings with it the risk of bacterial infections as well. We tend to find eutrophication in areas of the stream where water flow rate is very slow (as fast-flowing water dissolves fresh oxygen gas more quickly).

Nitrate fertilisers are very soluble. They are finding their way into our drinking water. People are starting to worry about the possible health risks. There is concern about stomach cancer and 'blue baby' disease (when a newborn baby's blood is starved of oxygen). However, others argue that there is no evidence. Links between the levels of nitrate in our water and disease have not been proven. Still, most people agree that it is wise to limit the amount of nitrate we drink.

Thermal pollution

Besides its use as a solvent, water is also used in industry as a coolant. It transfers energy away from a reaction. This raises the temperature of the water. An example is its use to transfer energy in *power stations*. The water is not polluted when it is passed out into a nearby river. However, it is warmer than the river water.

This can affect the delicate balance of life in the river. Remember that aquatic animals rely on oxygen gas dissolved in the water. Gases get less soluble in water as its temperature rises. So not as much oxygen dissolves in the warmer water and aquatic animals die.

Many coral reefs are also destroyed by thermal pollution as water used for cooling large machinery is expelled into the sea.

Pesticides

Pesticides in drinking water are another problem that water companies are tackling. Pesticide residues can get into waterways from crop spraying in nearby fields. The concentration of the toxic substances builds up in organisms the higher up the food chain you go. Our drinking water is now checked for acceptable levels of pesticides.

Oil spills

Crude oil is transported around the world in giant oil tankers. If these ships have an accident, the crude oil can escape. It floats on top of the sea, forming an oil slick.

Figure 17.4.2 This oil slick resulted from an accident on the seabed when drilling for oil in the Gulf of Mexico. It took months to stop the flow of oil into the sea.

Soapless detergents are used to clean up the mess. The detergent breaks up the slick. Then the oil is spread out by the action of the waves, but not before harming the aquatic ecosystem.

SUMMARY QUESTIONS

1 a What is the name of the type of pollution caused by excess fertiliser being leached out of the soil into a river?

  b Draw a flow chart to explain what happens when waterways are polluted by nitrates and/ or phosphates.

2 Why do you think that pesticide residues are found in higher proportions in the tissues of animals higher up the food chain?

3 Carry out some research into an oil spill. Find out about the harm it caused to the aquatic environment and how the oil slick was treated after the event.

Fishing is an important industry in the Caribbean. There is a great variety of fish in the seas, but caution is needed to guard against overfishing. Taking too many fish (especially young fish) will mean that stocks cannot recover. The industry, as well as the ecosystem, will suffer so fishing has to be sustainable. That is why government fisheries set rules, such as:

- banning foreign fishing vessels from their waters
- defining net sizes so that young fish can fit through
- setting limits on the catch taken.

They also take measures to avoid endangered species being killed when the target fish are caught. For example, nets can be fitted with devices that emit sounds to keep dolphins and porpoises away.

Here are some of the methods used to catch fish and shellfish.

By hand

This is a highly selective method as fish are caught one at a time and can be put back into the sea if they are not the target fish. The bait on the line can be chosen to attract certain fish. This is a time-consuming method, but useful for large fish, which command a high price, such as the bluefin tuna. The catch is good quality, as it comes aboard alive. Spears or harpoons can be used for larger fish.

Long-lining

This is a commercial version of fishing by hand, but many lines are set all at once, hanging from a main line (see Figure 17.5.1). The method is used to catch tuna and swordfish, or it can be set so the bait is near seabed depth for cod. However, it does kill sea birds and turtles, but it is not as destructive as some other methods, such as dredging.

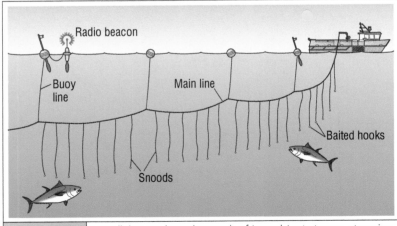

Figure 17.5.1 Long-lining can have thousands of 'snoods' set at once, at varying depths to target different species of fish

Purse seining

This method is used for fish that aggregate (swim in large shoals, quite near the surface), such as groupers and snappers.

The net is like a long fence with floats at the top and weights at the bottom. The bottom of the net also has rings, through which a rope is threaded. When the rope is pulled, the net acts like a drawstring purse, closing around the shoal of fish.

Trawling

In this method the net is dragged along a smooth seabed by a fishing boat called a trawler (see Figure 17.5.2). It targets fish that live at the bottom of the sea, for instance cod, plaice and sole. As in all netting methods, the size of the net mesh is critical. The net will catch fish whose head fits through the net, but whose body does not. Then, when the fish tries to 'back out', it gets trapped by its gills. Setting the mesh at a large enough size will ensure young fish can escape and go on to breed.

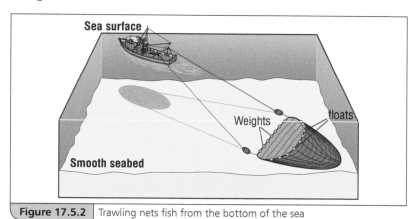

Figure 17.5.2 | Trawling nets fish from the bottom of the sea

Dredging

Dredging is used for gathering molluscs such as oysters, clams and scallops from the seabed. A dredge is a metal framed basket. Its bottom is made of iron rings or wire netting. The leading edge of the dredge has a raking bar. A small boat will drag a single dredge along the seabed. Larger boats will tow ten or more dredges over each side.

Shellfish, such as crab and lobsters, are also caught in traps or pots left on the seabed and lifted to the surface to check the catch.

Fish farming

Certain species of fish or shellfish are commercially 'farmed'. Species such as salmon are grown in enclosures with their food provided for them. Oysters can be cultivated on racks or lines lowered into the sea and raised when the oysters are mature.

Fish farming helps conserve natural stocks, but there are some environmental drawbacks. For instance, fishmeal is used to feed the fish. This is made from small fish that are not for human consumption. However, taking large quantities of these from near the bottom of the marine food chain disrupts the whole ecosystem.

KEY POINTS

1 There is a variety of ways to catch fish. Some are more indiscriminate than others, killing species that are not wanted for the market.

2 We have to have rules and regulations set to prevent over-fishing and to protect fish stocks for future generations.

SUMMARY QUESTIONS

1 Which method of fishing:
   a drags a metal cage along the seabed
   b traps shoals of fish
   c can ensure only the target fish is killed
   d is used to take fish at a variety of depths?

2 a Why is overfishing a problem?
   b What can be done to prevent overfishing?

Navigation and safety on the water

Navigational devices at sea

It is easy to get lost once you are out at sea. There are no features to distinguish where you are once you are out of sight of land. So sailors have used the Sun, stars and compasses to find their way around. Nowadays, there are more complex and accurate satellite systems to help.

The magnetic compass

A compass is a free-moving magnet that lines up with the Earth's magnetic field, so that it points north–south. The end that points north is called the North pole of the magnet, which in a compass is shaped like an arrowhead.

Sailors used compasses to set their course until more modern aids such as Global Positioning System (GPS) were invented.

Sonar and radar

Sonar is used on fishing vessels to locate shoals of fish. Pulses of sound are sent out from the boat beneath the water. The echo from the shoal is picked up by a detector, which tells the operator the depth of the shoal (see Figure 17.6.1).

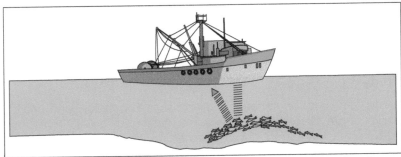

Figure 17.6.1 The time for the echo to return to the boat is shorter when the shoal of fish pass between the boat and the seabed

Radar uses radio waves instead of sound waves to detect objects, such as other ships at sea.

GPS

Modern vessels use GPS to locate their exact position. This uses radio signals to and from satellites in space, 12 000 miles above Earth, to give locations. The satellite signals from at least three satellites to your receiver can be used to calculate your position to great accuracy. Then the system will calculate your desired course when you set your destination. We call GPS global satellite navigation. It was first used on vessels in 1985 and has made the sea a much safer place to travel (see Figure 17.6.2).

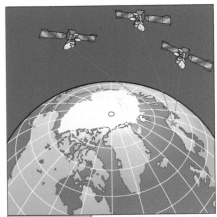

Figure 17.6.2 The time for the signal to return to the satellite gives an exact distance – so once there are three such distances, the receiver can be pin-pointed

Water safety

The sea can be a dangerous place when the weather turns stormy and the wind whips up large waves. That is why safety equipment is needed on vessels. Life jackets should be worn on rivers and lakes, as well as at sea when travelling on open boats where there is any danger of falling overboard. The life jackets are buoyancy aids, like inflatable rings, that people can use to float in water.

Modern life rafts inflate when a cord is pulled. They are self-righting and are almost impossible to turn over in the water.

Hazards of scuba-diving

With modern equipment and training, scuba-diving is a relatively safe activity. It is popular with tourists visiting the Caribbean. However, there are some risks associated with scuba-diving. Some of these are linked to changes in pressure; increasing too rapidly as you descend or decreasing too quickly as you come back up to the surface.

Changes in pressure can affect any cavity in the body that is sealed off and filled with gas. As pressure is increased when diving, gases contract or as pressure is decreased, they expand. The inner ear is one place affected, especially if you are blocked up with a cold or 'flu. In extreme cases the ear drum can burst. If you hold your breath when ascending from a dive, the alveoli in the lungs can expand rapidly and also be damaged as cell membranes burst.

We also have dissolved gases in our blood. More gas will dissolve as pressure is increased. Many divers use air, not pure oxygen, in their breathing tanks carried on their backs. The nitrogen gas from air, which dissolves in the blood, causes problems for divers. If they dive down too quickly, too much nitrogen dissolves in the blood. This leads to a condition called nitrogen narcosis. Its effects are similar to drinking too much alcohol. The diver becomes careless and will take risks, even ignoring safety procedures as their decision making is impaired.

Rising to the surface too quickly could be one mistake a diver suffering from nitrogen narcosis makes. If they do, the dissolved nitrogen comes out of the blood to form bubbles in blood vessels, called embolisms. This causes soreness, dizziness and nausea and is known as 'the bends'. It can be fatal if the air blockage reaches the heart or the brain.

A recompression chamber (also called a decompression chamber) is used to treat divers with the bends. It is a strong steel vessel which can withstand high pressure to re-dissolve any nitrogen bubbles in the blood. The pressure is gradually released to surface pressure in stages. Pure oxygen can be used inside the chamber, so no more nitrogen dissolves in the blood during recompression.

Figure 17.6.3 | An inflatable life raft

SUMMARY QUESTIONS

1 a Explain how the captain of a fishing boat can find a shoal of fish.

   b What could the captain use to return to exactly the same place to fish the next week?

2 If a vessel sinks at sea, which two pieces of safety equipment could keep people alive until rescuers arrive?

3 a Describe three conditions that scuba-divers could suffer from if they rise to the surface too quickly.

   b What is the function of a recompression chamber?

Formation of fossil fuels

Most of our common fuels are **fossil fuels**. Coal, crude oil (which gives us petrol) and natural gas are all fossil fuels. Peat is another fossil fuel.

Fossil fuels have taken millions of years to form. Coal came from trees and ferns that died and were buried beneath swamps about 300 million years ago.

Crude oil was formed from tiny animals and plants which lived in the sea about 150 million years ago. These were buried under layers of sand and silt on the sea bed. They did not decay normally as the bacteria feeding on them had little or no oxygen in these conditions. As the pressure and temperature slowly increased, they were changed into oil. Natural gas is usually found with the crude oil (see Figure 18.1.1).

The plants and animals got their energy from the Sun. This became stored (chemical) energy in the fossil fuel. So when you burn a fuel you are using energy that started off in the Sun (see Figure 18.1.2).

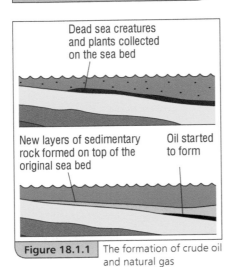

Dead sea creatures and plants collected on the sea bed

New layers of sedimentary rock formed on top of the original sea bed

Oil started to form

Figure 18.1.1 | The formation of crude oil and natural gas

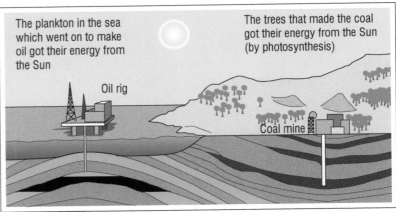

The plankton in the sea which went on to make oil got their energy from the Sun

The trees that made the coal got their energy from the Sun (by photosynthesis)

Oil rig

Coal mine

Figure 18.1.2 | The energy stored in fossil fuels originated from the Sun

Fossil fuels are called **non-renewable** fuels. That's because once we use up our supplies on Earth they cannot be replaced (at least not for millions of years).

Problems associated with fossil fuels

Most fossil fuels contain sulphur in compounds present as impurities. When we burn the fuel, the sulphur is oxidised. It turns into sulphur dioxide (SO_2) gas. Power stations burning coal or oil give off most sulphur dioxide.

Sulphur dioxide is the main cause of acid rain. The gas dissolves in rainwater, and reacts with oxygen in the air, to form sulphuric acid. Cars burning fuels distilled from crude oil also make our rain acidic. Most petrol is sulphur-free now. However, car exhausts give off nitrogen oxides. In the high temperatures inside an engine, even unreactive nitrogen gas will react with oxygen. These nitrogen oxides make nitric acid when it rains.

The effects of acid rain

- *Forests* – Trees are damaged and even killed.
- *Fish* – Hundreds of lakes now have no fish left in them at all. Aluminium, which is normally 'locked' in the soil, dissolves in acid rain. It then gets washed into the lakes, where it poisons the fish.
- *Buildings* – Acid rain attacks buildings and metal structures. Limestone buildings are most badly affected.

Global warming

The Earth's atmosphere acts like a greenhouse. It lets rays from the Sun through to warm the Earth. But gases, such as carbon dioxide and water vapour, absorb some of the heat energy given off as the Earth cools down. Therefore, the heat energy gets trapped and cannot escape out into space.

Without these so-called 'greenhouse gases', the Earth would be much colder and all our water would be frozen. How do you think that would affect life on Earth?

However, we are making more and more of these gases. Whenever we burn a fossil fuel we make carbon dioxide and we are now burning up fossil fuels at an incredible rate. This disturbs the natural balance of carbon dioxide.

Although plants absorb carbon dioxide, we are cutting down huge areas of forest every day. The trees are often just burned to clear land for farming. This makes even more carbon dioxide. The increased levels of carbon dioxide seem to be making the average temperature of the Earth hotter. We call this **global warming**. There is great concern in the Caribbean over the effects of global warming. People are worried by the predictions of increased frequency of hurricanes due to warmer seas and the rise in sea levels due to the melting of the polar ice caps.

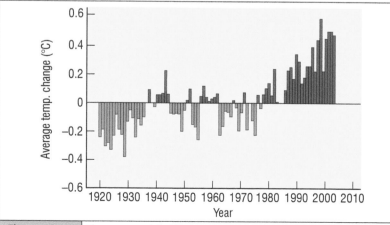

Figure 18.1.3 The average global temperature seems to be rising, but some people argue that these are just natural variations that have always happened. However, most scientists believe that human activities are contributing to global warming.

LINK

For more information on the carbon cycle, see 16.3 'Natural cycles'.

KEY POINTS

1 Coal, crude oil, natural gas and peat are all non-renewable fossil fuels.

2 Fossil fuels are stores of chemical energy that originated from the Sun.

3 Burning fossil fuels causes pollution problems, such as acid rain and global warming.

SUMMARY QUESTIONS

1 Describe how crude oil was formed using a flow diagram.

2 How can we say that when we burn a fossil fuel we are really using the Sun's energy?

3 Explain how burning petrol or diesel in a car engine can contribute to acid rain and global warming.

4 Find out how peat and coal are related.

LINK

You can find out more about using energy from the Sun in 18.3 'Solar energy'.

We have seen that fossil fuels are non-renewable sources of energy. As these start to run out, alternative forms of renewable energy will become increasingly important.

Solar energy

This is energy from the Sun. It can be used in solar cells which transfer the Sun's energy to electrical energy. Alternatively it can be used directly to heat water for use at home in solar panels.

Biofuels

Biofuels are derived from plants or animals, either directly or using their products. For example, wood-chip can be used to heat homes or generate electricity. New trees are planted to replace the ones cut down to burn as fuels.

Biogas is made from the waste products of farm animals and humans, as well as waste vegetation. The waste is collected into special biogas generators where microorganisms break down the waste materials (see Figure 18.2.1). In this process one of the gases they give off is methane, the main constituent of natural gas. This burns well, and can be used for heating and cooking in individual homes or rural villages. On a larger scale it can be used to generate electricity by using waste from huge herds of cattle.

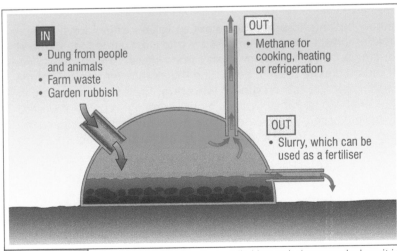

IN
- Dung from people and animals
- Farm waste
- Garden rubbish

OUT
- Methane for cooking, heating or refrigeration

OUT
- Slurry, which can be used as a fertiliser

Figure 18.2.1 A biogas generator can be installed beneath the ground where it is well insulated as the generators work best at about 30°C

Crops are also specially grown to make fuel for vehicles. Biodiesel is a fuel made from vegetable oils extracted from crops such as maize, oilseed rape and palm. This can be mixed with diesel from crude oil to make our limited supplies last longer or can be used as 'biodiesel' itself.

Ethanol is another biofuel. It is produced by the fermentation of sugar from crops such as sugar cane using yeast. The ethanol is an excellent fuel to replace petrol. Like biodiesel, it helps reduce carbon dioxide emissions overall. The plants it is made from absorb carbon dioxide as they grow, though they still give CO_2 off when they burn.

However, using crops to make fuels means there is less land for food crops. Also, if new land for growing the biofuel crops is created from forests, this will destroy habitats for wildlife.

Wind energy

On high ground, near the coast or even in the sea, wind turbines are becoming increasingly common. The huge blades of the wind turbines can rotate to face the wind and spin round. This provides the energy to generate electricity. The wind turbines only work when there is sufficient wind.

Wave energy

The movement of waves across the sea, caused by the wind, can be used to make electricity. Floats can rock up and down to harness the energy of the waves as they pass, but each one can only generate a small amount. So floats, stretching for several miles, would need to be coupled together, to generate the same power as a power station.

Geothermal energy

This uses energy from hot rocks beneath the Earth's surface. Water is piped down to areas where the hot rocks are not too deep and steam returns to the surface. The steam is used to drive the turbines to generate electricity as in conventional fossil fuel power stations.

Hydroelectric energy

Hydroelectric energy uses the gravitational potential energy stored in water held in a dam. Large areas of land are often flooded to create the dams. Hydroelectric plants are often in mountainous areas. The water is allowed to fall to a lower level and on the way down turns the turbines to generate electricity.

Figure 18.2.3 | A hydroelectric plant in Costa Rica

Figure 18.2.2 | More wind turbines are being sited offshore. They still have an impact on views, but issues of noise pollution are reduced as there are no near neighbours.

KEY POINTS

1. There are several options for countries wanting to generate electricity using renewable resources. These include solar, wind, wave, hydroelectric and geothermal energy as well as biofuels.

2. Each renewable source of energy has its own advantages and disadvantages.

SUMMARY QUESTIONS

1. What do we mean by a 'renewable energy source'?

2. Give a disadvantage of:
   a wind energy
   b hydroelectric energy
   c wave energy
   d biofuels.

3. Why do we need to find alternative sources of renewable energy?

Solar energy

LEARNING OUTCOMES

- Describe the uses of solar energy.
- Discuss the variables affecting solar energy.
- Appraise the usefulness of solar energy.

Uses of solar energy

The Sun provides us with energy that we do not have to pay for. We use it every time we hang clothes out to dry. In industry, salt can be extracted from seawater in shallow pools left to evaporate in the Sun's heat. Solar driers are also used to dry meat, fish, fruits or crops such as coffee beans in Costa Rica.

Scientists continue to develop more ways to use this free energy to do useful work.

Solar cells transfer energy from the Sun directly into electrical energy. The cells are called photovoltaic cells. They are used in solar powered calculators and for signs in remote areas that do not have mains electricity. Lots of photovoltaic cells linked together can even be used to generate electricity in a power station (see Figure 18.3.1).

Figure 18.3.1 In sunny places photovoltaic cells can be combined to generate mains electricity. However, you need a huge number of them as at present they are less than 20% efficient.

EXAM TIP

Solar energy can be stored as heat energy in substances with large heat capacities, such as rock or concrete.

Another way to generate electricity is to concentrate the Sun's energy to turn water into steam to turn turbines in generators. These power stations can use curved mirrors to track the path of the Sun across the sky and focus the light on to a tower. They can store heat energy in pressurised steam for a short time, but research continues to find better ways of storage, for example in molten salt.

On a smaller scale the same principle is used in solar cookers where the solar energy is concentrated by a shiny collecting dish onto a focal point to cook food.

Solar panels heat water that flows through pipes in the panels. The panels are often installed on south-facing roofs to supply hot water to a home. They are coloured black to absorb as much solar heat energy as possible (see Figure 18.3.2). Heating systems can also be run off solar power.

Figure 18.3.2 | Solar panels warm water that passes through them

Variables affecting solar energy transfer

To get the most out of solar power, any collection system must be set up for maximum exposure to sunlight. This exposure will be affected by:

- the time of day
- the seasons of the year
- the angle of tilt towards the Sun (perpendicular giving maximum exposure)
- the weather (high temperatures and clear skies are best)
- shading (for example by neighbouring trees)
- distance from the equator.

Advantages and disadvantages of solar energy

In the Caribbean, which lies near the equator and has plenty of hours of sunshine per year, solar energy is an attractive alternative source of energy. However at present it is the most expensive method of generating electricity of all the options available. It has high set up costs and is less than 20% efficient. Although the energy can be stored, research continues to find more efficient ways to do this and to make solar cells more effective.

SUMMARY QUESTIONS

1 Make a list of uses of solar energy.

2 Explain how a solar cooker works.

3 a There are two ways of using solar energy to generate electricity in a power station. What are they?

  b What would be the ideal location for a solar power station?

  c Why are solar cells on satellites the best way to supply their instruments with electrical energy?

4 Why is solar energy not more widely used at present?

19 Forces

19.1

Principles of forces

LEARNING OUTCOMES

- Define force.
- Discuss the principles of forces.

A force can cause a change in an object. The force may change its speed, the direction the object is moving in or its shape. But there are still forces acting on objects that are not moving or changing shape.

Whenever you push an object the object will push back on you with the same size force, but in the opposite direction. Newton called these forces the action force and the reaction force. Newton's third law of motions says that action and reaction are always equal and opposite.

If a plate is placed on a table, a force acts vertically downwards from the plate. This is the plate's weight, measured in the units of force, newtons (N). At the same time, the table pushes vertically upwards on the plate with an equal force. In order to move the plate to another position on the table, we must apply another force.

We can represent forces by arrows that point in the direction the force is acting. The length of the arrow is drawn to scale to represent the size of the force. The forces acting at a point can be added up to give a resultant force. If the forces cancel out to give a resultant force of zero, the object is either stationary or moving at a constant velocity.

A jet plane moves forward because its engines push hot gases backwards and the reaction force, called thrust, pushes the plane forward. A space vehicle changes direction in space in a similar way when it fires its booster rockets.

NEWTON'S FIRST LAW

Newton's first law states that an object will remain stationary or continue moving in the same direction, at the same speed, unless an external force acts on the object.

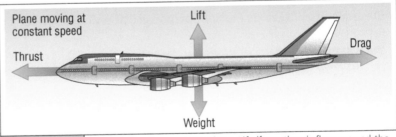

Figure 19.1.1 The forces acting on a jet plane. Lift (from the air-flow around the plane's wings) opposes the force of gravity (the plane's weight). Thrust (provided by the jet engines) opposes drag (friction of the air or air resistance). Planes travel faster with a strong tail-wind behind them, but the drag force also increases as velocity increases.

Friction is a hindrance in some ways, but is essential in others. We have seen how the moving parts of a machine waste energy because of the heat energy released through friction. However, we would not be able to walk without the force of friction between our feet and the ground. As your foot produces a force backwards, it is friction that stops it actually moving backwards and pushes you forward. If friction is reduced, such as walking on ice, your foot does move backwards and walking becomes difficult.

The same forces apply when a car moves along a road. If oil is spilt on a road, a tyre can no longer grip the road's surface and the force of friction is reduced. The wheels spin with no friction opposing their movement and the car skids. The same thing can happen on a wet or icy road or when the tread of a tyre is worn down.

Figure 19.1.2 | Wet road surfaces have less friction with tyres than a dry road surface

The drag experienced by cars is reduced by streamlining their shape. This is important as it saves fuel, reducing the energy needed to produce the same speed.

KEY POINTS

1 Forces can change an object's speed, its direction of motion or its shape.

2 Forces are balanced when an object is stationary or moving at constant speed in a straight line.

3 Friction is a force that opposes motion.

SUMMARY QUESTIONS

1 Two people on roller blades pull on either end of a rope. Explain what happens.

2 a What forces does a book on a desk experience?

   b Why does the book remain stationary on the desk even though it is experiencing forces?

3 Draw a diagram to show the forces acting on an aeroplane as it accelerates down a runway and is at the point of taking off. (There are four forces to consider.)

4 Explain one example of friction acting as a hindrance and one example of its usefulness.

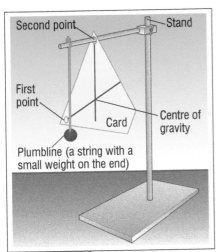

Figure 19.2.1 Experiment to find the centre of gravity of a piece of card. For symmetrical flat objects the centre of gravity will be their centre of symmetry.

Gravity

Any two objects tend to attract each other. The larger the mass of an object, the stronger its attraction for other objects. The objects we use in everyday life are too small to notice this attraction. But when you consider an object the size of a planet, then these forces become significant. It is the force of attraction between the objects on Earth and the Earth itself that keeps everything on the surface of the planet. We call this the force of gravity. This force always acts towards the centre of the Earth.

The force of gravity acting on us is called our weight, measured in newtons (N), where a mass of 1 kg has a weight of about 10 N. We can think of the force of gravity or an object's weight as acting through a single point. This point is called the object's **centre of gravity**.

We can find the centre of gravity of a flat object using a plumbline. Look at Figure 19.2.1.

As in the experiment in Figure 19.2.1, whenever we suspend an object it will always come to rest with its centre of gravity directly below the point of suspension. It is said to be in a position of stable equilibrium.

If we move the object sideways from its equilibrium position, it will experience a turning force. The object is unstable in this position. Its centre of gravity is raised and gravity will act to pull it down again. The turning force will return it to its position of equilibrium where it is stable again. Look at Figure 19.2.2.

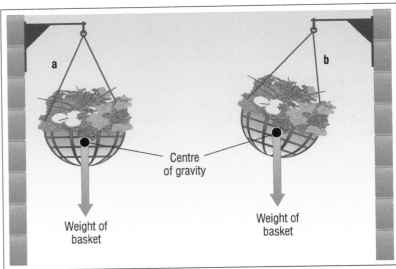

Figure 19.2.2 The hanging basket in **a** is in its position of stable equilibrium. In **b** it experiences a turning force as gravity tries to return it back to its stable equilibrium position.

An unstable equilibrium is one in which any movement of the balanced object makes its centre of gravity lower. The force of gravity then makes the object carry on falling. An example is a ball balanced on top of a hump. Once the ball is moved to one side, it will fall off – it will not return to its equilibrium position.

A third type of equilibrium is called neutral equilibrium. If a ball moves to one side on a flat surface, its centre of gravity does not rise or fall. It stays at the same level so the ball is displaced but remains in a position of equilibrium.

Stability and centre of gravity

The location of an object's centre of gravity affects its stability. Stability, in this case, is a measure of how difficult it is to make an object topple over. How far do you have to tilt an object before it falls over? Look at the block of wood in Figure 19.2.3.

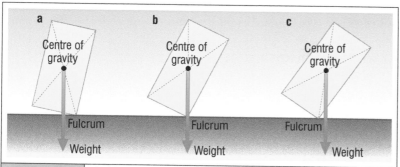

Figure 19.2.3 | The block of wood will topple over in **c**. In which position is the block of wood balanced?

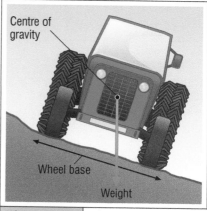

Figure 19.2.4 | What would happen if the tractor's centre of gravity was higher and its wheel base narrower?

An object topples as soon as the line of force of its weight acts outside its base.

In experiments like this we find that:

• the lower the centre of gravity, the more stable the object is
• the wider the base of the object, the more stable it is.

This is important in vehicle design as some off-road vehicles, such as tractors, have to travel across uneven land. That is why these have a wide wheel base and a low centre of gravity.

Turning forces

LEARNING OUTCOMES

- Calculate the moment of a force.
- Use the principle of moments to solve problems involving a balanced beam.

LINK

For more information about levers and force multipliers, see 12.1 'Simple machines'.

The moment of a force

We have seen how useful levers are already.

If you undo a tight wheel-nut on your bike, would you choose a short spanner or a long spanner? We can work out the turning force or moment that the long spanner and the short spanner have using this equation:

moment of force = force × perpendicular distance from the fulcrum to the line of action of the force

(in newton metres, Nm) (in newtons, N) (in metres, m)

We have two spanners and we apply the same force of 150 N to the end of each spanner.

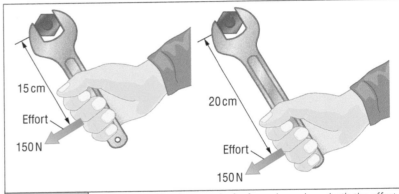

Figure 19.3.1 The turning effect (moment) of a force depends on both the effort applied and the distance of the effort from the fulcrum

Applying the equation above:

for the shorter spanner:
moment = 150 N × 0.15 m
       = **22.5 Nm**

for the longer spanner:
moment = 150 N × 0.2 m
       = **30 Nm**

So the longer spanner enables a greater turning force (moment) to be applied to the nut.

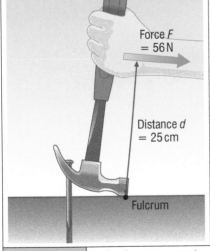

Figure 19.3.2 A claw hammer removing a nail

Worked example

A claw hammer is used to remove a nail from a piece of wood (see Figure 19.3.2).

What is the moment of the force applied to the nail?

Moment = force × distance to fulcrum
       = 56 N × 0.25 m
       = **14 Nm**

A balancing act

In the worked example with the hammer, the turning force is being applied in a clockwise direction around the fulcrum. When we have weights on either side of a balanced beam, we have turning forces of equal size acting downwards on either side of the fulcrum. On one side of the fulcrum the force will be tending to turn the beam clockwise and on the other side the force will be anticlockwise.

So when the beam is balanced we can say that:

$$\text{the sum of the clockwise moments} = \text{the sum of the anticlockwise moments}$$

We call this the **principle of moments**.

The turning force on each side of the fulcrum is calculated by the principle of moments equation. So in Figure 19.3.3 we can say that:

$$F_1 \times d_1 = F_2 \times d_2$$

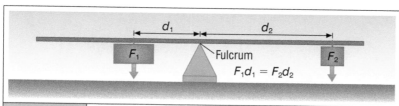

Figure 19.3.3 | Demonstrating the principle of moments

Worked example

In Figure 19.3.3, if $F_1 = 5.0\,\text{N}$, $d_1 = 0.2\,\text{m}$, and $F_2 = 4.0\,\text{N}$, how far from the fulcrum (d_2) is the weight F_2 applied in order to balance the beam?

$$F_1 \times d_1 = F_2 \times d_2$$
$$5.0\,\text{N} \times 0.2\,\text{m} = 4.0\,\text{N} \times d_2$$

Re-arranging the equation gives:

$$\frac{5.0\,\text{N} \times 0.2\,\text{m}}{4.0\,\text{N}} = d_2$$
$$\mathbf{0.25\,\text{m}} = d_2$$

KEY POINTS

1 We can calculate the turning effect of a force (called its moment) using the equation: moment = force × perpendicular distance from its line of action.

2 The principle of moments for a balanced object states that the sum of the clockwise moments equals the sum of the anticlockwise moments about a fulcrum ($F_1 \times d_1 = F_2 \times d_2$).

SUMMARY QUESTIONS

1 A girl uses a spanner to undo a nut. She applies a force of 75 N at a perpendicular distance of 15 cm from the nut. What is the moment of the force that she applies to the nut, in newton metres?

2 Look at the children on the see-saw opposite.

The girl weighs 450 N and sits 1 m from the fulcrum to balance her younger brother who weighs 300 N. How far from the fulcrum does her brother sit?

Vehicles have to be stable when they go around bends. They are in danger of toppling over if they take a sharp corner too quickly. When they go round a bend, they experience a **centripetal force** towards the centre of a circle. Their velocity is changing constantly as they are turning, so vehicles going round a bend are accelerating.

There is a natural tendency for any object travelling in a circular path to keep going in a straight line. However, the friction between the road and the tyres provides the inward centripetal force. Formula One racing cars have wide tyres to increase the centripetal force needed at high velocities. They are also low to the ground, with a wide wheel base, to prevent them rolling over.

An object tends to fly out of a circular path without a centripetal force pulling it toward the centre of the circle

Figure 19.4.1 A racing car has a low centre of gravity and a wide wheel base to keep it stable when cornering at high speed

You can feel the centripetal force when you whirl an object around your head on the end of a piece of string.

You are pulling inwards to keep the object flying around in a circle. This centripetal force always acts towards the centre of the circle. If at any point you let go of the string the object will fly off in a straight line at a tangent to its circular path. (Think of a hammer thrower in an athletics event.)

The centripetal force needed to keep an object travelling in a circular path is greater when:

- the speed is faster
- the circle is smaller
- the mass of the object is greater.

Figure 19.4.2 Whirling an object around on a piece of string

Satellites

Satellites are objects that orbit a larger object. The Moon is a satellite of the Earth. The Earth is a satellite of the Sun. The smaller object stays in orbit because centripetal force is provided by the gravitational attraction between the objects.

The speed at which a satellite orbits the larger object depends on their masses and the distance between them. The larger the distance, the slower the speed (as the gravitational attraction is weaker). The more distant planets from the Sun travel more slowly in larger orbits, so it takes them longer to circle the Sun.

While it takes Saturn 29.5 of our years to orbit the Sun, it takes Mercury (the nearest planet to the Sun) only about three months.

We also have man-made satellites orbiting the Earth. These are mainly used for communication, such as TV and GPS (global positioning satellites) receiving and transmitting signals from Earth. These communication satellites orbit at the same rate as the Earth spins round and in the same direction, so they stay in the same position relative to the Earth. They are called **geostationary satellites**.

Other satellites are used to monitor the Earth, for example for spying, to monitor weather patterns or pollution. They usually orbit from pole to pole so that they can take images of the whole Earth. They also tend to travel in lower orbits, taking two or three hours to complete each orbit.

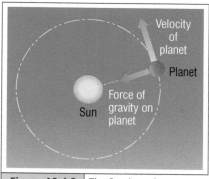

Figure 19.4.3 The Sun is at the centre of our Solar System. The Earth's orbit is an almost circular path.

Figure 19.4.4 The Hubble satellite orbits the Earth taking fantastic images of objects and events in outer space. As it orbits the Earth in space, there is no interference from the atmosphere to distort radiation detected by the telescope. The International Space Station is another satellite that adds to our scientific knowledge. Scientists can observe experiments in zero gravity on the space station.

KEY POINTS

1. Centripetal force acts towards the centre of a circular path and keeps an object in circular motion.

2. Satellites orbit larger objects. These can be planets orbiting the Sun, moons orbiting planets or man-made satellites launched into space at the correct speed to orbit the Earth.

SUMMARY QUESTIONS

1. Explain why a racing car can go round a tight corner much more quickly than a double-decker bus without toppling over.

2. a What is a satellite?

   b What force keeps a satellite in its orbit?

   c Explain why communication and monitoring satellites have different orbits around the Earth.

3. Why does Saturn take longer to orbit the Sun than Mercury?

SECTION C: Multiple-choice questions

1 What is responsible for day and night?

a   The position of the Sun relative to the other stars

b   The position of the Earth relative to the position of the Sun

c   The position of the Sun and the asteroids relative to the position of the Moon

d   The position of the Earth and the Sun relative to the position of the galaxies

2 The main reason not more wind energy is harnessed today is because

a   the wind does not blow enough at many places.

b   wind turbines are expensive and difficult to build.

c   no good way has been found to change wind energy to electricity.

d   wind turbines would pollute the atmosphere.

3 There are many ways to catch fish commercially. The method used depends on the habitat of the target species.

Which one of the following methods catches fish by surrounding them in a net?

a   Dredging

b   Trawling

c   Purse seining

d   Long-lining

4 An object has a mass of 200 g and a volume of 25 cm³. What is the object's density?

a   8 g/cm³

b   175 g/cm³

c   225 g/cm³

d   5000 g/cm³

5 What is the moment of the claw hammer shown in the diagram below?

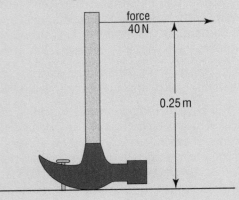

a   160 N

b   40.25 N

c   39.75 N

d   10 N

6 Polluted ponds and rivers can suffer from the effects of excess algae on the surface of the water. What can cause this type of pollution?

I   Fertilisers

II   Sewage

III   Detergents

IV   Oil spills

a   I only

b   I and III

c   II and IV

d   I, II and III

7 An object is travelling in a circular path. What do we call the name of the force that keeps it on its circular path?

a   Centripetal force

b   Kinetic force

c   Resultant force

d   Stability force

Further practice questions and examples can be found on the accompanying website.

8 The following chart compares a lunar and a solar eclipse. Write the words that belong in the lettered boxes.

		Lunar eclipse	Solar eclipse
a	Body that is hidden		
b	Body that causes the shadow		
c	Body where the shadow falls		
d	When it occurs (day or night)		
e	Size of shadow (large or small)		
f	Appearance of shadows edge (fuzzy or sharp)		

(12)

9 Most of the electricity produced at the present time comes from fossil fuel power stations.

a Name two fossil fuels. *(2)*

b State two examples of environmental problems caused by fossil fuel power stations. *(2)*

c Why are fossil fuels known as 'non-renewable sources of energy'? *(2)*

d Alternative forms of energy include the use of wind turbines to generate electricity.

  i Give one advantage and one disadvantage of using wind turbines to generate electricity. *(2)*

A research company was investigating how the height of a wind turbine affects its power output. Here is a table of the results of one of the investigations.

Height of turbine (m)	Power output (kW)
35	147
40	194
50	225
60	252
70	280
80	303
85	310

  ii What units are used to measure the power output? *(1)*

  iii What is the general pattern in the results obtained by the research company? *(1)*

  iv How would these results be best displayed? Choose one of the options below.

   A Bar chart

   B Line graph

   C Pie chart

   D Histogram *(1)*

  v What would be the main disadvantage of choosing to make wind turbines that give the maximum output? *(1)*

e The Sun's energy can also be used as a source of energy.

Give two examples of how we can use solar energy as an alternative source of energy in the home. *(2)*

f Geothermal energy is another source of energy. Explain how this energy could be used in a power station. *(2)*

Further practice questions and examples can be found on the accompanying website.

Index

Note: Key terms (glossary terms) are in **bold** type.

A

absorption 35
accidents 108
    avoiding accidents 108–9
acid rain 169
acids 124–5
active transport 8–9
aerobic respiration 58
AIDS 47
air masses 146
    how hurricanes form 149
    local weather fronts 148
    moving air masses 147
air pollution 60
    causes of air pollution 60–1
    respiratory disorders 61
alcohol 19
alcohol thermometers 89
alloys 121
aluminium 118–19
alveoli 54
    gaseous exchange at the alveoli 57
anaerobic respiration 58
    fermentation 58
    lactic acid production 59
animal cells 4
    functions of the cell parts 4
antibodies 44
antigens 44
arteries 42
    narrowing arteries 62
artificial light 71
asexual reproduction 10–11
assimilation 35
atherosclerosis 48

B

bacteria 20
balance 73
    principle of moments 179
bases 124–5
batteries 94
bimetallic strips 88
biodegradable waste 78
biofuels 170–1
biological waste 78
biological weathering 141
birth 15
birth control methods 16–17
blood 42
    blood groups 44
    blood pressure 48–9
    blood transfusions 44–5
    blood vessels 42
    rhesus factor 45

blue 70
brass 121
breastfeeding 18
    advantages 18
breathing 56–7
    breathing diseases 63
bungee jumping 94

C

cancers 63
capillaries 42
carbohydrases 34
carbohydrates 30
carbon cycle 145
carbon dioxide 60
carbon monoxide 60–1, 62
cells 4
    active transport 8–9
    animal cells 4
    cell membrane 4
    diffusion 6
    osmosis 6–7
    plant cells 5
centre of gravity 176
    stability and centre of gravity 177
centripetal force 180–1
chemical weathering 140
chlorophyll 24
chloroplasts 5
chromatography 71
chromosomes 4
ciliary muscles 68
circular motion 180
circulatory system 42–3
    blood 42
    blood vessels 42
    heart 43
clinical thermometers 89
cold fronts 148
colloids 126
colour 70
    colour of objects 71
    physically separating mixtures of pigments 71
compasses 166
compounds 124
computers 95
concentration gradients 6
conduction 84
conductors 98
conservation of energy 94
contraception 16–17
convection 86
    land and sea breezes 86–7
cornea 68
crop production 26–7
    crop rotation 27
current, electrical 98, 99

cyan 70
cytoplasm 4

D

decomposers 28–9
dental formulae 38–9
desalination 159
detergents 130
    soapy and soapless detergents 129
dialysis 65
diet 19
    balanced diet 30–1
    energy requirements 32–3
    food additives 33
    obesity 32
    protein energy malnutrition (PEM) 33
diffusion 6
digestion 34
    absorption and assimilation 35
    chemical digestion 34–5
    egestion 35, 64
    mechanical digestion 34
    teeth 38–9
    varying pH in the digestive system 34–5
digital thermometers 89
disease
    deficiency diseases 30
    diseases in pregnancy 19
    immunity 46–7
    respiratory disorders 61
    sexually transmitted infections (STIs) 20–1
    smoking 62–3
DNA 4
domestic waste 78
dredging 165
drugs 19, 50
    health and ethical issues 51
    performance-enhancing drugs 50–1
drying 37

E

ear 72
    hearing loss 73
    how we hear 73
    maintaining balance 73
    sound waves 72
Earth 134, 136
    day and night 138
    lunar eclipse 139
    solar eclipse 138–9
    tides 150
earthquakes 152–3
    measuring strength 153–4
eclipses 138–9
egestion 35, 64

electric shock 106–7
electricity
   conductors and insulators 98
   current, voltage and resistance 99
   energy consumption 102–3
   fuse as safety device 100
   plugs 100–1
   power 100, 102
   series and parallel circuits 98
electroplating 121, 123
emergencies 106–7
emulsifiers 130
endocrine system 76
   hormones 77
energy 94
   electricity 102–3
   energy interconversions 94–5
   forms of energy 94
   momentum 96–7
   moving energy 96
   renewable energy sources 170–1
   solar energy 170, 172–3
   unit of energy 95
energy requirements 32–3
energy transfer 84
   conduction 84
   fluids 86–7
   radiation 85
   variables affecting solar energy
      transfer 173
enzymes 34
erosion 26
eutrophication 162
evaporation 90–1
   cooling your body down 91
excretion 64
   kidneys 64–5
   plants 66–7
   skin 65
exercise 32, 49
exhalation 56
   comparing inhaled and exhaled air 56
eye 68
   defects 69
   eye lens 68
   focusing light 68–9
   ultraviolet or bright light 69

F
fats 30
   food tests 31
fermentation 58
fertilisation 12, 13
fibre 31
fire fighting 106
first aid 106–7
fish 55
fish farming 165

fishing 164
   fishing by hand 164
flotation 160–1
fluids 86–7
food additives 33
food chains 28
food preservation 36–7
food tests 31
food webs 29
forces 174–5
   centripetal force 180–1
   gravity 176–7
   turning forces 178–9
fossil fuels 168
   alternatives 170–1
   problems associated with fossil
      fuels 168–9
fungi 21
fuses 100

G
galaxies 134
galvanising 123
gaseous exchange 56–7
   fish 55
gases 2
geostationary satellites 181
geothermal energy 171
germination 22
gills 55
global warming 60, 169
glucose transport in plants 41
GPS (Global Positioning System) 166
gravity 176–7
   stability and centre of gravity 177
green 70
greenhouse farming 27
greenhouse gases 60

H
haemoglobin 42
hearing 73
   hearing loss 73
heart 43
heating 37
   cooling your body down 91
   overheating 92–3
high blood pressure 48
   effects 49
   reducing 49
HIV 47
homeostasis 64
hormones 14
   endocrine system 77
household appliances 88–9
household chemicals 124
   acids, bases and salts 124–5
   compounds and mixtures 124

household cleaners 130–1
human circulatory system 42–3
human ear 72–3
human eye 68–9
human growth 23
human reproduction 13
   birth control methods 16–17
   menopause 14
   menstrual cycle 14
   post-natal care 18
   pre-natal care 19
   pregnancy 15
   stages of labour and birth 15
human respiratory system 54, 56–7
human skeleton 52–3
humidity 92
humus 141
hurricanes 149
   hurricane precautions 149
hydroelectric energy 171
hydrophiles 130
hydrophobes 130
hydroponic farming 26
hygiene 79

I
immunity 46
   HIV/AIDS 47
   immunisation 46
   immunisation of the baby in
      pregnancy 46
   vaccination 46–7
inclined planes 111
industrial waste 79
inhalation 56
   comparing inhaled and exhaled
      air 56
inner planets 136–7
insulators 84, 98
involuntary actions 75
iris 68
iron 122, 123

J
joints 52–3
Jupiter 137

K
Kevlar 115
kidneys 64–5
   dialysis 65

L
laboratory thermometers 89
labour 15
lactic acid production 59
land breezes 86–7
latent heat of vaporisation 91

Index

lead 61
levers 110–11
   levers in the body 111
light 68–9
   colour of objects 71
   natural and artificial lighting 71
   primary and secondary colours 70
   visible spectrum 70
lighting 71
   display screens 104
   more efficient lighting 104–5
lipases 34
liquids 2
long-lining 164
long-sightedness 69
lunar eclipse 139

M

machines 110
   doing work 112
   inclined planes 111
   levers 110–11
   mechanical advantage 112–13
magenta 70
magnetic compasses 166
Mars 136–7
mass 96–7
maximum-minimum thermometers 89
menopause 14
menstrual cycle 14
Mercury 136
metals 114
   alloys 121
   cleaning metals 120
   electroplating 121
   reactivity of metals 116–19
methane 61
microorganisms 36–7
Milky Way 134
minerals 30
   transport in plants 41
mitochondria 4
mixtures 124
   classifying mixtures 126
moment of a force 178
   principle of moments 179
momentum 96–7
Moon 134, 138
   lunar eclipse 139
   tides 150
muscles 53

N

natural light 71
navigation at sea 166
Neptune 137
nervous system 74
   damage to the nervous system 75

endocrine system 76–7
   reflex (involuntary) actions 75
   voluntary actions 74
neurones 74
neutralisation 125
nicotine 62
nitrogen cycle 144
non-metallic materials 114–15
non-renewable fuels 168
nuclear power stations 95
nucleus 4

O

obesity 32
occluded fronts 148
Ohm's law 99
oil spills 163
oils 30
   food tests 31
opacity 70
optic nerve 68
osmoregulation 64
osmosis 6–7
outer planets 137
ovulation 14
oxidation 118
oxygen cycle 144–5
oxytocin 15

P

parallel circuits 98
parasites 79, 80
particle theory 2–3
passive smoking 63
pathogens 36
performance-enhancing
   drugs 50–1
peristalsis 34
pesticides 163
pests 80–1
pH in the digestive system 34–5
phloem 40
photochemical reactions 24
photosynthesis 24–5
physical weathering 140
   freezing and thawing 140
   temperature changes 140–1
pickling 37
planets 136–7
   planetary data 137
plant cells 5
   functions of the cell parts 5
plant reproduction 12
   fertilisation 13
   pollination 12
plants
   crop production 26–7
   excretion 66–7

photosynthesis 24–5
plant growth 22
soil 143
transport in plants 40–1
plasma 42
plastics 115
   plastics in sport 115
population growth 23
post-natal care 18
practice exam questions 82–3, 132–3,
   182–3
pre-natal care 19
pregnancy 15
   diseases in pregnancy and
     immunisation of the baby 19
preservatives 37
primary colours 70
producers 28
proteases 34
proteins 30
   food tests 31
   protein energy malnutrition
     (PEM) 33
pupil 68
purse seining 165

R

radar 166
radiation 85
reabsorption 65
red 70
red blood cells 42
reflex actions 75
refraction 70
refrigeration 37
relative humidity 92
reproduction 10
   asexual reproduction 10–11
   comparing asexual and sexual
     reproduction 11
   humans 13–15
   plants 12–13
   sexual reproduction 11
resistance 99
respiration 58
   aerobic respiration 58
   anaerobic respiration 58–9
respiratory system 54
   breathing 56–7
   gaseous exchange in fish 55
   respiratory disorders 61
   respiratory surfaces 54
resuscitation 106–7
retina 68
rhesus factor 45
ribosomes 4
rusting 122
   preventing rust 123

S

safety first 108–9
salting 36
salts 124–5
satellites 181
Saturn 137
scouring powders 131
scuba-diving 167
sea breezes 86–7
secondary colours 70
seismographs 153
series circuits 98
sexual reproduction 11
 humans 13–15
 plants 12–13
sexually transmitted infections
 (STIs) 20
 bacterial infections 20
 fungal infections 21
 viral infections 21
short-sightedness 69
skeleton 52
 muscles 53
 types of joints 52–3
skin 65
slopes 111
smoking 19, 62
 breathing diseases 63
 cancers 63
 harmful substances in tobacco
  smoke 62
 narrowing arteries 62
 passive smoking 63
soil 140–1, 142
 chemical properties of soil 142–3
 physical properties of soil 142
 soil conservation 26
 types of soil 141
solar eclipse 138–9
solar energy 170
 advantages and disadvantages 173
 solar cells 172
 solar panels 173
 uses 172–3
 variables affecting solar energy
  transfer 173
Solar System 136–9
solder 121
solids 2
solutions 126
solvents 127
sonar 166
sound waves 72
space exploration 134–5
spectrum of colour 70–1
stability 177
starch 25
 food tests 31

states of matter 2
 changing state 3
 particle theory 2–3
 properties of each state 2
stationary fronts 148
steel 121, 122, 123
stomata 40
sublimation 3
sugar 37
 reducing sugars 31
sulphur dioxide 60, 159
Sun 134, 136–7
 day and night 138
 solar eclipse 138–9
 tides 150
suspensions 126
suspensory ligaments 68
sweating 91

T

tarnishing 117
tars 62
teeth 38
 dental formulae 38–9
 function of different teeth 39
temperature changes 140–1
temperature control 84–5
 cooling your body down 91
 temperature control in the body 65
thermal conductors 84
thermal pollution 163
thermometers 89
thermos flasks 87
thermostats 88
 bimetallic strips 88
 household appliances 88–9
tides 150
 tidal waves 151
translucency 70
transparency 70
transport in plants 40
 transpiration 41
 water, mineral ions and glucose 41
trawling 165
trophic levels 28
tsunamis 151

U

ultrafiltration 64
ultraviolet light 69
Universe 134
 Solar System 136–9
upthrust 160–1
Uranus 137

V

vaccination 46–7
vacuole 5

vacuum flasks 87
veins 42
velocity 96–7
ventilation 93
Venus 136
viruses 21
vitamins 30
volcanoes 152
 Caribbean islands with live
  volcanoes 155
 types of volcano 154
voltage 99
voluntary actions 74

W

warm fronts 148
waste 78
 biological waste 78
 community and personal
  hygiene 79
 domestic waste 78
 industrial waste 79
 uses of waste 79
water 30, 156
 conserving water supplies 157
 hard and soft water 128
 properties of water 158
 removing hardness 128–9
 soapy and soapless
  detergents 129
 sources and treatment of drinking
  water 158–9
 transport in plants 41
 water cycle 156–7
 water purification 159
water navigation 166
water pollution 162
 eutrophication 162
 oil spills 163
 pesticides 163
 thermal pollution 163
water safety 167
wave energy 171
weather fronts 148
weathering 140–1
wetting agents 130
white blood cells 42
wind direction 86–7
wind energy 171
wood 114
work 112

X

X-rays 19
xylem 40

Y

yellow 70

Acknowledgements

Artworks by Cenveo

p3: Eaglet/Shutterstock; p5(T): Ed Reschke/Getty Images; p5(B): Power and Syred/ Science Photo Library; p10: Scimat/Science Photo Library; p12: Konrad Wothe / Look-Foto/Minden Pictures/Getty Images; p13: Art Directors & Trip/Alamy Stock Photo; p18: Choozyee/iStockphoto; p25: Sze Fei Wong/iStockphoto; p26: Art Directors & Trip/age fotostock; p27: Beat Bieler/iStockphoto; p31: Andrew Lambert Photography/Science Photo Library; p33: Sue Sharp; p36(T): Photocrew/Fotolia; p36(B): Sue Sharp; p39: iStockphoto; p44: AJ Photo/Science Photo Library; p47: Deloche/Science Photo Library; p48(T): Dann Tardif/Getty Images; p48(B): Science Photo Library; p49: Eye Ubiquitous/Alamy Stock Photo; p50: Alessandra Tarantino/ AP Photo; p51: Olivier Morin/AFP/Getty Images; p55: Peter Leahy/Shutterstock; p58: Sue Sharp; p59: Jeff Pachoud/AFP/Getty Images; p60: Sergiy Serdyuk/iStockphoto; p62: Miao Long/iStockphoto; p66: Nancy Nehring/iStockphoto; p67: Krystyna Szulecka/Alamy Stock Photo; p73: Lattapictures/iStockphoto; p77: Dzphotovideo/ iStockphoto; p78: David Nunuk/Science Photo Library; p79: Mediacolor's/ Alamy Stock Photo; p80: Henrik_L/iStockphoto; p81(T): Poresh/Fotolia; p81(C): Johncarnemolla/iStockphoto; p81(B): Ernie Janes/Alamy Stock Photo; p85: Cultura Rm/Alamy Stock Photo; p87: Phb.Cz Richard Semik/Shutterstock; p91: Paul Whitehill/Science Photo Library; p94: Ryan Johnson/iStockphoto; p95: SpaceKris/ Shutterstock; p96: Alan Dawson/age fotostock; p100: Robert Brook/Science Photo Library; p101: Lawrie Ryan; p103: D4Fish/iStockphoto; p104: Diego Cervo/ iStockphoto; p105: Loopall/Bigstock; p106: Intek1/iStockphoto; p115: Keith Ferris/ iStockphoto; p116: Charles D. Winters/Science Photo Library; p118: Amanda Heywood/DK Images; p121: D. Fabri/Fotolia; p123: Is_Imagesource/iStockphoto; p127: Martyn F. Chillmaid/Science Photo Library; p131: Emilio100/Shutterstock; p134: Alex Mit/Shutterstock; p135(R): Photodisc; p135(L): JPL/NASA; p135(BR): NASA; p136: NASA; p140: Jennifer Elizabeth/Fotolia; p143: Renee Keith/iStockphoto; p147: Jon Bower Dubai 2/Alamy Stock Photo; p151: The Yomiuri Shimbun/Hiroto Nomoto/ AP Photo; p153(T): Juan Barreto/AFP/Getty Images; p153(B): Ted Aljibe/AFP/Getty Images; p159: Eye Ubiquitous/Superstock; p161: Robert Harding/Alamy Stock Photo; p162: Dr. Jeremy Burgess/Science Photo Library; p163: U.S Coast Guard/Science Photo Library; p167: T.W. Van Urk/Shutterstock; p171(T): Tobias Schwarz/AFP/Getty Images; p171(B): Kryssia Campos/Getty Images; p172: Jonya/iStockphoto; p173: Jonya/iStockphoto; p175: Robert Cianflone/Getty Images; p180: Philippe Lopez/AFP/ Getty Images; p181: Cristian Andrei Matei/iStockphoto